Designing with type

Also by James Craig

Production for the Graphic Designer
Phototypesetting: A Design Manual
Basic Typography
Working with Graphic Designers
Graphic Design Career Guide
Thirty Centuries of Graphic Design

www.designingwithtype.com
www.designingwithtype.com/5

James Craig Irene Korol Scala
William Bevington

Designing with type

The Essential Guide to Typography

5

Watson-Guptill Publications
New York

Dedicated to a new generation of graphic designers.

This revised edition first published
in 2006 by Watson-Guptill Publications,
a division of VNU Business Media, Inc.,
770 Broadway, New York, NY 10003
www.wgpub.com

Library of Congress
Cataloging-in-Publication Data

Craig, James, 1930-
Designing with type: the essential guide to typography.—
5th ed. / by James Craig, Irene Korol Scala,
and William Bevington.
p. cm.
Includes bibliographical references and index.
ISBN 0-8230-1413-4 (alk. paper)
1. Graphic design (Typography)
I. Scala, Irene Korol. II. Bevington, William. III. Title.
Z246.C69 2006
686.2'2--dc22

2005029914

Printed in China

First Printing, 2006

1 2 3 4 5 6 7 8 / 13 12 11 10 09 08 07 06

Contents

Introduction

■ Typography, the art of designing with type, is probably the most important subject students will study in school. As professional graphic designers they will be called upon to perform many design tasks, most requiring a thorough knowledge of typography. Few assignments will be devoid of type, and many will consist entirely of type. Words will always remain central to communication.

Today's graphic design students will be the typographers of the future, and their success will be determined to a great degree by how well they are able to design with type.

Typography Today

Typography is a living art, with each generation of designers contributing something new and innovative. It is an art that continues to grow and change, drawing both praise and criticism.

This scrutiny is not unprecedented; typographic changes and experimentation have been criticized throughout history. Gutenberg's type was too cold and lacked the warmth of handwritten scripts. Subsequent typefaces designed over the centuries were criticized as having too much contrast and thereby causing eye strain and dizziness, while others lacking serifs were considered difficult to read.

The controversy continues. No longer is type required to be "invisible"—that is to serve as a quiet vehicle for enhancing the meaning of the text. Now type can be expressive, entertaining, challenging, outrageous, and in the best examples, fine art.

Some designers welcome change and the freedom to experiment, while others prefer a more traditional approach. Still others believe the old and the new can co-exist, which in the end will lead to a richer, more diverse world of typographic expression. However, there is no consensus when it comes to typography. Students should keep an open mind, embrace all forms of typographic expression, and from this perspective develop their own personal esthetic.

Hopefully, each new generation of graphic designers will continue to redefine the boundaries and conventions of their art. Some innovations will withstand the test of time, while others will simply represent passing fashions. All will add to the rich history of typography.

The Fifth Edition

Although typography can be taught in a number of ways, it is generally agreed that the most successful curricula are built around a knowledge of metal type because metal type is the source of our typographic vocabulary. This new edition of *Designing with Type* combines this rich foundation with today's technologies from which readers can acquire a deep and thorough understanding of typography.

In response to today's needs, we have completely redesigned and reorganized the contents, introduced full color throughout, and added much new information without omitting features that have made this book such a valuable tool.

Designing with Type was first published more than thirty-five years ago. The book has sold more than a quarter million copies and has been adopted by design schools around the world. All this would suggest that in spite of dramatic changes in the design industry, *Designing with Type* continues to educate and inspire. We believe this fifth edition will be a most useful companion to a new generation of graphic designers.

The Web Site: www.designingwithtype.com/5

A major innovation of this latest edition has been the integration of the book with the Web site www.designingwithtype.com/5, where students and faculty members can examine hundreds of solutions to design projects and explore a world of typographic information. ■

Basics of Typography

1

The art of designing with type began in the West around 1455 when Johannes Gutenberg perfected the craft of printing from individual pieces of type. From this early technology we draw a great deal of our current terminology. This section introduces the origins of the alphabet, and defines the terms and measurements that will form the basis of your typographic vocabulary. Once you are familiar with this information, you will be able to communicate your ideas clearly and work efficiently with type.

Origins of the Alphabet

1 | Pictographs

2 | Ideograph

Before proceeding with the more practical aspects of typography, let's first consider the twenty-six letters we call our alphabet. We tend to forget that the alphabet is composed of symbols, each representing sounds made in speech. The symbols we use today are derived from those used thousands of years ago. However, the ancient forms did not represent sounds but were pictures of things or symbols for ideas.

Pictographs

At some point in time, people began to communicate visually. They made simple drawings of the things that existed in their world—people, animals, tools, and weapons, for example. **These basic images, called *pictographs,* were symbols representing objects, such as an ox or a house (1).**

Ideographs

As the need to communicate more abstract thoughts developed, the symbols began to take on multiple meanings: ox, for example, could also mean food. **The new symbols would represent not objects, but ideas and are called *ideographs* (2).**

Abstract thoughts could also be communicated by combining different pictographs: for example, to communicate the idea of rest, pictographs of a man and a tree might be combined. A contemporary example of the ideograph is the warning symbol of the skull and crossbones, which is not seen for what it is, but for what it represents: danger, death, pirates, or poison.

This evolution from pictographs to ideographs represented a major step in the development of a written language. Early cultures used this system of picture-writing, combining symbols for the concrete (pictographs) and for the abstract (ideographs), to communicate and keep records. Today the Chinese still use an evolved version of this system.

There are some disadvantages to the picto-ideographic system: not only are the symbols complex, but their numbers run into the thousands, making learning more difficult and writing slow.

Phoenician Alphabet

As a nation of traders and merchants, the ancient Phoenicians needed a simplified writing form that would allow them to keep ledgers and communicate business transactions. Around 1200 B.C.E., a new concept in written communication evolved using symbols to represent the sounds of speech rather than ideas or objects.

To understand how this change came about, let's look at the first two letters of our alphabet, A and B, and see how they evolved (3). One of the primary spoken sounds the Phoenicians recorded was "A." This sound occurred at the beginning of their word *aleph*, meaning ox. Instead of devising a new symbol for the sound, they simply took the existing symbol for the ox.

They did the same for the sound "B," which was found in their word *beth*, meaning house. Again, they took the existing symbol for the house and applied it to the sound.

This process was continued until the Phoenicians had assigned a symbol for each sound. In all cases the symbols were of common objects or parts of the body, such as water, door, fish, hand, eye, or mouth. (See page 120.)

The Phoenician alphabet required far fewer symbols than the picto-ideographic system. Furthermore, the simplified letterforms could be written more rapidly, were easier to learn, and provided an ideal means of communication. By developing a standardized phonetic alphabet, the Phoenicians made a major contribution to Western civilization.

Greek Alphabet

The ancient Greek civilization gradually adopted the Phoenician alphabet for their use around 800 B.C.E. They recognized something quite different in the potential of this new system: in addition to its usefulness as a tool of trade, the alphabet also offered a valuable means of preserving knowledge. Along with adopting the alphabet, the Greeks adopted the Phoenician names for the letters, altering them only slightly. **For example, aleph became alpha, beth became beta (4).** From these two letters we derive our word *alphabet.*

The Phoenician alphabet contained no vowels, only consonants. Words formed from this alphabet would have looked similar to our abbreviations—Blvd. and Rte. Although this system worked well for business ledgers, its broader use was limited. Therefore the Greeks added five vowels and formalized the letterforms. A revised alphabet of only capital letters was adopted officially by Athens in 403 B.C.E.

Roman Alphabet

Just as the Greeks had altered the Phoenician alphabet, the Romans adopted and modified the Greek alphabet (5). Thirteen letters were left unchanged from the Greek: A, B, E, H, I, K, M, N, O, T, X, Y, and Z. Eight letters were revised: C, D, G, L, P, R,

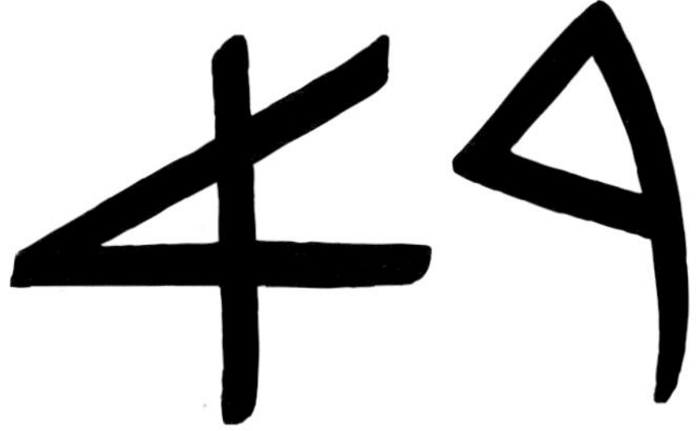

3 | Phoenician: aleph and beth

4 | Greek: alpha and beta

5 | Roman: A and B

S, and V. Two letters were added: F and Q. This gave the Romans a total of twenty-three letters. The Romans also dropped the Greek designations for the letters, such as *alpha, beta,* and *gamma,* and substituted simpler sounds to represent the letters, such as our ABCs of today. The letters U and W were added to the alphabet about a thousand years ago, and J was added five centuries later.

Small Letters

Up to now, we have been discussing capital (majuscule) letters only. Small (minuscule) letters were a natural outgrowth of writing and rewriting capital letters with a pen. At first only a few minuscules were consistently written, but eventually a full set of majuscules and minuscules was being used. As writing became common, greater economy was desired, and letters were compressed so that more words could fit on a line.

Prior to Gutenberg's invention of printing from movable type in the mid-fifteenth century, there were two popular schools of writing in western Europe: Gothic or Black Letter in Germany and the Northern nations and the round Humanistic hand in Italy.

The Black Letter forms (6) were used as the models for the typeface designed by Gutenberg in the mid-fifteenth century (7). The Humanistic script was a revival of the Carolingian minuscule of the ninth century and is the basis of our small letters (8). A flowing form of this same hand is the basis of our italic.

Examples of all three writing styles can be seen on the opposite page.

6 | Black Letter

7 | Gutenberg's type

AaBb

8 | Humanistic lettering

Punctuation

In early Greek and Roman writing, there was no punctuation as we know it. Words were either run together or separated with a dot or slash. This can be seen in the handwritten specimens of the Rustica, Half-Uncials, and Carolingian minuscules shown on the opposite page. It was not until the fifteenth century, with the advent of printing, that the rules of grammar and punctuation began to become formalized.

The Alphabet

As illustrated, our alphabet is made up of distinct symbols that represent thousands of years of evolution. As a designer, you can simplify or embellish the letterforms, but if you alter their basic shapes, you will reduce their ability to communicate effectively. Even within this seemingly fixed structure, you will find these symbols provide a lifetime of creative possibilities. ■

W T SH R Q TS P MUTE KS N M L K J TH H Z F H D G B A

Phoenician alphabet (circa 1000 B.C.E.) reads from right. Small letters indicate sounds.

ΑΒΓΔΕΖΗΘΙΚΛΜΝΞΟΠΡΣΤΥΦΧΨΩ

ALPHA BETA GAMMA DELTA EPSILON ZETA ETA THETA IOTA KAPPA LAMBDA MU NU XI OMICRON PI RHO SIGMA TAU UPSILON PHI CHI PSI OMEGA

Greek alphabet (circa 403 B.C.E.), adapted from Phoenician around 900 B.C.E.

ABCDEFGHIKLMNOPQRSTVXYZ

Roman alphabet (circa 100 C.E.), adapted from the Greek alphabet

AIQILLVMINPRAECEPSREMIGIISSV

Square capitals (fourth century), written with a reed pen

FELICESOPERVM·QVINIAMCOEVMOVE·LA

Rustica (fifth century), written with reed pen. Dots represent early punctuation

inſtauratio /nullatranſlati /nonaurum

Half-Uncials (seventh century), written with reed pen. Slashes indicate punctuation

búab quad uuétent· erſie thar tho mán

Carolingian minuscules (ninth century), written with reed pen

ſeniaam nutiga dans pecta in ſecula ſeculorum ant

Black Letter (fifteenth century), written with reed pen

uid loquar de ſecli hominibꝫ· tu apſtus paulus:vas de

Gutenberg typeface (circa 1455), derived from Black Letter above

igitur habet poteſtatem·ceſſe eſt eum qu

Humanistic Cursive writing (fifteenth century), based on Carolingian miniscule

Quidā eius libros nō ipſius eſſe ſed Dionyſii &Zophiri lophoniorū

Roman typeface designed by Nicholas Jensen (1475), based on Humanistic Cursive

P abula parua legens, nidisq; loquacibus eſcas, E t nunc porticibus

First italic typeface designed by Francesco Griffo (1501), also based on Humanistic Cursive

Type Terminology

As readers, we tend to see words in terms of the messages they convey, and are rarely conscious of the actual shape of individual letterforms. Only when we examine letters closely do we see how complex and visually elegant they are.

Have you ever taken the time to examine a letter closely? **Let's start right now by considering the many intricate shapes inside and around the letterforms and how they interrelate (1).**

1 | When the letters are reversed, the white areas become black and new shapes become apparent.

Anatomy of Type

Letterforms consist of many parts, and each has a specific name. **You should familiarize yourself with these names and with other typographic terms used by designers (2).** The following are the most common.

CHARACTERS | The individual letters, punctuation, numerals, and other elements that are used when setting type.

UPPERCASE | The capital letters, or caps, of the alphabet. The term derives from the early days of handset type when capital letters were stored in the upper section of the typecase. The small letters were kept in the lower portion and are called *lowercase.* When abbreviated, capital letters are indicated as *Caps, U.C.,* or simply *C*.

LOWERCASE | The small letters of the alphabet, often indicated as *lc*. When combined with uppercase, they are indicated as *U/lc, U&lc,* or *C/lc*.

BASELINE | An imaginary line upon which the characters seem to be standing.

MEANLINE | An imaginary line that runs along the top of most lowercase letters, such as a, c, e, i, m, n, u, v, w, and x.

X-HEIGHT | The height of the body, or main element, of the lowercase letterform, which falls between the meanline and baseline. This measurement is called the x-height because the strokes of the lowercase x terminate at the baseline and the meanline.

ASCENDER | The part of some lowercase letters, such as the strokes on the letters b, d, or h, that rises above the meanline.

DESCENDER | The part of some lowercase letters that falls below the baseline, such as the strokes on the letters p, y, and g.

COUNTER | The space entirely or partially enclosed within a letterform, such as the enclosed "bowl" of the letters b, d, and p.

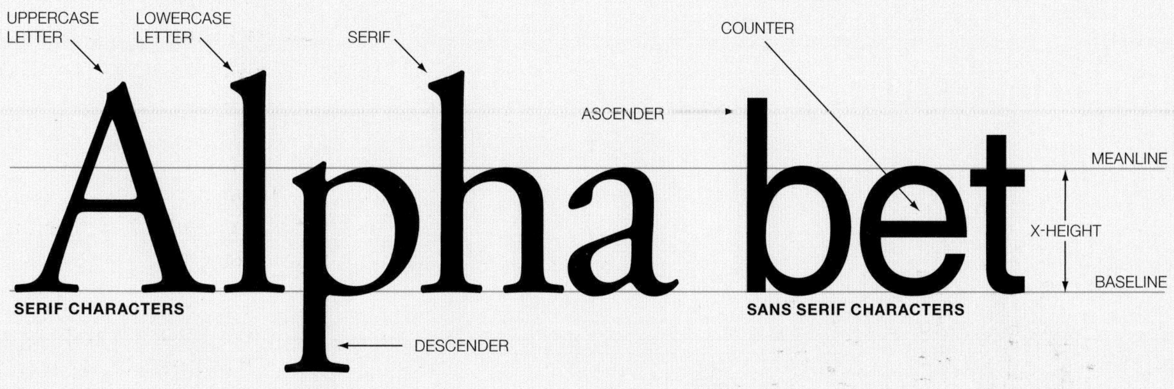

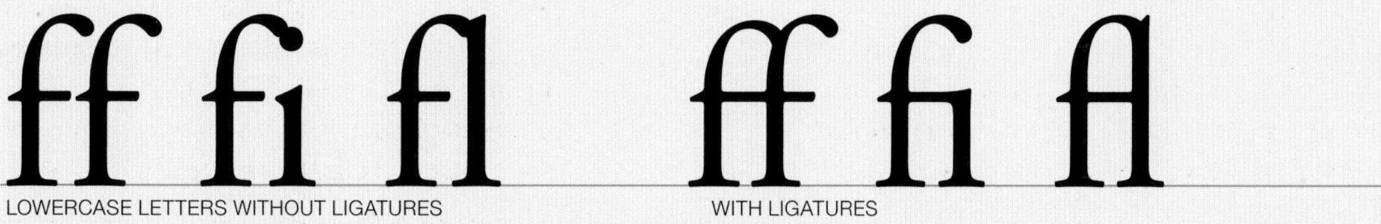

2 | The principle terms used to identify letterforms

Baskerville

Bodoni

Caslon

Gill Sans

Frutiger

Caledonia

Helvetica

Futura

Eurostyle

Modern

Century

3 | The names of specific typefaces

SERIF AND SANS SERIF | The finishing strokes that project from the main stroke of a letter are called the serifs. Serifs originated with the Roman masons, who terminated each stroke of a letter carved into a slab of stone with a serif to enhance its appearance. Not all type has serifs; type having no serifs at all is called *sans serif,* meaning without serif.

SMALL CAPS | A complete alphabet of caps that are the same size as the body, or x-height, of the lowercase letters: A, B, C, D, E, F, G, etc. Often used in text settings where regular capitals are required but might create unwanted emphasis. Small caps are compatible with lowercase letterforms in the weight of the strokes of the letter. A typical use is for acronyms like NASA or NATO.

MODERN FIGURES | Also called *lining figures,* these are numbers that resemble caps by being uniform in height: 1, 2, 3, 4, 5, 6, 7, 8, 9, 0. Modern figures are most often used for annual reports, charts, tables, and any application where numbers are meant to stand out or supply critical information. Another feature of modern figures is that they align vertically, making them preferable for setting tables and charts.

OLD STYLE FIGURES | Also called *nonlining figures,* these are similar to lowercase characters in the way they vary in size and may have ascenders and descenders: 1, 2, 3, 4, 5, 6, 7, 8, 9, 0. Primarily used when less obtrusive numerals are required, such as within the body of text. For the same reason, old style figures are often combined with small caps, for example, PT-109, or 2005 C.E.

LIGATURES | Two or more characters joined as a single unit. Ligatures are a typographic refinement that compensates for certain letters that set poorly when combined, such as ff, fi, fl, ffi, ffl.

Typefaces

***Typeface* refers to the specific design of an alphabet (3).** The difference between one typeface and another is often very subtle, no more than a slight modification in the shape of the letter, serifs, or the length of the ascenders and descenders. Regardless of how subtle the difference, the typeface you choose will greatly affect the appearance of the entire printed page.

Each typeface is identified by a name. A typeface may be named after the individual who designed it (Baskerville, Bodoni, Caslon, Gill, Frutiger) or refer to a country (Caledonia, Helvetica), or be named to describe its appearance or character (Futura, Eurostyle, Modern). The type you are now reading is Helvetica Neue.

Typestyles

Today an incredible number of typestyles are available to graphic designers. The number and variety have developed over time to accommodate diverse trends and uses. **Most of these typestyles are simply variations in the weight or width of the letterforms (4)**. Although some typefaces are available in a wide variety of styles, the majority of typefaces offer only a few variations, such as roman, italic, and bold.

ROMAN | The upright letterforms derived from the historic characters developed by the Romans. The majority of typeset copy is roman. It is the first typestyle we learn and the most comfortable to read. The letterforms of this sentence are set as roman.

ITALIC | The second most common typestyle. A true italic typeface is not merely roman characters slanted to the right but is specifically created to be a companion to the roman. Italic is used mainly for quiet emphasis. *These words are set in italic.* If a roman typeface is simply slanted to the right (or left), it is referred to as *oblique*. *These words are set in oblique.*

REGULAR | The standard weight of a typeface, also referred to as *normal*. Regular is the basic form and weight from which all the other variations are derived.

BOLD | A thicker, heavier version of the regular typeface, commonly used for increased emphasis. Among the various designations for bold typestyles and heavier weights are *semibold, heavy, black, extrabold,* and *ultra*.

LIGHT | A lighter or thinner version of the regular typeface. An extremely light version is often referred to as *thin*.

CONDENSED | A narrower version of the regular typeface. Condensed type is particularly desirable if it is important to fit more letters or a larger type size into a given space. Also referred to as *compressed*.

EXTENDED | A wider version of the regular typeface. Also known as *expanded*.

In addition to the typestyles mentioned above, are combinations of styles such as *light condensed* and *bold extended*, to name just a few.

To better understand the typestyles available in a single typeface, study the many variations of Helvetica on page 59.

Roman

Italic

Thin

Light

Regular

Semibold

Bold

Extrabold

Condensed

Extended

Light Condensed

Bold Extended

4 | Variations of weights and styles

ABCDEFGHIJKL
MNOPQRSTUV
WXYZ&
abcdefghijklmnop
qrstuvwxyz
1234567890
1234567890
ff fi fl ffi ffl . , " " - : ; ! ?

5 | Traditional font, one size of one typeface

Garamond Roman

Garamond Italic

Garamond Semibold

Garamond Semibold Italic

Garamond Bold

Garamond Bold Italic

6 | A family of type

Fonts

Traditionally, a font was one size of one typestyle in a particular typeface (5). Garamond roman was one font and Garamond italic another. A font consisted of all the characters required to set type in a single size: uppercase and lowercase letters, punctuation marks, numerals, and special reference marks. A familiar example of a font is the keyboard of a typewriter. If you were to strike every key a single time, you would produce a font.

Today the term *font* is used more loosely. A font still refers to a specific typeface and typestyle but no longer refers to a particular type size. This is because technology is able to generate type in any number of sizes.

Fonts may vary in both the number and variety of characters they contain. In addition to having the alphabet and punctuation marks, some fonts are drawn to include special characters, such as small caps, ligatures, old style figures, mathematical symbols, and diacritical marks.

Type Families

If we combine all the fonts of all the typestyles of a given typeface (roman, italic, bold, condensed, etc.) we have a family of type (6). By selecting fonts within the same family, a designer maintains typographic consistency. Since all typestyles within a family share common characteristics, such as design, x-height, cap height, and length of ascenders and descenders, they will appear harmonious when combined.

Most type families are relatively small, containing roman, italic, and bold typestyles. Some families—Helvetica, for example—are exceptionally large, with variations ranging from thin condensed to bold extended, plus unique display faces such as outline and drop shadow.

For a few of the many Helvetica variations, see page 59.

Type Classifications

In an effort to bring some measure of order to the thousands of typefaces created over the centuries, scholars and historians of typography have placed all typefaces within several categories or classifications. A typical classification contains typefaces sharing similar visual characteristics. The most familiar type classifications are Old Style, Transitional, Modern, Egyptian/Slab Serif, Sans Serif, Decorative/Novelty, Script, and Black Letter. (These classifications are discussed and illustrated in detail in *Part Eight: Type Specimens*. See pages 145 to 154.) ■

Type Measurements

■ Just as a great deal of our typographic terminology is derived from the early days of printing, so too is our system of measuring type. For this reason, a knowledge of metal type provides an excellent means of understanding the terminology and measuring systems in use today.

Points and Picas

You should be familiar with two basic units of measurement: *points* and *picas*. These two measurements are to the designer what inches and feet are to the architect, and with these measurements the designer determines the appearance of a printed piece. Points are very small units used to measure both the type size and the size of the space between lines of type. Picas, which are the larger unit, are used to measure the length of a line of type. There are 12 points in 1 pica (and approximately 6 picas in 1 inch). **By comparing an inch to a point and a pica, you can get a good idea of their relative sizes (1).**

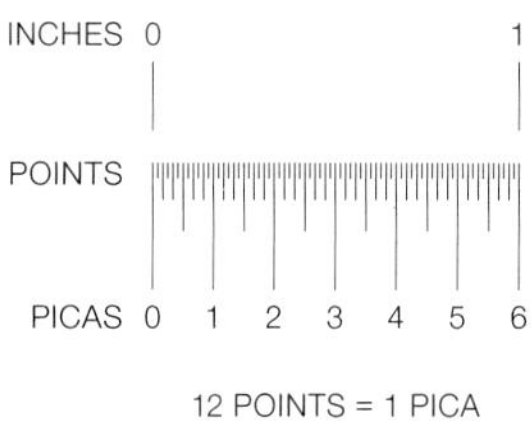

1 | Points and picas

Measuring Type in Points

Our present method of measuring type in points is derived from the traditional typesetting practice in which each character was cast as an individual block of metal. (See *Typesetting Methods* on page 158.)

Two dimensions of a piece of type are relevant to today's designer: the width and the depth (2). The width, called the *set-width*, is determined by the particular letterform itself. The M and W are the widest, and the i and punctuation marks are the most narrow. Digital typesetting systems still use set-widths in determining the amount of space characters occupy. (See *Units* on page 22.)

The depth of the type block designates the size of metal type. This dimension is generally referred to as *type size* or *point size*. So if a piece of metal type measures 10 points, then the type size is 10 points. If the metal type measures 60 points, the type size is 60 points. The type you are now reading is 8.5 points.

To see the relationship between the point size of a piece of type and the character it produces, study the three pieces of type along with the three printed letters they produce (3). Notice that although the body size of the metal type is consistent, the printed letters themselves vary in size. Since no individual letter fills the entire body, you can see why merely measuring the printed letter will not reveal the point size.

Although type is no longer cast in metal, we continue to use metal type for basic measurements and terminology.

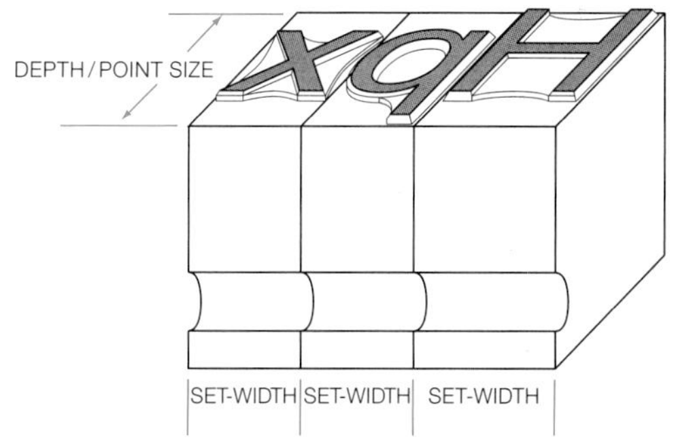

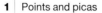

2 | Point size and set-width

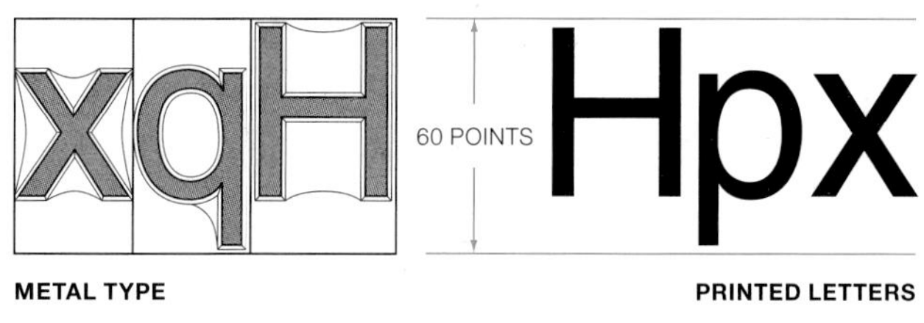

3 | Point size cannot be determined by measuring the printed letter.

5-point type
6-point type
7-point type
8-point type
9-point type
10-point type
11-point type
12-point type
14-point type

TEXT TYPE

16-point type
18-point type
20-point type
24-point type
30-point type
36-point type
42-point typ
48-point ty
60-point
72-poin

DISPLAY TYPE

4 | Traditional text and display sizes.

Type Sizes

Metal type was cast in a range of specific sizes between 5 and 72 points. Sizes below 5 points were extremely difficult to cast (and extremely difficult to read), and sizes above 72 points weighed too much. If sizes larger than 72 points were required, the letterforms were carved on lighter wooden blocks.

Type sizes were divided into two categories: *text type* and *display type* (4). The text type sizes, designed for general reading, were 5, 6, 7, 8, 9, 10, 11, 12, and 14 points. Although the difference of a single point may seem insignificant, in smaller sizes it can be very noticeable. The traditional display sizes, designed primarily for headlines, were 16, 18, 20, 24, 30, 36, 42, 48, 60, and 72 points.

With today's digital equipment, type is no longer limited to these specific sizes but can be generated in any size or fraction thereof. However, the terms *text* and *display* are still used in a general way for type sizes below and above 14 points. Furthermore, type manufacturers still use the traditional sizes when displaying type specimens.

X-height

Earlier we learned that the x-height is the height of the lowercase letter exclusive of ascenders and descenders. Although the x-height is not a fixed unit of measurement, as are points and picas, it is of great significance to the designer because the x-height—not the point size of a typeface—conveys the visual impression of the type size.

Different typefaces having the same point size may appear larger or smaller because of variations in their x-height. To understand this, compare the five display type specimens on the opposite page. **Although they are all 60 points, the x-height of each typeface varies (5).** Garamond and Bodoni have smaller x-heights, while Century Expanded and Helvetica have larger x-heights. Notice that typefaces with a small x-height generally have longer ascenders and descenders and vice versa. Design decisions, such as x-heights, are made by the typeface designers for practical and esthetic reasons.

The effects of the x-height are very noticeable when type is set as text (6). Although all are set in 10-point type the Garamond appears smaller than either the Century Expanded or the Helvetica with their larger x-heights. Also notice how the x-height affects the number of characters per line and the amount of space between lines. Typefaces with small x-heights appear to have more space between lines than do typefaces with large x-heights.

1

hpx hpx hpx hpx hpx

GARAMOND BASKERVILLE BODONI CENTURY EXPANDED HELVETICA

5 All display specimens are 60-point type.

The x-height is the height of the lowercase letter exclusive of ascenders and descenders. Although this is not a unit of measurement, it is significant because it is the x-height of the letter that conveys the visual impact of the type size. Therefore typefaces that are the same point size may appear smaller or larger because of variations in the x-height. Study these five samples closely: Garamond, with its small x-height, appears much smaller than Century Expanded and Helvetica with their larger

GARAMOND

The x-height is the height of the lowercase letter exclusive of ascenders and descenders. Although this is not a unit of measurement, it is significant because it is the x-height of the letter that conveys the visual impact of the type size. Therefore typefaces that are the same point size may appear smaller or larger because of variations in the x-height. Study these five samples closely: Garamond, with its small x-height, appears much smaller than Century

BASKERVILLE

The x-height is the height of the lowercase letter exclusive of ascenders and descenders. Although this is not a unit of measurement, it is significant because it is the x-height of the letter that conveys the visual impact of the type size. Therefore typefaces that are the same point size may appear smaller or larger because of variations in the x-height. Study these five samples closely: Garamond, with its small x-height, appears much smaller than Century Expanded and

BODONI

The x-height is the height of the lowercase letter exclusive of ascenders and descenders. Although this is not a unit of measurement, it is significant because it is the x-height of the letter that conveys the visual impact of the type size. Therefore typefaces that are the same point size may appear smaller or larger because of variations in the x-height. Study these five samples closely: Garamond, with its small x-height, appears

CENTURY EXPANDED

The x-height is the height of the lowercase letter exclusive of ascenders and descenders. Although this is not a unit of measurement, it is significant because it is the x-height of the letter that conveys the visual impact of the type size. Therefore typefaces that are the same point size may appear smaller or larger because of variations in the x-height. Study these five samples closely: Garamond, with its small x-height,

HELVETICA

6 All text specimens are 10-point type.

1/4 POINT (HAIRLINE)

1/2 POINT

1 POINT

2 POINTS

4 POINTS

6 POINTS

8 POINTS

12 POINTS

7 | Linespacing is measured in points and fractions of points.

Points, and fractions of points, are used to separate lines of type.

18 POINTS BASELINE TO BASELINE

18-POINT TYPE, SET SOLID, 18/18

Points, and fractions of points, are used to separate lines of type.

24 POINTS BASELINE TO BASELINE

18-POINT TYPE WITH 6 POINTS LEADING, 18/24

Points, and fractions of points, are used to separate lines of type.

16 POINTS BASELINE TO BASELINE

18-POINT TYPE MINUS 2 POINTS LEADING, 18/16

8 | Type set solid, plus linespacing, and minus linespacing

Linespacing or Leading

Points are used not only to measure the type size, but also to measure the space between lines of type. With traditional metal typesetting the lines of type were stacked one over the other to create a column of type. If the setting appeared too dense, additional space was added between the lines to make the printed text more open and therefore easier to read.

To add space, strips of *lead* were placed between the lines of type (7). This process was called *leading* (pronounced ledding). The metal strips, or *leads* (pronounced leds), were lower in height than the type and therefore did not print; their function was merely to separate the lines of type. Today leading is commonly referred to as *linespacing*; in this book we will use both terms.

To help you understand linespacing and its effect on a setting, examine the settings of 18-point Helvetica (8). The first is set solid, that is, with no linespacing. This setting is called 18 on 18 (written 18/18). The first figure indicates the point size of the type; the second number indicates the point size plus any additional linespace. In this example, the figures are the same, which indicates that no additional linespacing has been added. Therefore the lines of type measure 18 points from baseline to baseline, or *B-to-B*.

The next block is set with 6 points of linespacing, which is indicated as 18/24. This setting measures 24 points from baseline to baseline. Again, the first number indicates the point size of the type and the second indicates the point size plus the linespacing. Although leading does not print, it has been indicated with rules of 6 points between the lines to better demonstrate the amount of space that has been added.

The third block is set with minus 2 points of linespacing. Since typesetting is no longer constrained by the mechanics of metal type, lines of type can be set even closer than solid: this is referred to as *minus leading* or *minus linespacing*, such as 18/16. Be aware that there is a limit to just how close lines of type can be set before the ascenders and descenders start overlapping.

Linespacing greatly affects the appearance of a setting. As a general rule, when more linespacing is added, the blocks of text appear lighter and more open on the page. This can be seen more clearly in the type specimens shown throughout Part Two.

The type you are now reading is 8.5/12 Helvetica Neue and therefore has 3.5 points of linespacing. It measures 12 points baseline to baseline.

Letterspacing and Wordspacing

The terms letterspacing and wordspacing refer to the space between letters and words respectively. **Adjusting the spacing between letters and words not only affects the number of characters that can be set on a line, but also readability (9).** The looser the setting, the fewer characters per line; the tighter the setting, the more characters per line. In turn, this adjustment affects the amount of space copy will occupy and the "color" of the printed piece. The tighter the setting, the darker the lines appears on the page and vice versa.

Spacing was traditionally specified with the following general terms: *normal, loose (or open), tight, very tight,* or *touching*. Today many designers use the same vocabulary when referring to letterspacing and wordspacing.

Normal spacing, as the name suggests, is the standard setting, with no extra space added or deleted. Normal spacing is generally the easiest to read and the recommended setting for most applications. With loose settings, space is added; with tight settings space is deleted.

Letterspacing and wordspacing can be modified by "tracking" and "kerning" to affect the space between specific letters, words, or text on an entire page. Adjusting the spacing equally between all the letters is referred to as tracking. **Adjusting the spacing between specific letters is referred to as kerning (10).** Generally, only a minimal adjustment is required for problematic letter combinations such as Wo, Te, AT, etc. Kerning is particularity critical when setting large type sizes and all caps.

See page 64 for additional information on letterspacing and wordspacing.

Line length in Picas

The pica is used to indicate the length of a line of type—called the *line length* or *measure* (11). Although inches and centimeters may also be employed to measure line lengths, picas remain the standard. The column you are now reading is set in 8.5-point Helvetica Neue on 12 points by 17.5 picas. This is written as 8.5/12 Helvetica Neue x 17p6.

Just as the type size you select is important, so too is the line length. It is the type size in conjunction with the line length that determines, to a great degree, the ease with which you read.

NOTE | A pica rule has been printed on the inside of both cover flaps that can be used for measuring line lengths.

Letterspacing and wordspacing can drastically affect readability, the number of characters per line, and the "color" of the setting of text.

LOOSE SETTING

Letterspacing and wordspacing can drastically affect readability, the number of characters per line, and the "color" of the setting of text.

NORMAL SETTING

Letterspacing and wordspacing can drastically affect readability, the number of characters per line, and the "color" of the setting of text.

VERY TIGHT SETTING

9 | Letterspacing and wordspacing are variable.

Wo Te V. AT

WITHOUT KERNING

Wo Te V. AT

WITH KERNING

10 | Some letter combinations may require kerning.

Lines are measured in picas.

11 | Points measure type sizes and picas measure line lengths.

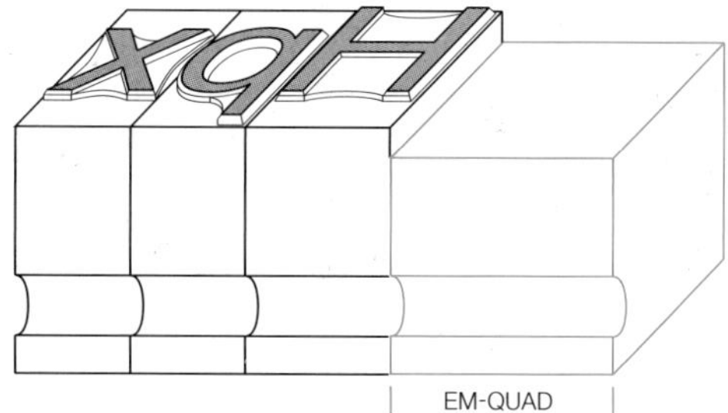

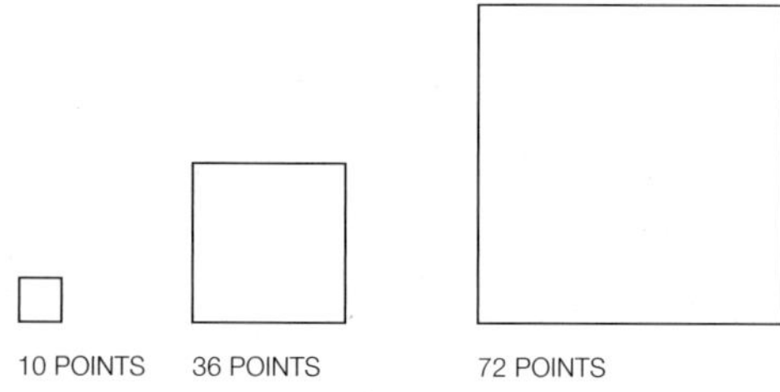

12 | The em-quad is the square of the type size.

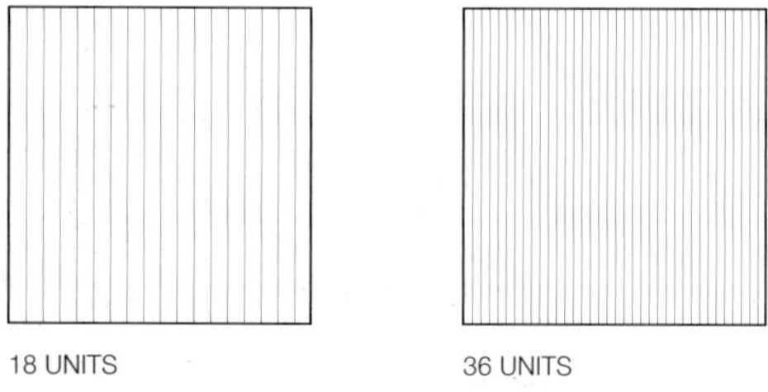

13 | The em quad is divided into units.

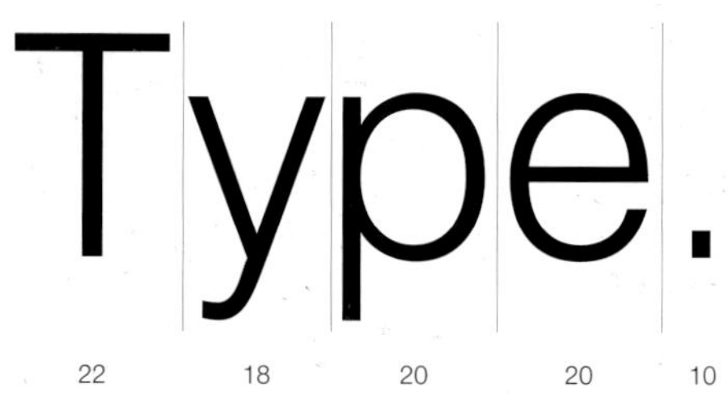

14 | Each character has a unit-value or set-width.

Em-Quads, Units, and Set-Widths

Today most type measurements are automatically measured in units. Once again, the concept of units is based on a metal type measurement called an *em-quad,* or simply an *em*.

EM-QUADS | **The em-quad is the square of a specific type size and therefore varies according to type size (12).** For example, if the type is 10 points, the em-quad is a square that occupies a space of 10 points by 10 points. If the type is 72 points, the em-quad is 72 points square. As the em varies with the type size, any visual effect created by a one em space will be consistent regardless of type size.

In traditional metal typesetting, em-quads, like leads, did not print but were simply used for spacing. Since 1-em was too much space to leave between words, the em-quad was subdivided to produce smaller spaces for wordspacing. (See *Letterspacing and Wordspacing* on page 64.) With the exception of the em, these metal type designations for spacing are no longer used.

A 1-em space is still utilized as the standard paragraph indent and is called a 1-em indent. To get an idea of what a 1-em space looks like, just check the beginning of this paragraph. Since the type size is 8.5 points, the 1-em indent is also 8.5 points.

UNITS | **For today's technologies the em-quad was further subdivided into segments called units (13).** The number of units varies with the typesetting system. The greater the number of units to the em, the greater the possibilities of typographic refinement.

SET-WIDTH | In computer typesetting programs, every character occupies a specific amount of space, measurable in units. This dimension, called the *set-width,* includes a small amount of space on either side to prevent the characters from touching one another.

The wider the character, the greater the set-width; hence, more units required. **For example, based upon a 36-unit system, a cap T may be 22 units wide, while a lowercase y is 18 units wide, and a lowercase e is 20 units wide (14).** A period might require 10 units. The set-width, when expressed in units, is referred to as the *unit value.*

Computer programs for typography allow you to make fine adjustments in the spacing between letters and words. By increasing the number of units (to add space) or reducing the number of units (to delete space) text can be visually refined, thereby granting the designer complete control over the setting.

Five Classic Typefaces

Until now we have dealt with type terminology and measurements. Now we shall study five classic typefaces in detail to learn what distinguishes one typeface from another. This will lead to an enhanced awareness of type design and a greater confidence in your type selection.

Each of the five typefaces represents a distinct stage in the evolution of type design and they remain among the most popular and widely used typefaces today. Below are the names of the typefaces with their classification and approximate date of design.

Garamond (France)	Old Style	1615
Baskerville (England)	Transitional	1757
Bodoni (Italy)	Modern	1788
Century Expanded (U.S.)	Egyptian	1894
Helvetica (Switzerland)	Sans Serif	1957

Classifications

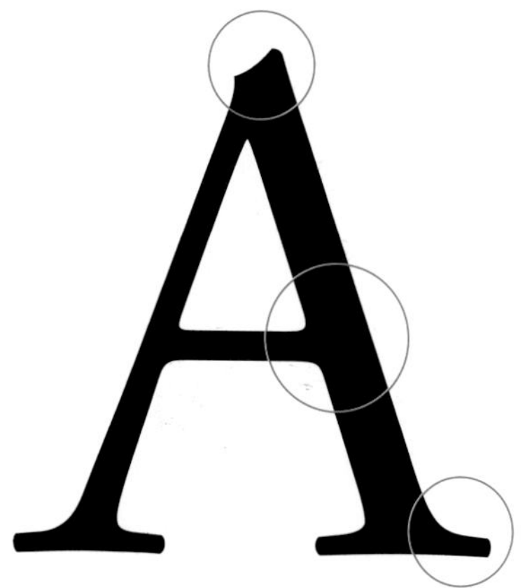

1 | Garamond: Old Style

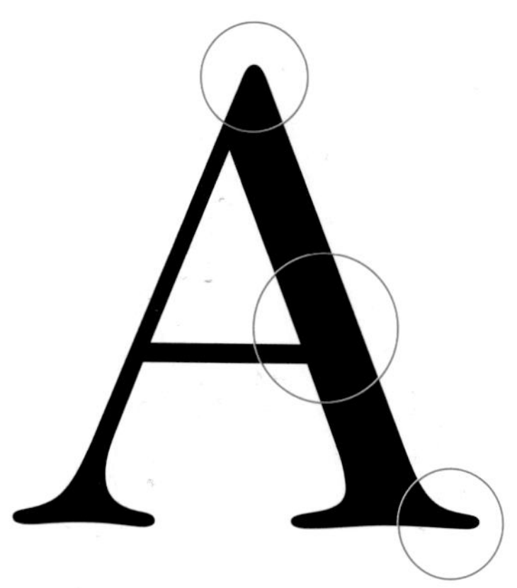

2 | Baskerville: Transitional

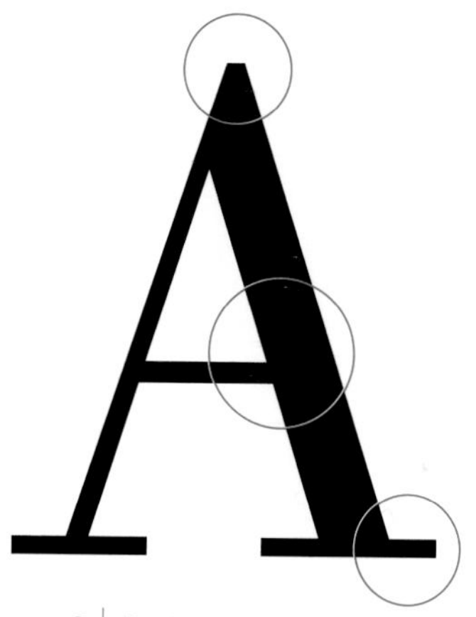

3 | Bodoni: Modern

■ There is no better way to train the eye to discern typographic subtleties than by studying the changing forms in typeface design through the centuries. Just as the great arts — painting, music, and literature — may be classified historically and by style, so too can typefaces.

Listed below are the names of the five classic typefaces with their classifications and approximate dates of design.

Garamond (France)	Old Style	1615
Baskerville (England)	Transitional	1757
Bodoni (Italy)	Modern	1788
Century Expanded (U.S.)	Egyptian (Slab Serif)	1894
Helvetica (Switzerland)	Sans Serif	1957

Understanding these historical divisions is not as important as appreciating the significance of how seemingly small changes in type design can affect both the character of the typeface and how each typeface appears as text on a page.

Old Style, Transitional, and Modern

Perhaps the easiest way to understand the various historical classifications is to consider the first three as one group: Old Style, Transitional, and Modern (1, 2, 3).

OLD STYLE | In Claude Garamond's time (the early 1600s), all papers were hand made and printing technology was still somewhat primitive. A typestyle that we now call "Old Style" was created that complimented the technology. The Old Style typefaces had relatively thick strokes and heavily bracketed serifs (bracketed refers to the curved part where the serif connects with the main stroke).

TRANSITIONAL | By John Baskerville's time (around 1750), technological advances made it possible to produce smoother papers, better printing presses, and improved inks. Therefore Transitional typefaces reflect a trend toward greater refinement; there is an increased contrast between the thick and thin strokes, and the serifs are more sculpted.

MODERN | The extremes of typographic refinement were achieved in the late eighteenth century when the Italian typographer Giambattista Bodoni further reduced the thin strokes and serif to fine hairlines and virtually eliminated the brackets. This modification created an elegant typeface with extreme contrast between the thin and thick strokes.

It is important to note that Claude Garamond did not consider himself a designer of Old Style typefaces, any more than Baskerville considered himself a designer of Transitional typefaces. It is only by studying these faces in retrospect that type scholars came to categorize Garamond as an Old Style typeface and Bodoni as a Modern typeface. Therefore Baskerville, which bridged the gap between Old Style and Modern, became a Transitional typeface.

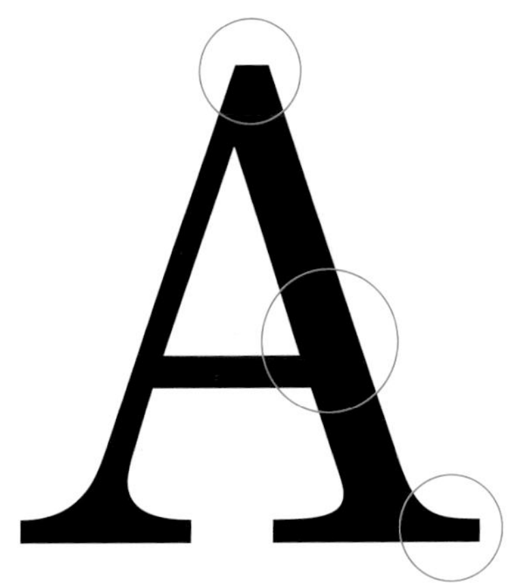

4 | Century Expanded: Egyptian or Slab Serif

Egyptian or Slab Serif

After Bodoni, type design became eclectic. In search of new forms of typographic expression, often to satisfy the need of advertisers, designers began experimenting. They created bold, extended, condensed, and decorative typefaces, producing a greater variety than in any previous century.

One of the typestyles to emerge was Egyptian, also referred to as slab serif or square serif, in which the letterforms are characterized by heavy serifs (4). These typefaces show a return to very little contrast between the thick and thin strokes.

Century Expanded, based on an 1894 design by Linn Boyd Benton, is a refined version of this style. The heavy slab serifs are lighter in weight and modified by the addition of brackets. (Specimens of true slab serif typefaces can be found on page 150.)

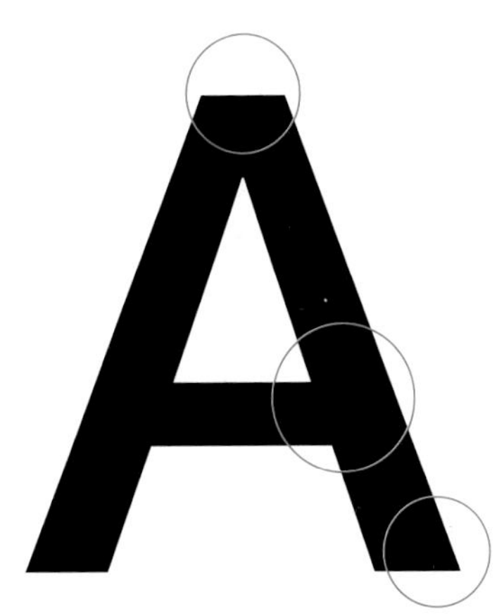

5 | Helvetica: Sans Serif

Sans Serif

Prior to the twentieth century, sans serif typefaces were seldom used, and then usually limited to display purposes and classified advertisements. By the mid-twentieth century, however, sans serif typefaces became popular. The new sans serif designs were refined and contemporary in appearance, but still considered inappropriate for general text purposes. Today sans serif typefaces are commonly used for text as well as for display.

Helvetica, developed in 1957 by Max Miedinger and Eduard Hoffmann, is a well-designed, popular sans serif typeface (5). Helvetica is the most widely used of all sans serif typefaces, and the Helvetica family of typestyles is probably the most diverse.

Helvetica Neue, the typeface you are now reading, was chosen for this book because of its popularity and legibility. ■

NOTE | This section features extensive settings of the five typefaces in varying sizes and linespacing. Take time to study their individual characteristics critically to become familiar with the typefaces and to understand how type size and linespacing can affect readability.

Characteristics

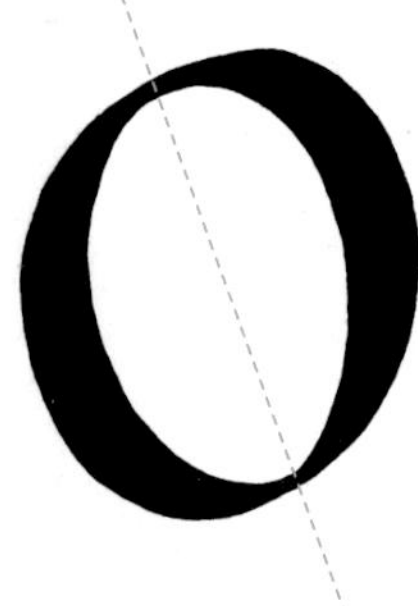

DIAGONAL STRESS OF A PENNED LETTER

On the opposite page, specific letterforms of the five classic typefaces are illustrated. Study these typefaces closely. Each has certain common characteristics and individual characteristics that greatly affect the way that type appears on the printed page.

Common Characteristics

Common characteristics fall into three categories: variations in stress, strokes, and serifs.

VARIATIONS IN STRESS | Basing their designs on the written letterforms of the scribes, early type designers tried to capture as much of the character of this written form as possible. Study the letter O at left, which has been drawn with a calligraphy pen. Notice how the pen has created a thick stroke in the upper right and the lower left, and a thin stroke in the upper left and the lower right of the letter. This distribution of weight creates a diagonal stress through the thin parts of the letterform (as indicated by the dotted line).

This feature was one of the characteristics early type designers followed when designing typefaces, as can be seen quite clearly in Garamond. As type evolved and designers were less influenced by handwriting, the stress became more vertical—as can be seen in Baskerville. Later, with Bodoni, the stress became totally vertical. Century Expanded shows a return to a slight diagonal stress. In Helvetica you will find no noticeable stress at all.

VARIATIONS IN STROKES | Typefaces also vary in the weight of the strokes, that is, in the degree of contrast between the thick and thin parts of the letters. In Garamond we see a prominent characteristic of Old Style faces: relatively little contrast between the weight of the thick and thin strokes of a letter. As we move toward Transitional typefaces, there is a tendency toward refinement and a greater contrast between the thicks and thins. Modern typefaces, such as Bodoni, present the maximum contrast between thick and thin strokes.

After the Modern typefaces, there was a return to less contrast between thick and thin strokes, as can be seen in Century Expanded. In Helvetica there is an absence of any noticeable variation; there is uniformity of strokes.

VARIATIONS IN SERIFS | Serifs also vary from one typeface to another in weight and bracketing, that is, in the way in which the serif meets the vertical stroke of the letter. Once again you can see the evolution of type from the heavy Old Style serif of Garamond through the Transitional serif of Baskerville to the hairline serif of Bodoni.

While Modern typefaces demonstrated the most extreme serif refinement, Century Expanded marked a return to the use of heavy serifs. Helvetica and other trend setting sans serif typefaces of the twentieth century eliminated serifs altogether.

Individual Characteristics

Although the common characteristics are what allow designers to place a typeface in its historic classification, it is the individual characteristics that enable us to identify specific typefaces. As you become more familiar with numerous typefaces, you will be able to distinguish the subtle differences that give a typeface its individuality and character.

When trying to identify an unknown typeface, always look to the individual characters that contain the most design information, such as the uppercase R, T, or W and the lowercase a, e, g, h, or o. These characters provide more visual clues than such letters as the uppercase L or the lowercase i.

Take the time to study the five specimens provided here and familiarize yourself with the individual characteristics that make each face unique.

Notes on Typeface Design

The design of a specific typeface may vary from one manufacturer to another. For this reason, one Garamond may look quite different from another Garamond, not only in design but also in x-height, the number of characters per pica, and even the name. A typeface identical to Helvetica may be named Helios, Vega, or ITC Helvetica, depending on the manufacturer.

Generally speaking, this lack of standardization can be a problem, especially if you need to share files with other designers, service bureaus, or clients. To minimize this problem, always be certain that everyone working on your project is using exactly the same fonts produced by the same manufacturer, and owns a license to use them. Keep in mind that specific fonts are protected by copyright.

The following are the specific versions of the five classic typefaces used in this book along with the names of the foundries or manufacturers.

Adobe Garamond	Linotype Library
Baskerville MT	AGFA Monotype
Bauer Bodoni	Bauer Types, Linotype Library
Century Expanded	Bitstream
Neue Helvetica	Heidelberger Druckmaschinen AG, Linotype Library

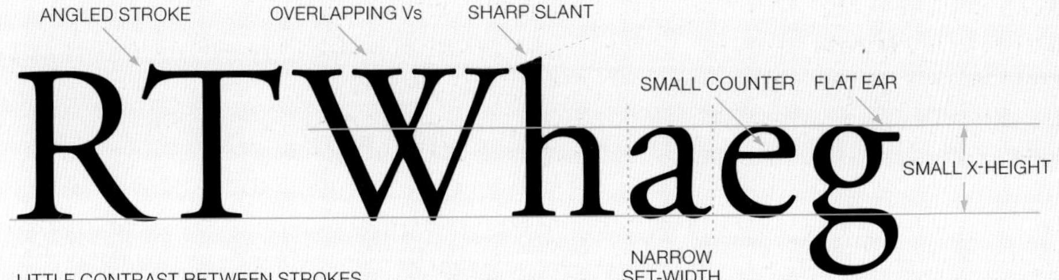

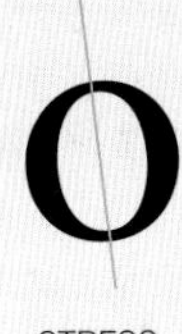

GARAMOND
OLD STYLE

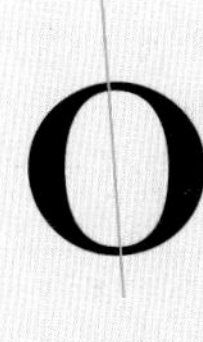

BASKERVILLE
TRANSITIONAL

BODONI
MODERN

FLOPPY EAR

RTWhaeg

LARGE X-HEIGHT

o

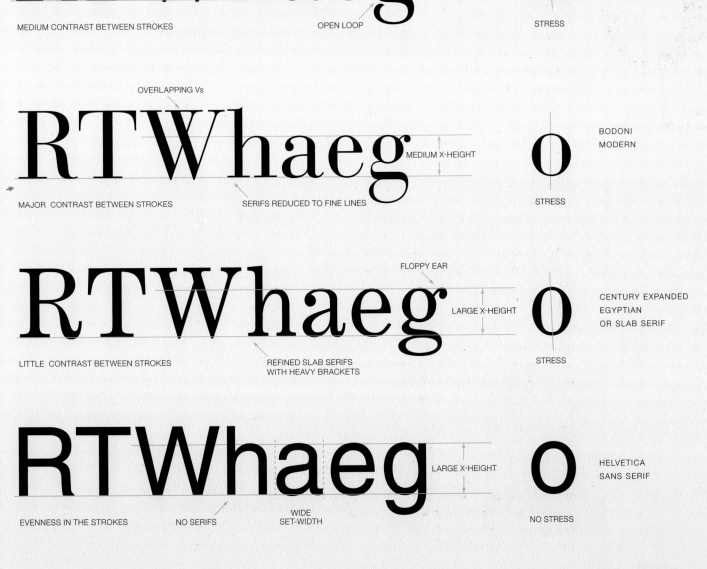

LITTLE CONTRAST BETWEEN STROKES

REFINED SLAB SERIFS
WITH HEAVY BRACKETS

STRESS

CENTURY EXPANDED
EGYPTIAN
OR SLAB SERIF

RTWhaeg

LARGE X-HEIGHT

o

EVENNESS IN THE STROKES

NO SERIFS

WIDE
SET-WIDTH

NO STRESS

HELVETICA
SANS SERIF

Garamond is a classic Old Style typeface. Claude Garamond, who died in 1561, was originally credited with the design of this elegant French typeface; however, it has recently been discovered that this typeface was designed by Jean Jannon in 1615. Many of the present-day versions of this elegant typeface may be either Garamond or Jannon designs, although they are all called Garamond. This is a typical Old Style face, having very little contrast between the thicks and thins, heavily bracketed serifs, and oblique stress. The capital letters are shorter than the ascenders of the lowercase letters. *The letterforms are open and round, making the face extremely readable.*

20/30 GARAMOND

Claude Garamond (1480–1561) was born in Paris, France, and worked for the scholar and printer Robert Estienne, where he learned to cut punches and cast typefaces. Garamond later established himself as a punch cutter, printer, and operator of a type foundry. Garamond is credited with being among the first printers who designed and cast typefaces to be sold to other printers. Perhaps Garamond's greatest contribution was the freeing of type design from its dependence on calligraphic forms. Instead of trying to make type look like writing, he allowed the metal to dictate the letterforms.

2

ABCDEFGHIJKLMNO
PQRSTUVWXYZ&
abcdefghijklmnopqrstuvwxyz
1234567890.,“ ” ‘ ’; : ! ? fi fl

LINING FIGURES LIGATURES

ABCDEFGHIJKLMNOPQRSTU

SMALL CAPS

VWXYZ 1234567890

48-POINT GARAMOND OLD STYLE FIGURES

ABCDEFGHIJKLMNOP
QRSTUVWXYZ& fi fl
abcdefghijklmnopqrstuvwxyz
1234567890.,“ ” ‘ ’; : ! ?
1234567890

48-POINT GARAMOND ITALIC

72-POINT Designing with Ty

60-POINT Designing with Typ

48-POINT Designing with Type

36-POINT Designing with Type

30-POINT Designing with Type

24-POINT Designing with Type

18-POINT Designing with Type

72-POINT *Designing with Ty*

60-POINT *Designing with Type*

48-POINT *Designing with Type*

36-POINT *Designing with Type*

30-POINT *Designing with Type*

24-POINT *Designing with Type*

18-POINT *Designing with Type*

14/14

Garamond is a classic Old Style typeface. Claude Garamond, who died in 1561, was originally credited with the design of this elegant French typeface; however, it has recently been discovered that this typeface was designed by Jean Jannon in 1615. Many of the present-day versions of this elegant typeface may be either Garamond or Jannon designs, although they are all called Garamond. This is a typical Old Style face, having very little contrast between the thicks and thins, heavily bracketed serifs, and oblique stress. The capital letters are shorter than the ascenders of the lowercase letters. *The letterforms are open and round, making the face extremely readable.*

12/12

Garamond is a classic Old Style typeface. Claude Garamond, who died in 1561, was originally credited with the design of this elegant French typeface; however, it has recently been discovered that this typeface was designed by Jean Jannon in 1615. Many of the present-day versions of this elegant typeface may be either Garamond or Jannon designs, although they are all called Garamond. This is a typical Old Style face, having very little contrast between the thicks and thins, heavily bracketed serifs, and oblique stress. The capital letters are shorter than the ascenders of the lowercase letters. *The letterforms are open and round, making the face extremely readable.*

11/11

Garamond is a classic Old Style typeface. Claude Garamond, who died in 1561, was originally credited with the design of this elegant French typeface; however, it has recently been discovered that this typeface was designed by Jean Jannon in 1615. Many of the present-day versions of this elegant typeface may be either Garamond or Jannon designs, although they are all called Garamond. This is a typical Old Style face, having very little contrast between the thicks and thins, heavily bracketed serifs, and oblique stress. The capital letters are shorter than the ascenders of the lowercase letters. *The letterforms are open and round, making the face extremely readable.*

10/10

Garamond is a classic Old Style typeface. Claude Garamond, who died in 1561, was originally credited with the design of this elegant French typeface; however, it has recently been discovered that this typeface was designed by Jean Jannon in 1615. Many of the present-day versions of this elegant typeface may be either Garamond or Jannon designs, although they are all called Garamond. This is a typical Old Style face, having very little contrast between the thicks and thins, heavily bracketed serifs, and oblique stress. The capital letters are shorter than the ascenders of the lowercase letters. *The letterforms are open and round, making the face extremely readable.*

9/9

Garamond is a classic Old Style typeface. Claude Garamond, who died in 1561, was originally credited with the design of this elegant French typeface; however, it has recently been discovered that this typeface was designed by Jean Jannon in 1615. Many of the present-day versions of this elegant typeface may be either Garamond or Jannon designs, although they are all called Garamond. This is a typical Old Style face, having very little contrast between the thicks and thins, heavily bracketed serifs, and oblique stress. The capital letters are shorter than the ascenders of the lowercase letters. *The letterforms are open and round, making the face extremely readable.*

8/8

Garamond is a classic Old Style typeface. Claude Garamond, who died in 1561, was originally credited with the design of this elegant French typeface; however, it has recently been discovered that this typeface was designed by Jean Jannon in 1615. Many of the present-day versions of this elegant typeface may be either Garamond or Jannon designs, although they are all called Garamond. This is a typical Old Style face, having very little contrast between the thicks and thins, heavily bracketed serifs, and oblique stress. The capital letters are shorter than the ascenders of the lowercase letters. *The letterforms are open and round, making the face extremely readable.*

Garamond | Old Style

14/15 Garamond is a classic Old Style typeface. Claude Garamond, who died in 1561, was originally credited with the design of this elegant French typeface; however, it has recently been discovered that this typeface was designed by Jean Jannon in 1615. Many of the present-day versions of this elegant typeface may be either Garamond or Jannon designs, although they are all called Garamond. This is a typical Old Style face, having very little contrast between the thicks and thins, heavily bracketed serifs, and oblique stress. The capital letters are shorter than the ascenders of the lowercase letters. *The letterforms are open and round, making the face extremely readable.*

12/13 Garamond is a classic Old Style typeface. Claude Garamond, who died in 1561, was originally credited with the design of this elegant French typeface; however, it has recently been discovered that this typeface was designed by Jean Jannon in 1615. Many of the present-day versions of this elegant typeface may be either Garamond or Jannon designs, although they are all called Garamond. This is a typical Old Style face, having very little contrast between the thicks and thins, heavily bracketed serifs, and oblique stress. The capital letters are shorter than the ascenders of the lowercase letters. *The letterforms are open and round, making the face extremely readable.*

11/12 Garamond is a classic Old Style typeface. Claude Garamond, who died in 1561, was originally credited with the design of this elegant French typeface; however, it has recently been discovered that this typeface was designed by Jean Jannon in 1615. Many of the present-day versions of this elegant typeface may be either Garamond or Jannon designs, although they are all called Garamond. This is a typical Old Style face, having very little contrast between the thicks and thins, heavily bracketed serifs, and oblique stress. The capital letters are shorter than the ascenders of the lowercase letters. *The letterforms are open and round, making the face extremely readable.*

10/11 Garamond is a classic Old Style typeface. Claude Garamond, who died in 1561, was originally credited with the design of this elegant French typeface; however, it has recently been discovered that this typeface was designed by Jean Jannon in 1615. Many of the present-day versions of this elegant typeface may be either Garamond or Jannon designs, although they are all called Garamond. This is a typical Old Style face, having very little contrast between the thicks and thins, heavily bracketed serifs, and oblique stress. The capital letters are shorter than the ascenders of the lowercase letters. *The letterforms are open and round, making the face extremely readable.*

9/10 Garamond is a classic Old Style typeface. Claude Garamond, who died in 1561, was originally credited with the design of this elegant French typeface; however, it has recently been discovered that this typeface was designed by Jean Jannon in 1615. Many of the present-day versions of this elegant typeface may be either Garamond or Jannon designs, although they are all called Garamond. This is a typical Old Style face, having very little contrast between the thicks and thins, heavily bracketed serifs, and oblique stress. The capital letters are shorter than the ascenders of the lowercase letters. *The letterforms are open and round, making the face extremely readable.*

8/9 Garamond is a classic Old Style typeface. Claude Garamond, who died in 1561, was originally credited with the design of this elegant French typeface; however, it has recently been discovered that this typeface was designed by Jean Jannon in 1615. Many of the present-day versions of this elegant typeface may be either Garamond or Jannon designs, although they are all called Garamond. This is a typical Old Style face, having very little contrast between the thicks and thins, heavily bracketed serifs, and oblique stress. The capital letters are shorter than the ascenders of the lowercase letters. *The letterforms are open and round, making the face extremely readable.*

14/16

Garamond is a classic Old Style typeface. Claude Garamond, who died in 1561, was originally credited with the design of this elegant French typeface; however, it has recently been discovered that this typeface was designed by Jean Jannon in 1615. Many of the present-day versions of this elegant typeface may be either Garamond or Jannon designs, although they are all called Garamond. This is a typical Old Style face, having very little contrast between the thicks and thins, heavily bracketed serifs, and oblique stress. The capital letters are shorter than the ascenders of the lowercase letters. *The letterforms are open and round, making the face extremely readable.*

12/14

Garamond is a classic Old Style typeface. Claude Garamond, who died in 1561, was originally credited with the design of this elegant French typeface; however, it has recently been discovered that this typeface was designed by Jean Jannon in 1615. Many of the present-day versions of this elegant typeface may be either Garamond or Jannon designs, although they are all called Garamond. This is a typical Old Style face, having very little contrast between the thicks and thins, heavily bracketed serifs, and oblique stress. The capital letters are shorter than the ascenders of the lowercase letters. *The letterforms are open and round, making the face extremely readable.*

11/13

Garamond is a classic Old Style typeface. Claude Garamond, who died in 1561, was originally credited with the design of this elegant French typeface; however, it has recently been discovered that this typeface was designed by Jean Jannon in 1615. Many of the present-day versions of this elegant typeface may be either Garamond or Jannon designs, although they are all called Garamond. This is a typical Old Style face, having very little contrast between the thicks and thins, heavily bracketed serifs, and oblique stress. The capital letters are shorter than the ascenders of the lowercase letters. *The letterforms are open and round, making the face extremely readable.*

10/12

Garamond is a classic Old Style typeface. Claude Garamond, who died in 1561, was originally credited with the design of this elegant French typeface; however, it has recently been discovered that this typeface was designed by Jean Jannon in 1615. Many of the present-day versions of this elegant typeface may be either Garamond or Jannon designs, although they are all called Garamond. This is a typical Old Style face, having very little contrast between the thicks and thins, heavily bracketed serifs, and oblique stress. The capital letters are shorter than the ascenders of the lowercase letters. *The letterforms are open and round, making the face extremely readable.*

9/11

Garamond is a classic Old Style typeface. Claude Garamond, who died in 1561, was originally credited with the design of this elegant French typeface; however, it has recently been discovered that this typeface was designed by Jean Jannon in 1615. Many of the present-day versions of this elegant typeface may be either Garamond or Jannon designs, although they are all called Garamond. This is a typical Old Style face, having very little contrast between the thicks and thins, heavily bracketed serifs, and oblique stress. The capital letters are shorter than the ascenders of the lowercase letters. *The letterforms are open and round, making the face extremely readable.*

8/10

Garamond is a classic Old Style typeface. Claude Garamond, who died in 1561, was originally credited with the design of this elegant French typeface; however, it has recently been discovered that this typeface was designed by Jean Jannon in 1615. Many of the present-day versions of this elegant typeface may be either Garamond or Jannon designs, although they are all called Garamond. This is a typical Old Style face, having very little contrast between the thicks and thins, heavily bracketed serifs, and oblique stress. The capital letters are shorter than the ascenders of the lowercase letters. *The letterforms are open and round, making the face extremely readable.*

Baskerville, an elegant, well-designed typeface created by the Englishman John Baskerville in 1757, is an excellent example of a Transitional typeface. Transitional typefaces are so called because they form a bridge between the Old Style and the Modern faces. Compared to the Old Style, Transitional typefaces show greater contrast between the thicks and thins, serifs are less heavily bracketed, and the stress is almost vertical. Baskerville characters are very wide for their x-height, are closely fitted, and are of excellent proportions. *Baskerville is considered one of the most pleasant and readable typefaces.*

20/30 BASKERVILLE

John Baskerville (1706–1775) was born in Wolverley, England, and began his career as a writing master, but gave it up to make his fortune in the japanning business in Birmingham. After retiring at the age of forty-four, Baskerville returned to his first love, letterforms, and began printing as a wealthy amateur.

Extremely dissatisfied with the state of English printing and typography, Baskerville decided to print his own books, to show by example what could be done when one took pains with every stage of production.

Baskerville is also credited by some with being the first to print on "wove" paper, a smoother surface that allowed for finer detail than the traditional "laid" paper with its rougher surface.

ABCDEFGHIJKLMN
OPQRSTUVWXYZ&
abcdefghijklmnopqrstu
vwxyz 1234567890 fi fl

LINING FIGURES LIGATURES

. , " " ' ' ; : ! ?

48-POINT BASKERVILLE

ABCDEFGHIJKLMN
OPQRSTUVWXYZ&
abcdefghijklmnopqrstu
vwxyz 1234567890 fi fl
. , " " ' ' ; : ! ?

48-POINTBASKERVILLE ITALIC

Baskerville | Transitional

72-POINT Designing with Ty

60-POINT Designing with Typ

48-POINT Designing with Type

36-POINT Designing with Type

30-POINT Designing with Type

24-POINT Designing with Type

18-POINT Designing with Type

72-POINT *Designing with Type*

60-POINT *Designing with Type*

48-POINT *Designing with Type*

36-POINT *Designing with Type*

30-POINT *Designing with Type*

24-POINT *Designing with Type*

18-POINT *Designing with Type*

Baskerville, an elegant, well-designed typeface created by the Englishman John Baskerville in 1757, is an excellent example of a Transitional typeface. Transitional typefaces are so called because they form a bridge between the Old Style and the Modern faces. Compared to the Old Style, Transitional typefaces show greater contrast between the thicks and thins, serifs are less heavily bracketed, and the stress is almost vertical. Baskerville characters are very wide for their x-height, are closely fitted, and are of excellent proportions. *Baskerville is considered one of the most pleasant and readable typefaces.* 14/14

Baskerville, an elegant, well-designed typeface created by the Englishman John Baskerville in 1757, is an excellent example of a Transitional typeface. Transitional typefaces are so called because they form a bridge between the Old Style and the Modern faces. Compared to the Old Style, Transitional typefaces show greater contrast between the thicks and thins, serifs are less heavily bracketed, and the stress is almost vertical. Baskerville characters are very wide for their x-height, are closely fitted, and are of excellent proportions. *Baskerville is considered one of the most pleasant and readable typefaces.* 12/12

Baskerville, an elegant, well-designed typeface created by the Englishman John Baskerville in 1757, is an excellent example of a Transitional typeface. Transitional typefaces are so called because they form a bridge between the Old Style and the Modern faces. Compared to the Old Style, Transitional typefaces show greater contrast between the thicks and thins, serifs are less heavily bracketed, and the stress is almost vertical. Baskerville characters are very wide for their x-height, are closely fitted, and are of excellent proportions. *Baskerville is considered one of the most pleasant and readable typefaces.* 11/11

Baskerville, an elegant, well-designed typeface created by the Englishman John Baskerville in 1757, is an excellent example of a Transitional typeface. Transitional typefaces are so called because they form a bridge between the Old Style and the Modern faces. Compared to the Old Style, Transitional typefaces show greater contrast between the thicks and thins, serifs are less heavily bracketed, and the stress is almost vertical. Baskerville characters are very wide for their x-height, are closely fitted, and are of excellent proportions. *Baskerville is considered one of the most pleasant and readable typefaces.* 10/10

Baskerville, an elegant, well-designed typeface created by the Englishman John Baskerville in 1757, is an excellent example of a Transitional typeface. Transitional typefaces are so called because they form a bridge between the Old Style and the Modern faces. Compared to the Old Style, Transitional typefaces show greater contrast between the thicks and thins, serifs are less heavily bracketed, and the stress is almost vertical. Baskerville characters are very wide for their x-height, are closely fitted, and are of excellent proportions. *Baskerville is considered one of the most pleasant and readable typefaces.* 9/9

Baskerville, an elegant, well-designed typeface created by the Englishman John Baskerville in 1757, is an excellent example of a Transitional typeface. Transitional typefaces are so called because they form a bridge between the Old Style and the Modern faces. Compared to the Old Style, Transitional typefaces show greater contrast between the thicks and thins, serifs are less heavily bracketed, and the stress is almost vertical. Baskerville characters are very wide for their x-height, are closely fitted, and are of excellent proportions. *Baskerville is considered one of the most pleasant and readable typefaces.* 8/8

Baskerville | Transitional

14/15 Baskerville, an elegant, well-designed typeface created by the Englishman John Baskerville in 1757, is an excellent example of a Transitional typeface. Transitional typefaces are so called because they form a bridge between the Old Style and the Modern faces. Compared to the Old Style, Transitional typefaces show greater contrast between the thicks and thins, serifs are less heavily bracketed, and the stress is almost vertical. Baskerville characters are very wide for their x-height, are closely fitted, and are of excellent proportions. *Baskerville is considered one of the most pleasant and readable typefaces.*

12/13 Baskerville, an elegant, well-designed typeface created by the Englishman John Baskerville in 1757, is an excellent example of a Transitional typeface. Transitional typefaces are so called because they form a bridge between the Old Style and the Modern faces. Compared to the Old Style, Transitional typefaces show greater contrast between the thicks and thins, serifs are less heavily bracketed, and the stress is almost vertical. Baskerville characters are very wide for their x-height, are closely fitted, and are of excellent proportions. *Baskerville is considered one of the most pleasant and readable typefaces.*

11/12 Baskerville, an elegant, well-designed typeface created by the Englishman John Baskerville in 1757, is an excellent example of a Transitional typeface. Transitional typefaces are so called because they form a bridge between the Old Style and the Modern faces. Compared to the Old Style, Transitional typefaces show greater contrast between the thicks and thins, serifs are less heavily bracketed, and the stress is almost vertical. Baskerville characters are very wide for their x-height, are closely fitted, and are of excellent proportions. *Baskerville is considered one of the most pleasant and readable typefaces.*

10/11 Baskerville, an elegant, well-designed typeface created by the Englishman John Baskerville in 1757, is an excellent example of a Transitional typeface. Transitional typefaces are so called because they form a bridge between the Old Style and the Modern faces. Compared to the Old Style, Transitional typefaces show greater contrast between the thicks and thins, serifs are less heavily bracketed, and the stress is almost vertical. Baskerville characters are very wide for their x-height, are closely fitted, and are of excellent proportions. *Baskerville is considered one of the most pleasant and readable typefaces.*

9/10 Baskerville, an elegant, well-designed typeface created by the Englishman John Baskerville in 1757, is an excellent example of a Transitional typeface. Transitional typefaces are so called because they form a bridge between the Old Style and the Modern faces. Compared to the Old Style, Transitional typefaces show greater contrast between the thicks and thins, serifs are less heavily bracketed, and the stress is almost vertical. Baskerville characters are very wide for their x-height, are closely fitted, and are of excellent proportions. *Baskerville is considered one of the most pleasant and readable typefaces.*

8/9 Baskerville, an elegant, well-designed typeface created by the Englishman John Baskerville in 1757, is an excellent example of a Transitional typeface. Transitional typefaces are so called because they form a bridge between the Old Style and the Modern faces. Compared to the Old Style, Transitional typefaces show greater contrast between the thicks and thins, serifs are less heavily bracketed, and the stress is almost vertical. Baskerville characters are very wide for their x-height, are closely fitted, and are of excellent proportions. *Baskerville is considered one of the most pleasant and readable typefaces.*

Baskerville, an elegant, well-designed typeface created by the Englishman John Baskerville in 1757, is an excellent example of a Transitional typeface. Transitional typefaces are so called because they form a bridge between the Old Style and the Modern faces. Compared to the Old Style, Transitional typefaces show greater contrast between the thicks and thins, serifs are less heavily bracketed, and the stress is almost vertical. Baskerville characters are very wide for their x-height, are closely fitted, and are of excellent proportions. *Baskerville is considered one of the most pleasant and readable typefaces.* 14/16

Baskerville, an elegant, well-designed typeface created by the Englishman John Baskerville in 1757, is an excellent example of a Transitional typeface. Transitional typefaces are so called because they form a bridge between the Old Style and the Modern faces. Compared to the Old Style, Transitional typefaces show greater contrast between the thicks and thins, serifs are less heavily bracketed, and the stress is almost vertical. Baskerville characters are very wide for their x-height, are closely fitted, and are of excellent proportions. *Baskerville is considered one of the most pleasant and readable typefaces.* 12/14

Baskerville, an elegant, well-designed typeface created by the Englishman John Baskerville in 1757, is an excellent example of a Transitional typeface. Transitional typefaces are so called because they form a bridge between the Old Style and the Modern faces. Compared to the Old Style, Transitional typefaces show greater contrast between the thicks and thins, serifs are less heavily bracketed, and the stress is almost vertical. Baskerville characters are very wide for their x-height, are closely fitted, and are of excellent proportions. *Baskerville is considered one of the most pleasant and readable typefaces.* 11/13

Baskerville, an elegant, well-designed typeface created by the Englishman John Baskerville in 1757, is an excellent example of a Transitional typeface. Transitional typefaces are so called because they form a bridge between the Old Style and the Modern faces. Compared to the Old Style, Transitional typefaces show greater contrast between the thicks and thins, serifs are less heavily bracketed, and the stress is almost vertical. Baskerville characters are very wide for their x-height, are closely fitted, and are of excellent proportions. *Baskerville is considered one of the most pleasant and readable typefaces.* 10/12

Baskerville, an elegant, well-designed typeface created by the Englishman John Baskerville in 1757, is an excellent example of a Transitional typeface. Transitional typefaces are so called because they form a bridge between the Old Style and the Modern faces. Compared to the Old Style, Transitional typefaces show greater contrast between the thicks and thins, serifs are less heavily bracketed, and the stress is almost vertical. Baskerville characters are very wide for their x-height, are closely fitted, and are of excellent proportions. *Baskerville is considered one of the most pleasant and readable typefaces.* 9/10

Baskerville, an elegant, well-designed typeface created by the Englishman John Baskerville in 1757, is an excellent example of a Transitional typeface. Transitional typefaces are so called because they form a bridge between the Old Style and the Modern faces. Compared to the Old Style, Transitional typefaces show greater contrast between the thicks and thins, serifs are less heavily bracketed, and the stress is almost vertical. Baskerville characters are very wide for their x-height, are closely fitted, and are of excellent proportions. *Baskerville is considered one of the most pleasant and readable typefaces.* 8/10

Bodoni is a Modern typeface, designed in the late 1700s by the Italian typographer Giambattista Bodoni. At the end of the eighteenth century, a fashion grew for faces with a stronger contrast between the thicks and thins, unbracketed serifs, and a strong vertical stress. These were called Modern typefaces. All the older faces became known as Old Style, while the more recent faces—just prior to the change—were referred to as Transitional. Although Bodoni has a small x-height, it appears very wide and black. *Because of the strong vertical stress, accentuated by its heavy thicks and hairline thins, Bodoni should be well leaded.*

20/30 BODONI

Galleria Nazionale, Parma

Giambattista Bodoni (1740–1813) was born in Saluzzo, Italy, and became his country's most renowned type designer and printer. At the age of twenty-eight, Bodoni was invited by Duke Ferdinand of Parma to set up a private press and type foundry. The operation was called Stamperia Reale and it was here that Bodoni designed many of his famous typefaces. By using smooth, hard-surfaced paper, rich black ink, large type, and generous leading, Bodoni created layouts that were open, formal, and free of unnecessary decoration.

A great part of Bodoni's fame rests on the superb printing of the works of Horace and Virgil and the two-volume edition of his *Manuele Typographica*, designed by him, but issued by his wife, Margherita Dall'Aglio, after his death.

ABCDEFGHIJKLMN
OPQRSTUVWXYZ&
abcdefghijklmnopqr
stuvwxyz 1234567890

LINING FIGURES

ﬁ ﬂ ABCDEFGHIJKLMNOPQ

LIGATURES SMALL CAPS

RSTUVWXYZ 1234567890

OLD STYLE FIGURES

. , " " ' ' ; : ! ?

48-POINT BODONI

ABCDEFGHIJKLMNO
PQRSTUVWXYZ&
abcdefghijklmnopqrstuv
wxyz 1234567890 ﬁ ﬂ
1234567890 . , " " ' ' ; : ! ?

48-POINT BODONI ITALIC

72-POINT Designing with Ty

60-POINT Designing with Typ

48-POINT Designing with Type

36-POINT Designing with Type

30-POINT Designing with Type

24-POINT Designing with Type

18-POINT Designing with Type

72-POINT *Designing with T*

60-POINT *Designing with Typ*

48-POINT *Designing with Type*

36-POINT *Designing with Type*

30-POINT *Designing with Type*

24-POINT *Designing with Type*

18-POINT *Designing with Type*

2

Bodoni is a Modern typeface, designed in the late 1700s by the Italian typographer GIAMBATTISTA BODONI. At the end of the eighteenth century, a fashion grew for faces with a stronger contrast between the thicks and thins, unbracketed serifs, and a strong vertical stress. These were called Modern typefaces. All the older faces became known as Old Style, while the more recent faces—just prior to the change—were referred to as Transitional. Although Bodoni has a small x-height, it appears very wide and black. *Because of the strong vertical stress, accentuated by its heavy thicks and hairline thins, Bodoni should be well leaded.* 14/14

Bodoni is a Modern typeface, designed in the late 1700s by the Italian typographer GIAMBATTISTA BODONI. At the end of the eighteenth century, a fashion grew for faces with a stronger contrast between the thicks and thins, unbracketed serifs, and a strong vertical stress. These were called Modern typefaces. All the older faces became known as Old Style, while the more recent faces—just prior to the change—were referred to as Transitional. Although Bodoni has a small x-height, it appears very wide and black. *Because of the strong vertical stress, accentuated by its heavy thicks and hairline thins, Bodoni should be well leaded.* 12/12

Bodoni is a Modern typeface, designed in the late 1700s by the Italian typographer GIAMBATTISTA BODONI. At the end of the eighteenth century, a fashion grew for faces with a stronger contrast between the thicks and thins, unbracketed serifs, and a strong vertical stress. These were called Modern typefaces. All the older faces became known as Old Style, while the more recent faces—just prior to the change—were referred to as Transitional. Although Bodoni has a small x-height, it appears very wide and black. *Because of the strong vertical stress, accentuated by its heavy thicks and hairline thins, Bodoni should be well leaded.* 11/11

Bodoni is a Modern typeface, designed in the late 1700s by the Italian typographer GIAMBATTISTA BODONI. At the end of the eighteenth century, a fashion grew for faces with a stronger contrast between the thicks and thins, unbracketed serifs, and a strong vertical stress. These were called Modern typefaces. All the older faces became known as Old Style, while the more recent faces—just prior to the change—were referred to as Transitional. Although Bodoni has a small x-height, it appears very wide and black. *Because of the strong vertical stress, accentuated by its heavy thicks and hairline thins, Bodoni should be well leaded.* 10/10

Bodoni is a Modern typeface, designed in the late 1700s by the Italian typographer GIAMBATTISTA BODONI. At the end of the eighteenth century, a fashion grew for faces with a stronger contrast between the thicks and thins, unbracketed serifs, and a strong vertical stress. These were called Modern typefaces. All the older faces became known as Old Style, while the more recent faces—just prior to the change—were referred to as Transitional. Although Bodoni has a small x-height, it appears very wide and black. *Because of the strong vertical stress, accentuated by its heavy thicks and hairline thins, Bodoni should be well leaded.* 9/9

Bodoni is a Modern typeface, designed in the late 1700s by the Italian typographer GIAMBATTISTA BODONI. At the end of the eighteenth century, a fashion grew for faces with a stronger contrast between the thicks and thins, unbracketed serifs, and a strong vertical stress. These were called Modern typefaces. All the older faces became known as Old Style, while the more recent faces—just prior to the change—were referred to as Transitional. Although Bodoni has a small x-height, it appears very wide and black. *Because of the strong vertical stress, accentuated by its heavy thicks and hairline thins, Bodoni should be well leaded.* 8/8

Bodoni | Modern

14/15 Bodoni is a Modern typeface, designed in the late 1700s by the Italian typographer Giambattista Bodoni. At the end of the eighteenth century, a fashion grew for faces with a stronger contrast between the thicks and thins, unbracketed serifs, and a strong vertical stress. These were called Modern typefaces. All the older faces became known as Old Style, while the more recent faces—just prior to the change—were referred to as Transitional. Although Bodoni has a small x-height, it appears very wide and black. *Because of the strong vertical stress, accentuated by its heavy thicks and hairline thins, Bodoni should be well leaded.*

12/13 Bodoni is a Modern typeface, designed in the late 1700s by the Italian typographer Giambattista Bodoni. At the end of the eighteenth century, a fashion grew for faces with a stronger contrast between the thicks and thins, unbracketed serifs, and a strong vertical stress. These were called Modern typefaces. All the older faces became known as Old Style, while the more recent faces—just prior to the change—were referred to as Transitional. Although Bodoni has a small x-height, it appears very wide and black. *Because of the strong vertical stress, accentuated by its heavy thicks and hairline thins, Bodoni should be well leaded.*

11/12 Bodoni is a Modern typeface, designed in the late 1700s by the Italian typographer Giambattista Bodoni. At the end of the eighteenth century, a fashion grew for faces with a stronger contrast between the thicks and thins, unbracketed serifs, and a strong vertical stress. These were called Modern typefaces. All the older faces became known as Old Style, while the more recent faces—just prior to the change—were referred to as Transitional. Although Bodoni has a small x-height, it appears very wide and black. *Because of the strong vertical stress, accentuated by its heavy thicks and hairline thins, Bodoni should be well leaded.*

10/11 Bodoni is a Modern typeface, designed in the late 1700s by the Italian typographer Giambattista Bodoni. At the end of the eighteenth century, a fashion grew for faces with a stronger contrast between the thicks and thins, unbracketed serifs, and a strong vertical stress. These were called Modern typefaces. All the older faces became known as Old Style, while the more recent faces—just prior to the change—were referred to as Transitional. Although Bodoni has a small x-height, it appears very wide and black. *Because of the strong vertical stress, accentuated by its heavy thicks and hairline thins, Bodoni should be well leaded.*

9/10 Bodoni is a Modern typeface, designed in the late 1700s by the Italian typographer Giambattista Bodoni. At the end of the eighteenth century, a fashion grew for faces with a stronger contrast between the thicks and thins, unbracketed serifs, and a strong vertical stress. These were called Modern typefaces. All the older faces became known as Old Style, while the more recent faces—just prior to the change—were referred to as Transitional. Although Bodoni has a small x-height, it appears very wide and black. *Because of the strong vertical stress, accentuated by its heavy thicks and hairline thins, Bodoni should be well leaded.*

8/9 Bodoni is a Modern typeface, designed in the late 1700s by the Italian typographer Giambattista Bodoni. At the end of the eighteenth century, a fashion grew for faces with a stronger contrast between the thicks and thins, unbracketed serifs, and a strong vertical stress. These were called Modern typefaces. All the older faces became known as Old Style, while the more recent faces—just prior to the change—were referred to as Transitional. Although Bodoni has a small x-height, it appears very wide and black. *Because of the strong vertical stress, accentuated by its heavy thicks and hairline thins, Bodoni should be well leaded.*

Bodoni is a Modern typeface, designed in the late 1700s by the Italian typographer GIAMBATTISTA BODONI. At the end of the eighteenth century, a fashion grew for faces with a stronger contrast between the thicks and thins, unbracketed serifs, and a strong vertical stress. These were called Modern typefaces. All the older faces became known as Old Style, while the more recent faces—just prior to the change—were referred to as Transitional. Although Bodoni has a small x-height, it appears very wide and black. *Because of the strong vertical stress, accentuated by its heavy thicks and hairline thins, Bodoni should be well leaded.* 14/16

Bodoni is a Modern typeface, designed in the late 1700s by the Italian typographer GIAMBATTISTA BODONI. At the end of the eighteenth century, a fashion grew for faces with a stronger contrast between the thicks and thins, unbracketed serifs, and a strong vertical stress. These were called Modern typefaces. All the older faces became known as Old Style, while the more recent faces—just prior to the change—were referred to as Transitional. Although Bodoni has a small x-height, it appears very wide and black. *Because of the strong vertical stress, accentuated by its heavy thicks and hairline thins, Bodoni should be well leaded.* 12/14

Bodoni is a Modern typeface, designed in the late 1700s by the Italian typographer GIAMBATTISTA BODONI. At the end of the eighteenth century, a fashion grew for faces with a stronger contrast between the thicks and thins, unbracketed serifs, and a strong vertical stress. These were called Modern typefaces. All the older faces became known as Old Style, while the more recent faces—just prior to the change—were referred to as Transitional. Although Bodoni has a small x-height, it appears very wide and black. *Because of the strong vertical stress, accentuated by its heavy thicks and hairline thins, Bodoni should be well leaded.* 11/13

Bodoni is a Modern typeface, designed in the late 1700s by the Italian typographer GIAMBATTISTA BODONI. At the end of the eighteenth century, a fashion grew for faces with a stronger contrast between the thicks and thins, unbracketed serifs, and a strong vertical stress. These were called Modern typefaces. All the older faces became known as Old Style, while the more recent faces—just prior to the change—were referred to as Transitional. Although Bodoni has a small x-height, it appears very wide and black. *Because of the strong vertical stress, accentuated by its heavy thicks and hairline thins, Bodoni should be well leaded.* 10/12

Bodoni is a Modern typeface, designed in the late 1700s by the Italian typographer GIAMBATTISTA BODONI. At the end of the eighteenth century, a fashion grew for faces with a stronger contrast between the thicks and thins, unbracketed serifs, and a strong vertical stress. These were called Modern typefaces. All the older faces became known as Old Style, while the more recent faces—just prior to the change—were referred to as Transitional. Although Bodoni has a small x-height, it appears very wide and black. *Because of the strong vertical stress, accentuated by its heavy thicks and hairline thins, Bodoni should be well leaded.* 9/10

Bodoni is a Modern typeface, designed in the late 1700s by the Italian typographer GIAMBATTISTA BODONI. At the end of the eighteenth century, a fashion grew for faces with a stronger contrast between the thicks and thins, unbracketed serifs, and a strong vertical stress. These were called Modern typefaces. All the older faces became known as Old Style, while the more recent faces—just prior to the change—were referred to as Transitional. Although Bodoni has a small x-height, it appears very wide and black. *Because of the strong vertical stress, accentuated by its heavy thicks and hairline thins, Bodoni should be well leaded.* 8/10

Century, the first major American typeface, was designed in 1894 by Linn Boyd Benton for Theodore Lowe DeVinne, the printer of *The Century Magazine*. After Bodoni, type designers began to search for new forms of typographic expression. Around 1815 a typestyle appeared that was characterized by thick slab serifs and thick main strokes with little contrast between the thicks and thins. This style was called Egyptian. Century Expanded is an excellent example of a refined Egyptian, or slab serif, typeface. *The large x-height and simple forms combine to make this a very legible typeface.*

20/30 CENTURY EXPANDED

Linn Boyd Benton (1844–1932) was born in the United States at Little Falls, New Jersey, at a time when type designers were experimenting with many forms of typographic expression, often to satisfy the needs of advertisers. Merchants wanted typefaces that were new, big, and eye-catching.

The type designers rose to the challenge, producing the wildest assortment of typefaces ever seen—from condensed to expanded, from simple to elaborate. One of the more popular typestyles to emerge was Egyptian, also referred to as slab serif or square serif.

Benton is also credited with the invention of the pantographic punch cutter, which revolutionized type production.

ABCDEFGHIJKLMN
OPQRSTUVWXYZ&
abcdefghijklmnopqrstu
vwxyz 1234567890 fi fl

LINING FIGURES LIGATURES

. , “ ” ‘ ’ ; : ! ?

48-POINT CENTURY EXPANDED

ABCDEFGHIJKLMN
OPQRSTUVWXYZ&
abcdefghijklmnopqrst
uvwxyz 1234567890 fi fl
. , “ ” ‘ ’ ; : ! ?

48-POINT CENTURY EXPANDED ITALIC

Century Expanded | Egyptian

72-POINT Designing with T

60-POINT Designing with Typ

48-POINT Designing with Type

36-POINT Designing with Type

30-POINT Designing with Type

24-POINT Designing with Type

18-POINT Designing with Type

72-POINT *Designing with T*

60-POINT *Designing with Ty*

48-POINT *Designing with Type*

36-POINT *Designing with Type*

30-POINT *Designing with Type*

24-POINT *Designing with Type*

18-POINT *Designing with Type*

2

Century, the first major American typeface, was designed in 1894 by Linn Boyd Benton for Theodore Lowe DeVinne, the printer of *The Century Magazine*. After Bodoni, type designers began to search for new forms of typographic expression. Around 1815 a typestyle appeared that was characterized by thick slab serifs and thick main strokes with little contrast between the thicks and thins. This style was called Egyptian. Century Expanded is an excellent example of a refined Egyptian, or slab serif, typeface. *The large x-height and simple forms combine to make this a very legible typeface.* 14/14

Century, the first major American typeface, was designed in 1894 by Linn Boyd Benton for Theodore Lowe DeVinne, the printer of *The Century Magazine*. After Bodoni, type designers began to search for new forms of typographic expression. Around 1815 a typestyle appeared that was characterized by thick slab serifs and thick main strokes with little contrast between the thicks and thins. This style was called Egyptian. Century Expanded is an excellent example of a refined Egyptian, or slab serif, typeface. *The large x-height and simple forms combine to make this a very legible typeface.* 12/12

Century, the first major American typeface, was designed in 1894 by Linn Boyd Benton for Theodore Lowe DeVinne, the printer of *The Century Magazine*. After Bodoni, type designers began to search for new forms of typographic expression. Around 1815 a typestyle appeared that was characterized by thick slab serifs and thick main strokes with little contrast between the thicks and thins. This style was called Egyptian. Century Expanded is an excellent example of a refined Egyptian, or slab serif, typeface. *The large x-height and simple forms combine to make this a very legible typeface.* 11/11

Century, the first major American typeface, was designed in 1894 by Linn Boyd Benton for Theodore Lowe DeVinne, the printer of *The Century Magazine*. After Bodoni, type designers began to search for new forms of typographic expression. Around 1815 a typestyle appeared that was characterized by thick slab serifs and thick main strokes with little contrast between the thicks and thins. This style was called Egyptian. Century Expanded is an excellent example of a refined Egyptian, or slab serif, typeface. *The large x-height and simple forms combine to make this a very legible typeface.* 10/10

Century, the first major American typeface, was designed in 1894 by Linn Boyd Benton for Theodore Lowe DeVinne, the printer of *The Century Magazine*. After Bodoni, type designers began to search for new forms of typographic expression. Around 1815 a typestyle appeared that was characterized by thick slab serifs and thick main strokes with little contrast between the thicks and thins. This style was called Egyptian. Century Expanded is an excellent example of a refined Egyptian, or slab serif, typeface. *The large x-height and simple forms combine to make this a very legible typeface.* 9/9

Century, the first major American typeface, was designed in 1894 by Linn Boyd Benton for Theodore Lowe DeVinne, the printer of *The Century Magazine*. After Bodoni, type designers began to search for new forms of typographic expression. Around 1815 a typestyle appeared that was characterized by thick slab serifs and thick main strokes with little contrast between the thicks and thins. This style was called Egyptian. Century Expanded is an excellent example of a refined Egyptian, or slab serif, typeface. *The large x-height and simple forms combine to make this a very legible typeface.* 8/8

Century Expanded | Egyptian

14/15 Century, the first major American typeface, was designed in 1894 by Linn Boyd Benton for Theodore Lowe DeVinne, the printer of *The Century Magazine*. After Bodoni, type designers began to search for new forms of typographic expression. Around 1815 a typestyle appeared that was characterized by thick slab serifs and thick main strokes with little contrast between the thicks and thins. This style was called Egyptian. Century Expanded is an excellent example of a refined Egyptian, or slab serif, typeface. *The large x-height and simple forms combine to make this a very legible typeface.*

12/13 Century, the first major American typeface, was designed in 1894 by Linn Boyd Benton for Theodore Lowe DeVinne, the printer of *The Century Magazine*. After Bodoni, type designers began to search for new forms of typographic expression. Around 1815 a typestyle appeared that was characterized by thick slab serifs and thick main strokes with little contrast between the thicks and thins. This style was called Egyptian. Century Expanded is an excellent example of a refined Egyptian, or slab serif, typeface. *The large x-height and simple forms combine to make this a very legible typeface.*

11/12 Century, the first major American typeface, was designed in 1894 by Linn Boyd Benton for Theodore Lowe DeVinne, the printer of *The Century Magazine*. After Bodoni, type designers began to search for new forms of typographic expression. Around 1815 a typestyle appeared that was characterized by thick slab serifs and thick main strokes with little contrast between the thicks and thins. This style was called Egyptian. Century Expanded is an excellent example of a refined Egyptian, or slab serif, typeface. *The large x-height and simple forms combine to make this a very legible typeface.*

10/11 Century, the first major American typeface, was designed in 1894 by Linn Boyd Benton for Theodore Lowe DeVinne, the printer of *The Century Magazine*. After Bodoni, type designers began to search for new forms of typographic expression. Around 1815 a typestyle appeared that was characterized by thick slab serifs and thick main strokes with little contrast between the thicks and thins. This style was called Egyptian. Century Expanded is an excellent example of a refined Egyptian, or slab serif, typeface. *The large x-height and simple forms combine to make this a very legible typeface.*

9/10 Century, the first major American typeface, was designed in 1894 by Linn Boyd Benton for Theodore Lowe DeVinne, the printer of *The Century Magazine*. After Bodoni, type designers began to search for new forms of typographic expression. Around 1815 a typestyle appeared that was characterized by thick slab serifs and thick main strokes with little contrast between the thicks and thins. This style was called Egyptian. Century Expanded is an excellent example of a refined Egyptian, or slab serif, typeface. *The large x-height and simple forms combine to make this a very legible typeface.*

8/9 Century, the first major American typeface, was designed in 1894 by Linn Boyd Benton for Theodore Lowe DeVinne, the printer of *The Century Magazine*. After Bodoni, type designers began to search for new forms of typographic expression. Around 1815 a typestyle appeared that was characterized by thick slab serifs and thick main strokes with little contrast between the thicks and thins. This style was called Egyptian. Century Expanded is an excellent example of a refined Egyptian, or slab serif, typeface. *The large x-height and simple forms combine to make this a very legible typeface.*

Century, the first major American typeface, was designed in 1894 by 14/16
Linn Boyd Benton for Theodore Lowe DeVinne, the printer of *The
Century Magazine.* After Bodoni, type designers began to search for
new forms of typographic expression. Around 1815 a typestyle
appeared that was characterized by thick slab serifs and thick main
strokes with little contrast between the thicks and thins. This style
was called Egyptian. Century Expanded is an excellent example of a
refined Egyptian, or slab serif, typeface. *The large x-height and
simple forms combine to make this a very legible typeface.*

Century, the first major American typeface, was designed in 1894 by Linn Boyd 12/14
Benton for Theodore Lowe DeVinne, the printer of *The Century Magazine.*
After Bodoni, type designers began to search for new forms of typographic
expression. Around 1815 a typestyle appeared that was characterized by thick
slab serifs and thick main strokes with little contrast between the thicks and
thins. This style was called Egyptian. Century Expanded is an excellent
example of a refined Egyptian, or slab serif, typeface. *The large x-height and
simple forms combine to make this a very legible typeface.*

Century, the first major American typeface, was designed in 1894 by Linn Boyd Benton 11/13
for Theodore Lowe DeVinne, the printer of *The Century Magazine.* After Bodoni, type
designers began to search for new forms of typographic expression. Around 1815 a
typestyle appeared that was characterized by thick slab serifs and thick main strokes
with little contrast between the thicks and thins. This style was called Egyptian.
Century Expanded is an excellent example of a refined Egyptian, or slab serif, typeface.
The large x-height and simple forms combine to make this a very legible typeface.

Century, the first major American typeface, was designed in 1894 by Linn Boyd Benton for 10/12
Theodore Lowe DeVinne, the printer of *The Century Magazine.* After Bodoni, type designers
began to search for new forms of typographic expression. Around 1815 a typestyle appeared that
was characterized by thick slab serifs and thick main strokes with little contrast between the
thicks and thins. This style was called Egyptian. Century Expanded is an excellent example of a
refined Egyptian, or slab serif, typeface. *The large x-height and simple forms combine to make
this a very legible typeface.*

Century, the first major American typeface, was designed in 1894 by Linn Boyd Benton for Theodore Lowe 9/11
DeVinne, the printer of *The Century Magazine.* After Bodoni, type designers began to search for new
forms of typographic expression. Around 1815 a typestyle appeared that was characterized by thick slab
serifs and thick main strokes with little contrast between the thicks and thins. This style was called
Egyptian. Century Expanded is an excellent example of a refined Egyptian, or slab serif, typeface. *The
large x-height and simple forms combine to make this a very legible typeface.*

Century, the first major American typeface, was designed in 1894 by Linn Boyd Benton for Theodore Lowe DeVinne, the 8/10
printer of *The Century Magazine.* After Bodoni, type designers began to search for new forms of typographic expression.
Around 1815 a typestyle appeared that was characterized by thick slab serifs and thick main strokes with little contrast
between the thicks and thins. This style was called Egyptian. Century Expanded is an excellent example of a refined
Egyptian, or slab serif, typeface. *The large x-height and simple forms combine to make this a very legible typeface.*

Helvetica is a sans serif typeface of Swiss origin. Although typefaces without serifs were used in the nineteenth century, it was not until the twentieth century that they became popular. In 1957 the Haas foundry introduced Haas Grotesk, designed by Max Miedinger (with Eduard Hoffmann), later to become known internationally as Helvetica. Helvetica's large x-height, slightly condensed letters, and clean design make it a very readable typeface. *In general, sans serif typefaces have relatively little stress, with optically equal strokes, and should always be leaded.*

22/28 HELVETICA NEUE

Max Miedinger (1910–1980) was born in Zurich, Switzerland. He began his career as a typesetter in Zurich and next as a typographer in an advertising studio. He achieved his greatest success as a design developer for Haas Schriftgiesserei in Munich.

After the Second World War there was a great demand for new typefaces, especially sans serifs. In 1957, Eduard Hoffmann, another Swiss, took an old typeface, Neue Haas Grotesk, and had it redrawn by Max Miedinger. The result was Helvetica, which quickly became the favorite typeface of Swiss designers and many others around the world. Today, Helvetica is still one of the most widely used typefaces and the Helvetica family one of the most diverse.

ABCDEFGHIJKLMNO
PQRSTUVWXYZ&
abcdefghijklmnopqrs
tuvwxyz 1234567890

LINING FIGURES

. , " " ' ' ; : ! ?

48-POINT HELVETICA

ABCDEFGHIJKLMN
OPQRSTUVWXYZ&
abcdefghijklmnopqrst
uvwxyz 1234567890
. , " " ' ' ; : ! ?

48-POINT HELVETICA ITALIC

Helvetica | Sans Serif

72-POINT Designing with T

60-POINT Designing with Typ

48-POINT Designing with Type

36-POINT Designing with Type

30-POINT Designing with Type

24-POINT Designing with Type

18-POINT Designing with Type

72-POINT *Designing with T*

60-POINT *Designing with Typ*

48-POINT *Designing with Type*

36-POINT *Designing with Type*

30-POINT *Designing with Type*

24-POINT *Designing with Type*

18-POINT *Designing with Type*

Helvetica is a sans serif typeface of Swiss origin. Although typefaces without serifs were used in the nineteenth century, it was not until the twentieth century that they became popular. In 1957 the Haas foundry introduced Haas Grotesk, designed by Max Miedinger (with Eduard Hoffmann), later to become known internationally as Helvetica. Helvetica's large x-height, slightly condensed letters, and clean design make it a very readable typeface. *In general, sans serif typefaces have relatively little stress, with optically equal strokes, and should always be leaded.* 14/14

Helvetica is a sans serif typeface of Swiss origin. Although typefaces without serifs were used in the nineteenth century, it was not until the twentieth century that they became popular. In 1957 the Haas foundry introduced Haas Grotesk, designed by Max Miedinger (with Eduard Hoffmann), later to become known internationally as Helvetica. Helvetica's large x-height, slightly condensed letters, and clean design make it a very readable typeface. *In general, sans serif typefaces have relatively little stress, with optically equal strokes, and should always be leaded.* 12/12

Helvetica is a sans serif typeface of Swiss origin. Although typefaces without serifs were used in the nineteenth century, it was not until the twentieth century that they became popular. In 1957 the Haas foundry introduced Haas Grotesk, designed by Max Miedinger (with Eduard Hoffmann), later to become known internationally as Helvetica. Helvetica's large x-height, slightly condensed letters, and clean design make it a very readable typeface. *In general, sans serif typefaces have relatively little stress, with optically equal strokes, and should always be leaded.* 11/11

Helvetica is a sans serif typeface of Swiss origin. Although typefaces without serifs were used in the nineteenth century, it was not until the twentieth century that they became popular. In 1957 the Haas foundry introduced Haas Grotesk, designed by Max Miedinger (with Eduard Hoffmann), later to become known internationally as Helvetica. Helvetica's large x-height, slightly condensed letters, and clean design make it a very readable typeface. *In general, sans serif typefaces have relatively little stress, with optically equal strokes, and should always be leaded.* 10/10

Helvetica is a sans serif typeface of Swiss origin. Although typefaces without serifs were used in the nineteenth century, it was not until the twentieth century that they became popular. In 1957 the Haas foundry introduced Haas Grotesk, designed by Max Miedinger (with Eduard Hoffmann), later to become known internationally as Helvetica. Helvetica's large x-height, slightly condensed letters, and clean design make it a very readable typeface. *In general, sans serif typefaces have relatively little stress, with optically equal strokes, and should always be leaded.* 9/9

Helvetica is a sans serif typeface of Swiss origin. Although typefaces without serifs were used in the nineteenth century, it was not until the twentieth century that they became popular. In 1957 the Haas foundry introduced Haas Grotesk, designed by Max Miedinger (with Eduard Hoffmann), later to become known internationally as Helvetica. Helvetica's large x-height, slightly condensed letters, and clean design make it a very readable typeface. *In general, sans serif typefaces have relatively little stress, with optically equal strokes, and should always be leaded.* 8/8

Helvetica | Sans Serif

14/15 Helvetica is a sans serif typeface of Swiss origin. Although typefaces without serifs were used in the nineteenth century, it was not until the twentieth century that they became popular. In 1957 the Haas foundry introduced Haas Grotesk, designed by Max Miedinger (with Eduard Hoffmann), later to become known internationally as Helvetica. Helvetica's large x-height, slightly condensed letters, and clean design make it a very readable typeface. *In general, sans serif typefaces have relatively little stress, with optically equal strokes, and should always be leaded.*

12/13 Helvetica is a sans serif typeface of Swiss origin. Although typefaces without serifs were used in the nineteenth century, it was not until the twentieth century that they became popular. In 1957 the Haas foundry introduced Haas Grotesk, designed by Max Miedinger (with Eduard Hoffmann), later to become known internationally as Helvetica. Helvetica's large x-height, slightly condensed letters, and clean design make it a very readable typeface. *In general, sans serif typefaces have relatively little stress, with optically equal strokes, and should always be leaded.*

11/12 Helvetica is a sans serif typeface of Swiss origin. Although typefaces without serifs were used in the nineteenth century, it was not until the twentieth century that they became popular. In 1957 the Haas foundry introduced Haas Grotesk, designed by Max Miedinger (with Eduard Hoffmann), later to become known internationally as Helvetica. Helvetica's large x-height, slightly condensed letters, and clean design make it a very readable typeface. *In general, sans serif typefaces have relatively little stress, with optically equal strokes, and should always be leaded.*

10/11 Helvetica is a sans serif typeface of Swiss origin. Although typefaces without serifs were used in the nineteenth century, it was not until the twentieth century that they became popular. In 1957 the Haas foundry introduced Haas Grotesk, designed by Max Miedinger (with Eduard Hoffmann), later to become known internationally as Helvetica. Helvetica's large x-height, slightly condensed letters, and clean design make it a very readable typeface. *In general, sans serif typefaces have relatively little stress, with optically equal strokes, and should always be leaded.*

9/10 Helvetica is a sans serif typeface of Swiss origin. Although typefaces without serifs were used in the nineteenth century, it was not until the twentieth century that they became popular. In 1957 the Haas foundry introduced Haas Grotesk, designed by Max Miedinger (with Eduard Hoffmann), later to become known internationally as Helvetica. Helvetica's large x-height, slightly condensed letters, and clean design make it a very readable typeface. *In general, sans serif typefaces have relatively little stress, with optically equal strokes, and should always be leaded.*

8/9 Helvetica is a sans serif typeface of Swiss origin. Although typefaces without serifs were used in the nineteenth century, it was not until the twentieth century that they became popular. In 1957 the Haas foundry introduced Haas Grotesk, designed by Max Miedinger (with Eduard Hoffmann), later to become known internationally as Helvetica. Helvetica's large x-height, slightly condensed letters, and clean design make it a very readable typeface. *In general, sans serif typefaces have relatively little stress, with optically equal strokes, and should always be leaded.*

Helvetica is a sans serif typeface of Swiss origin. Although typefaces without serifs were used in the nineteenth century, it was not until the twentieth century that they became popular. In 1957 the Haas foundry introduced Haas Grotesk, designed by Max Miedinger (with Eduard Hoffmann), later to become known internationally as Helvetica. Helvetica's large x-height, slightly condensed letters, and clean design make it a very readable typeface. *In general, sans serif typefaces have relatively little stress, with optically equal strokes, and should always be leaded.* 14/16

Helvetica is a sans serif typeface of Swiss origin. Although typefaces without serifs were used in the nineteenth century, it was not until the twentieth century that they became popular. In 1957 the Haas foundry introduced Haas Grotesk, designed by Max Miedinger (with Eduard Hoffmann), later to become known internationally as Helvetica. Helvetica's large x-height, slightly condensed letters, and clean design make it a very readable typeface. *In general, sans serif typefaces have relatively little stress, with optically equal strokes, and should always be leaded.* 12/14

Helvetica is a sans serif typeface of Swiss origin. Although typefaces without serifs were used in the nineteenth century, it was not until the twentieth century that they became popular. In 1957 the Haas foundry introduced Haas Grotesk, designed by Max Miedinger (with Eduard Hoffmann), later to become known internationally as Helvetica. Helvetica's large x-height, slightly condensed letters, and clean design make it a very readable typeface. *In general, sans serif typefaces have relatively little stress, with optically equal strokes, and should always be leaded.* 11/13

Helvetica is a sans serif typeface of Swiss origin. Although typefaces without serifs were used in the nineteenth century, it was not until the twentieth century that they became popular. In 1957 the Haas foundry introduced Haas Grotesk, designed by Max Miedinger (with Eduard Hoffmann), later to become known internationally as Helvetica. Helvetica's large x-height, slightly condensed letters, and clean design make it a very readable typeface. *In general, sans serif typefaces have relatively little stress, with optically equal strokes, and should always be leaded.* 10/12

Helvetica is a sans serif typeface of Swiss origin. Although typefaces without serifs were used in the nineteenth century, it was not until the twentieth century that they became popular. In 1957 the Haas foundry introduced Haas Grotesk, designed by Max Miedinger (with Eduard Hoffmann), later to become known internationally as Helvetica. Helvetica's large x-height, slightly condensed letters, and clean design make it a very readable typeface. *In general, sans serif typefaces have relatively little stress, with optically equal strokes, and should always be leaded.* 9/11

Helvetica is a sans serif typeface of Swiss origin. Although typefaces without serifs were used in the nineteenth century, it was not until the twentieth century that they became popular. In 1957 the Haas foundry introduced Haas Grotesk, designed by Max Miedinger (with Eduard Hoffmann), later to become known internationally as Helvetica. Helvetica's large x-height, slightly condensed letters, and clean design make it a very readable typeface. *In general, sans serif typefaces have relatively little stress, with optically equal strokes, and should always be leaded.* 8/10

Type Families

GARAMOND ROMAN	Designing with Type
GARAMOND ITALIC	*Designing with Type*
GARAMOND SEMIBOLD	**Designing with Type**
GARAMOND SEMIBOLD ITALIC	***Designing with Type***
GARAMOND BOLD	**Designing with Type**
GARAMOND BOLD ITALIC	***Designing with Type***
BASKERVILLE ROMAN	Designing with Type
BASKERVILLE ITALIC	*Designing with Type*
BASKERVILLE SEMIBOLD	Designing with Type
BASKERVILLE SEMIBOLD ITALIC	*Designing with Type*
BASKERVILLE BOLD	**Designing with Type**
BASKERVILLE BOLD ITALIC	***Designing with Type***
BODONI ROMAN	Designing with Type
BODONI ITALIC	*Designing with Type*
BODONI BOOK	Designing with Type
BODONI BOOK ITALIC	*Designing with Type*
BODONI BOLD	**Designing with Type**
BODONI BOLD ITALIC	***Designing with Type***
BODONI POSTER	**Designing with Type**
BODONI POSTER ITALIC	***Designing with Type***

CENTURY EXPANDED	Designing with Type
CENTURY EXPANDED ITALIC	*Designing with Type*
CENTURY EXPANDED BOLD	**Designing with Type**
CENTURY EXPANDED BOLD ITALIC	***Designing with Type***

25 HELVETICA ULTRALIGHT	Designing with Type
26 HELVETICA ULTRALIGHT ITALIC	*Designing with Type*
35 HELVETICA THIN	Designing with Type
36 HELVETICA THIN ITALIC	*Designing with Type*
45 HELVETICA LIGHT	Designing with Type
46 HELVETICA LIGHT ITALIC	*Designing with Type*
55 HELVETICA ROMAN	Designing with Type
56 HELVETICA ITALIC	*Designing with Type*
65 HELVETICA MEDIUM	**Designing with Type**
66 HELVETICA MEDIUM ITALIC	***Designing with Type***
75 HELVETICA BOLD	**Designing with Type**
76 HELVETICA BOLD ITALIC	***Designing with Type***
85 HELVETICA HEAVY	**Designing with Type**
86 HELVETICA HEAVY ITALIC	***Designing with Type***
95 HELVETICA BLACK	**Designing with Type**
96 HELVETICA BLACK ITALIC	***Designing with Type***

Exercise | Identify Typefaces

I am the voice of today, the herald of tomorrow. I am type! Of my earliest ancestry neither history nor relics remain. The wedge-shaped symbols impressed in plastic clay by Babylonian builders in the dim past foreshadowed me: from them, on through the hieroglyphs of the ancient Egyptians, down to the beautiful manuscript letters of the medieval scribes, I was in the making. The ingenious JOHANNES GUTENBERG—with a dream most golden—first applied the principle of casting me in metal.

I am the voice of today, the herald of tomorrow. I am type! Of my earliest ancestry neither history nor relics remain. The wedge-shaped symbols impressed in plastic clay by Babylonian builders in the dim past foreshadowed me: from them, on through the hieroglyphs of the ancient Egyptians, down to the beautiful manuscript letters of the medieval scribes, I was in the making. The ingenious Johannes Gutenberg—with a dream most golden—first applied the principle of casting me in metal.

I am the voice of today, the herald of tomorrow. I am type! Of my earliest ancestry neither history nor relics remain. The wedge-shaped symbols impressed in plastic clay by Babylonian builders in the dim past foreshadowed me: from them, on through the hieroglyphs of the ancient Egyptians, down to the beautiful manuscript letters of the medieval scribes, I was in the making. The ingenious Johannes Gutenberg—with a dream most golden—first applied the principle of casting me in metal.

I am the voice of today, the herald of tomorrow. I am type! Of my earliest ancestry neither history nor relics remain. The wedge-shaped symbols impressed in plastic clay by Babylonian builders in the dim past foreshadowed me: from them, on through the hieroglyphs of the ancient Egyptians, down to the beautiful manuscript letters of the medieval scribes, I was in the making. The ingenious JOHANNES GUTENBERG—with a dream most golden—first applied the principle of casting me in metal.

I am the voice of today, the herald of tomorrow. I am type! Of my earliest ancestry neither history nor relics remain. The wedge-shaped symbols impressed in plastic clay by Babylonian builders in the dim past foreshadowed me: from them, on through the hieroglyphs of the ancient Egyptians, down to the beautiful manuscript letters of the medieval scribes, I was in the making. The ingenious Johannes Gutenberg—with a dream most golden—first applied the principle of casting me in metal.

Designing with Text Type

Designing text is the process of selecting a typeface, deciding which words or phrases should be emphasized, and determining how the type should be arranged on a page. The final design will be influenced by the copy you work with, the intended audience, your understanding of the principles of typography, and consideration of how we read. This holds true whether your goal is to make the experience of reading as comfortable as possible or to challenge accepted typographic conventions.

how do we read?

1 | The upper half is more easily recognizable than the lower half.

how do we read?

HOW DO WE READ?

2 | Lowercase letters are more easily recognizable than all caps.

How We Read

Since we learn to read at such an early age, we often take this valuable asset for granted. We generally give little thought to how spoken words and ideas are converted into the twenty-six letters of the alphabet and arranged on the page to communicate effectively. For the casual reader, this lack of awareness is acceptable, but a graphic designer must understand that our reading habits are formed early in life and are not easily modified.

As children, we are introduced to the alphabet, we memorize the basic letterforms, and learn to read from left to right, line by line, top to bottom. As we mature, these reading habits are formulated, modified, and reinforced until we have formed specific preferences.

Generally speaking, we tend to be very conservative in our reading habits, regardless of how radical we may be in other aspects of our lives. For serious reading, we prefer what is familiar: black type on white paper, roman typefaces in regular weight, and set in uppercase and lowercase. Anytime a designer departs from these criteria, the reader may be challenged.

To better understand the mechanics of reading, we have taken a line of type and split it through the center. **Notice that reading the upper half is relatively easy, while the bottom half is far more difficult to discern (1).** The eye scans the upper half of the letters and recognizes them almost instinctively.

The more distinct the outline, the more easily the eye recognizes the words. **When words of a similar size are set in both uppercase and lowercase, the lowercase words being more familiar are quickly recognizable and more comfortable to read (2).** For this reason, most of what we read is set in uppercase and lowercase.

We generally expect to be able to read entire passages effortlessly, without being distracted by poorly designed type or self-conscious typography. In other words, the type should not call attention to itself, intruding between the reader and the thought expressed on the printed page.

In all cases, when designing with type, ask yourself some basic questions: how much copy is being read, who is the audience, and under what conditions? Reading one or two words on a billboard is a far different activity from reading a novel or a full-page advertisement in a magazine.

Legibility and Readability

Legibility is the quality of the typeface design and readability with the design of the printed page. Designers aim to achieve excellence in both.

The typeface you choose should be legible, that is, it should be read without effort. Sometimes legibility is simply a matter of type size; more often, however, it is a matter of typeface design. Generally speaking, typefaces that are true to the basic letterforms are more legible than typefaces that have been condensed, expanded, embellished, or abstracted. Therefore always start with a legible typeface.

Keep in mind, however, that even a legible typeface can become unreadable through poor setting and placement, just as a less legible typeface can be made more readable through good design.

Esthetics

There is no formula for defining beauty in a typeface or type arrangement, but there are standards of typographic excellence that have been established over the centuries. For example, early typesetters and printers would always strive for the highest level of legibility and readability through careful consideration of typeface design, letterspacing, wordspacing, linespacing, and other typographic refinements that will be discussed in this part.

Today these considerations continue to play a significant role in determining excellence in typography. Esthetic choices tend to be dictated by these standards, as well as the designer's taste and experience.

Appropriateness

Designers often begin a project by choosing a typeface that appeals to them. This choice is highly personal; Bodoni may appeal to one designer, Helvetica to another. Regardless of your choice, be certain that the typeface is not only well designed but also appropriate to both the audience and the project.

Typefaces have personalities and convey different moods. While a single, well-drawn typeface can be utilized for a variety of jobs, there are occasions when specific projects seem to dictate a particular typeface or typestyle. For example, an advertisement for cosmetics may suggest an elegant typeface such as Bodoni rather than a bold sans serif. A logo for industrial machinery might call for the opposite.

Consider the audience. If the reader is either very young or very old, you should choose a simple, well-designed typeface that is easy to read and set in a large size—larger than the type you are now reading. On the other hand, young people, such as teenagers and college students, are generally more receptive to experimental—or even outlandish—typography.

The length of the copy is another factor: an appropriate typeface for a caption or blurb may not be a practical choice for a lengthy novel or vice versa.

Eventually, through use and experimentation and by researching examples of fine typography in design publications and exhibitions, you will develop an eye for the typographic qualities that are effective and appealing to both you and your audience. ■

Legibility and readability

involve not only typeface selection,

but also how the type is set.

Letterspacing and Wordspacing

Whatisthedesirableamountofspacebetween words?Toomuchortoolittlemakesreadingdifficult. Wordsplacedtooclosetogetherforcethereaderto workhardertodistinguishonewordfromanother. Ontheotherhand,wordsplacedtoofarapartcreate whitespacesthatrundownthepageas“rivers”and disruptthenaturalmovementoftheeyefromleftto right.Properwordspacingnotonlyimprovesreadabilitybutismorepleasingesthetically.

1 | Too tight

What is the desirable amount of space between words? Too much or too little makes reading difficult. Words placed too close together force the reader to work harder to distinguish one word from another. On the other hand, words placed too far apart create white spaces that run down the page as “rivers” and disrupt the natural movement of the eye from left to right. Proper wordspacing not only improves readability but is more pleasing esthetically.

2 | Too loose

What is the desirable amount of space between words? Too much or too little makes reading difficult. Words placed too close together force the reader to work harder to distinguish one word from another. On the other hand, words placed too far apart create white spaces that run down the page as “rivers” and disrupt the natural movement of the eye from left to right. Proper wordspacing not only improves readability but is more pleasing esthetically.

3 | Normal

■ Type can be letterspaced and wordspaced to produce *normal, tight, very tight,* or *open settings.* The spacing you select will depend very much on the typeface, typestyle, and type size.

Although the letterspacing and wordspacing you choose are based on personal preference, your first priority should be readability. Most text is set normal, that is, without additional spacing considerations.
If you choose to customize the setting, consider that regular text sizes can be set with either normal or tight spacing, while smaller text sizes require slightly more open spacing. A condensed typeface can be set tighter than a regular or extended typeface. In nearly all cases, designers are consistent in their specifications; if they tighten the letterspacing, they also consider tightening the wordspacing.

If you decide to use tight letterspacing, remember that there is a limit to how much space can be removed before the letters start to touch or overlap. Check the round letters first, such as the o and c; they will overlap before the straight letters, such as the i and l.

Besides overall letterspacing, there is also selective letterspacing, or *kerning*. This affects only certain letter combinations that are improved with a reduction of space, such as AT, TI, LV, Te, Wo, and Ya. (See page 21.)

Spacing can have a dramatic effect on the “color” of the typesetting. The tighter the spacing, the blacker the setting; conversely, the looser the spacing, the grayer the effect. The majority of jobs are set with either normal or tight spacing.

Optimal Spacing

What is the desirable amount of space between letters and words? Type that runs together and type that is too far apart are both unsatisfactory.
In general, too much or too little wordspacing is conspicuous: it diverts attention away from the text to the way words are placed.

Words placed too close together force the reader to work harder to distinguish one word from another (1). In text settings, words placed too far apart leave large spaces that look like “rivers” running down the page — creating a vertical emphasis that disrupts the movement of the eye from left to right (2). These rivers are especially apparent in newspapers, where narrow columns make even wordspacing difficult. **Proper wordspacing improves readability and is more pleasing esthetically (3).** The page of text appears as orderly lines of black and white instead of looking like a field full of potholes.

Justified and Unjustified Settings

The two most common typesetting arrangements are generally referred to as *justified* or *unjustified*. Justified settings have lines of equal length, with each of the lines aligning on both the left and the right sides of a column. Unjustified settings have lines of unequal length that are usually aligned on the left, such as the type you are now reading. (In cases where the copy is rather brief, such as captions, the lines can also be aligned on the right.)

One critical difference between unjustified and justified type that is worth noting is the effect the setting has on wordspacing, and therefore readability.

UNJUSTIFIED TYPE | Ideally, type should be set with uniform wordspacing. **When type is set unjustified (flush left or flush right), this is the case (4).** This arrangement assures an even texture throughout the setting.

JUSTIFIED TYPE | When type is set justified, equal wordspacing is no longer possible because extra space must be inserted between the words in the shorter lines to extend them to the same length as the longer lines. **As a result, the wordspacing is no longer equal (5).**

If the lines of type are of sufficient length, the unequal wordspacing is not noticeable. Unequal wordspacing is less apparent in long lines of type because the extra space is distributed between many words, whereas in short lines the space is distributed between fewer words and therefore more noticeable.

When setting type justified, you may be tempted to introduce additional letterspacing in order to compensate for overly generous wordspacing (6). Resist the temptation. While this method may improve the wordspacing, it may also draw unwanted attention to the irregular letterspacing, which can be even more objectionable than the irregular wordspacing.

When wordspacing of justified type presents a problem, there are more appropriate options than tampering with the letterspacing. First, you might try increasing the measure to allow more characters per line, which helps to equalize the wordspacing. If the problem exists only on one or two lines, the solution may simply be to introduce some hyphenation. Or you may even want to consider an unjustified setting, which will ensure even wordspacing.

Finally, if all else fails, you might attempt to have the copy rewritten or edited to fit, provided you are not setting Shakespeare!

What is the desirable amount of space between words? Too much or too little makes reading difficult. Words placed too close together force the reader to work harder to distinguish one word from another. On the other hand, words placed too far apart create white spaces that run down the page as "rivers" and disrupt the natural movement of the eye from left to right. Proper wordspacing not only improves readability but is more pleasing esthetically.

4 | Unjustified setting: equal wordspacing

What is the desirable amount of space between words? Too much or too little makes reading difficult. Words placed too close together force the reader to work harder to distinguish one word from another. On the other hand, words placed too far apart create white spaces that run down the page as "rivers" and disrupt the natural movement of the eye from left to right. Proper wordspacing not only improves readability but is more pleasing esthetically.

5 | Justified setting: unequal wordspacing

What is the desirable amount of space between words? Too much or too little makes reading difficult. Words placed too close together force the reader to work harder to distinguish one word from another. On the other hand, words placed too far apart create white spaces that run down the page as "rivers" and disrupt the natural movement of the eye from left to right. Proper wordspacing not only improves readability but is more pleasing esthetically.

6 | Inconsistent letterspacing can be distracting.

Linespacing | Leading

Linespacing, or leading, like wordspacing and letterspacing, can be used to improve readability. Your choice of typeface, type size, line length, and copy will all affect the amount of linespacing. With so many factors involved, you can see why proper linespacing is more a matter of visual judgment than of mathematics.

1 | Small type benefits from additional linespacing.

Linespacing, or leading, like wordspacing and letterspacing, can be used to improve readability. Your choice of typeface, type size, line length, and copy will all affect the amount of linespacing. With so many factors involved, you can see why proper linespacing is more a matter of visual judgment than of mathematics.

2 | Large x-heights require additional linespacing.

■ As a general guide, text settings are improved with the addition of one or two points of linespacing. It is important, however, to avoid excessive leading because the lines tend to drift apart, which makes the setting appear grayer and affects the pace at which the type is read. In shorter settings, such as in advertisements, this effect can be desirable, but it is not recommended for sustained reading. Alternatively, if your choice is minus linespacing, be aware that when too much space is removed between lines of type, the ascenders and descenders may overlap. The settings will also become very dense, which will affect readability.

Factors Affecting Linespacing

Proper linespacing not only improves readability but has an important esthetic function. Unfortunately, there is no formula to determine optimal linespacing. If you consider the following factors involved in determining linespacing, you can see why the decision is more a matter of visual judgment than of mathematics.

TYPE SIZE | Average text sizes are usually set with one or two points of linespacing. **A smaller text size generally requires more linespacing to make it readable (1).**

X-HEIGHT | Some typefaces, such as Helvetica and Century Expanded, have large x-heights and therefore have very little white space between lines when set solid. **Such typefaces require more linespacing than those with small x-heights (2).**

LINE LENGTH | When long lines are set too close, there is a tendency to read the same line twice, called *doubling.* **Increasing linespacing for lines longer than approximately 75 characters helps to prevent doubling (3).**

Linespacing, or leading, like wordspacing and letterspacing, can be used to improve readability. Your choice of typeface, type size, line length, and copy will all affect the amount of linespacing. With so many factors involved, you can see why proper linespacing is more a matter of visual judgment than of mathematics.

3 | Long lines require extra linespacing.

VERTICAL STRESS | The strong vertical stress caused by the extreme thick and thin strokes of typefaces such as Bodoni draws the eye down the page. This tends to compete with the horizontal flow required of comfortable reading. **Letters with strong vertical stress also require more linespacing (4).**

This is also the case with condensed typefaces, which tend to have even greater vertical emphasis and therefore may require additional linespacing.

SANS SERIF | Some sans serif typefaces, such as Helvetica, may require more linespacing because of their large x-height and lack of serifs. **Additional linespacing helps promote a stronger horizontal flow to facilitate reading (5).** Even sans serif typefaces with smaller x-heights, such as Futura and Univers, benefit from additional leading.

Perhaps the most extreme case is a condensed sans serif with a large x-height, such as Helvetica Condensed. You must take into account not only the x-height and lack of serifs but also the extreme vertical stress.

COPY LENGTH | The amount of copy to be set can also affect linespacing decisions. **Obviously you can fit more copy into a given area if the type is set either solid or with minus linespacing (6).**

This can be helpful on jobs where space is a consideration, such as classified ads. If a great deal of copy must fit in a small space, the designer must carefully consider the choice of typeface and arrangement in order to maintain maximum readability.

On the other hand, short copy can be made to fit a larger area simply by increasing the linespacing. This is a common practice in advertising, where the designer wishes to slow down the reader while adding a touch of elegance.

Be aware, when dealing with overly generous linespacing, that there is a point beyond which excessive linespacing will cause the setting to lose its sense of unity and to simply appear as a page full of scattered lines.

Designers must often deal with situations in which the copy is simply too lengthy for the allotted space. In such cases where no design solution is acceptable, you may suggest to the client that the copy be edited or reworked in order to resolve the problem. ■

Linespacing, or leading, like wordspacing and letterspacing, can be used to improve readability. Your choice of typeface, type size, line length, and copy will all affect the amount of linespacing. With so many factors involved, you can see why proper linespacing is more a matter of visual judgment than of mathematics.

4 | Typeface with strong vertical stress

Linespacing, or leading, like wordspacing and letterspacing, can be used to improve readability. Your choice of typeface, type size, line length, and copy will all affect the amount of linespacing. With so many factors involved, you can see why proper linespacing is more a matter of visual judgment than of mathematics.

5 | Sans serif typeface

Linespacing, or leading, like wordspacing and letterspacing, can be used to improve readability. Your choice of typeface, type size, line length, and copy will all affect the amount of linespacing. With so many factors involved, you can see why proper linespacing is more a matter of visual judgment than of mathematics.

Linespacing, or leading, like wordspacing and letterspacing, can be used to improve readability. Your choice of typeface, type size, line length, and copy will all affect the amount of linespacing. With so many factors involved, you can see why proper linespacing is more a matter of visual judgment than of mathematics.

6 | Linespacing affects depth of setting.

Line Length | Measure

In general, the length of a line of type should be comfortable to read: too short and it breaks up words or phrases; too long and the reader must search for the beginning of each line, which can be tiring (1, 2). If you have ever found yourself reading the same line twice, the lines were probably too long and the text insufficiently linespaced.

From a design point of view, line length is dictated by such factors as type size and the amount of copy to be set. In general, the larger the type, the longer the measure should be. For example, a 30-pica line of 11-point type would be acceptable, whereas a 30-pica line of 6-point type would be difficult to read. A reasonable amount of copy set on a very short or very long measure will not present a problem for most readers.

If you are uncertain about line length, a good rule of thumb is to set the type with 35 to 70 characters per line. **Settings within this range are the most comfortable to read (3).**

The length
of a line
should be
comfortable
to read:
too short
and it
breaks up
words or
phrases;
too long
and the
reader must
search for the
beginning of
each line.

1 | Line too short

The length of a line should be comfortable to read: too short and it breaks up words or phrases; too long and the reader must search for the beginning of each line. If you are uncertain about line length, a good rule of thumb is to set the type with 35 to 70 characters per line.

2 | Line too long

The length of a line should be comfortable to read: too short and it breaks up words or phrases; too long and the reader must search for the beginning of each line. If you are uncertain about line length, a good rule of thumb is to set the type with 35 to 70 characters per line.

3 | Better line length

Orphans and Widows

Among the most distracting — and easily corrected — situations in typography are settings in which words (or short phrases) are isolated at the top of a column or left dangling at the end of a paragraph. These are referred to as orphans and widows.

Not everyone agrees on just how many words constitutes and orphan or widow, but they agree it is not good typography and should be corrected.

ORPHAN | **An orphan is a short line that appears at the top of a column (4).** It is usually the last line of a paragraph from the preceding column.

Because of its position on the page orphans are not only distracting, but as the line is separated from the rest of the paragraph, it confuses the reader.

Just as one should never leave the last line of a paragraph at the top of a column, avoid leaving the first line of a paragraph at the bottom of a column. This is not only esthetically distracting, but is particularly annoying for the reader of a book to find that after reading one line of a paragraph at the bottom of a page, that the entire thought is continued on the following page. Although not a typical orphan, a situation such as this can destroy continuity for the reader.

WIDOW | **A widow, on the other hand, is a short line at the end of a paragraph (5).** There is no rule for just how few words constitute a widow. It may be a single word, a short phrase, or the last syllable of a hyphenated word, but they are easily recognizable and typographically distracting.

What also determines a widow is often the line length in relationship to the amount of copy. The longer the measure, the more noticeable a short line will be. Widows are also more noticeable in small amounts of copy with few paragraphs, such as advertisements, as compared to widows buried in books or lengthy magazine articles.

Widows, like orphans, are avoidable and usually easily corrected. This may require resetting a number of lines within the paragraph, or, in some cases, rewriting the copy.

Ignoring widows and orphans is not an option. ■

to read.

Two unforgivable sins for designers are leaving uncorrected widows and orphans in a setting.

An orphan is a short line that appears at the top of the page. It is usually the last line of a paragraph from the preceding column or page. It is more obvious and therefore distracting.

4 | An orphan is a short line at the top of a page.

There is no rule for just how few words or letters constitute a widow as much depends upon the line length. The longer the line the more noticeable the widow.

5 | A widow is a short line at the end of a paragraph.

Type Arrangements

■ With an understanding of wordspacing, line length, and linespacing, we can now consider ways of arranging lines of type on a page. Whether type aligns on the left, the right, or both may at first appear to be a subtlety, but in fact this choice has a great impact on how viewers respond to a design. How you choose to arrange type is a critical decision that affects all typographic communication.

Nearly all settings are variations or combinations of five basic arrangements. Let us consider the advantages and disadvantages of each.

1. Justified (flush left, flush right)
2. Flush left, ragged right
3. Flush right, ragged left
4. Centered
5. Random, or asymmetrical

Justified (Flush Left, Flush Right)

The most common method of arranging lines of type is called justified. **In this arrangement all the lines of text are the same length, so that they align on both left and right (1).**

Because all the lines of type are the same length and the margins are even, a page of justified type assumes a quiet look. Most lengthy reading matter is set justified because this arrangement is best suited for sustained reading comfort. The text does not distract the reader. Its predictability allows for concentration on content rather than design. Justified type is usually employed for material that is lengthy or serious, such as in books, newspapers, or magazines.

One drawback of justified type is the possibility of uneven wordspacing, which can result in "rivers" running down the column of text. This can be avoided if the lines are of sufficient length and the type is properly set. However, if the pica measure is too narrow, wordspacing is difficult to control.

Flush Left, Ragged Right

When type is set with even wordspacing, such as with typewritten copy, the lines will vary in length. If we align the lines of type on the left, the edges on the right will appear ragged, or "feathered." **This arrangement is referred to as unjustified, or simply flush left, ragged right (2).** Besides type-written copy, poems and most captions normally appear this way.

Because of the equal wordspacing, the type has an even texture. The risk of white rivers flowing down the page is eliminated. This is especially appealing when the type is to be set in narrow columns. Moreover, since the lines can run either short or long, the need for hyphen-ating words is reduced. As with justified type, the reader has no difficulty locating the beginning of a new line because the lines are aligned at the left. The ragged edge on the right also adds visual interest to the page.

It is important that the ragged edge creates a pleasing silhouette, with no adjacent lines set the same length, or that the text is set in such a way that a long line is followed by an extremely short one, or is predictably stepped.

Be aware that copy set unjustified runs slightly longer than justified type due to the short lines that do not fill the measure.

Flush Right, Ragged Left

In this instance, the lines are aligned at the right, so that the left side is ragged. **This arrangement is referred to as flush right, ragged left (3).**

Because it is used infrequently, this arrangement may create an interesting layout, particularly for short copy such as a caption running along the side of an illustration. As with flush left, ragged right, you have the advantage of maintaining even wordspacing.

Although visually interesting, this setting is more demanding of the reader. Since we are accustomed to reading from left to right, a ragged left edge forces us to pause momentarily in search of the beginning of each line, which is why this arrangement is usually reserved for very short copy.

Centered

Another way to arrange type is by centering lines of uneven length, one over the other, so that both left and right edges are ragged (4). Like other ragged settings, centered type has even wordspacing and visual interest. Centered type can give the page a look of quiet dignity.

Centered lines should vary enough to create an interesting silhouette, so avoid stacking lines of the same or similar lengths. Generous linespacing is also recommended—it adds to the dignity of the setting and assists the reader in locating the beginning of each line.

Reading centered lines is demanding, which means it is better suited to small amounts of copy, such as announcements and invitations. Try to break the lines for sense. Keeping phrases and related thoughts on separate lines facilitates comprehension and creates a pleasing shape.

There are five ways of arranging lines of type
on a page. The first is justified: all the lines
are the same length and align both on the left
and on the right. The second is unjustified:
the lines are of different lengths and align on
the left and are ragged on the right. The third
is a similar arrangement, except now the
lines align on the right and are ragged on
the left. The fourth possibility is centered: the
lines are of unequal lengths with both sides
ragged. The fifth possibility is a random,
or asymmetric, arrangement with no predictable pattern in the placement of the lines,
limited only by the designer's imagination.

1 | Justified

There are five ways of arranging lines of
type on a page. The first is justified:
all the lines are the same length and align
both on the left and on the right.
The second is unjustified: the lines are
of different lengths and align on the
left and are ragged on the right. The third is
a similar arrangement, except now the
lines align on the right and are ragged
on the left. The fourth possibility is centered:
the lines are of unequal lengths with
both sides ragged. The fifth possibility
is a random, or asymmetric, arrangement
with no predictable pattern in the
placement of the lines, limited only by
the designer's imagination.

2 | Flush left, ragged right

There are five ways of arranging lines of
type on a page. The first is justified:
all the lines are the same length and align
both on the left and on the right.
The second is unjustified: the lines are
of different lengths and align on the
left and are ragged on the right. The third is
a similar arrangement, except now the
lines align on the right and are ragged on the
left. The fourth possibility is centered:
the lines are of unequal lengths with
both sides ragged. The fifth possibility
is a random, or asymmetric, arrangement
with no predictable pattern in the
placement of the lines, limited only by
the designer's imagination.

2 | Flush left, ragged right

There are five ways
of arranging lines of type on a page.
The first is justified: all the lines are the same length
and align both on the left and on
the right. The second is unjustified:
the lines are of different lengths and align on the left
and are ragged on the right. The third is a similar
arrangement, except now the lines align
on the right and are ragged on the left.
The fourth possibility is centered:
the lines are of unequal lengths with both
sides ragged. The fifth possibility
is a random, or asymmetric, arrangement
with no predictable pattern in the placement
of the lines, limited only
by the designer's imagination.

4 | Centered

There are five ways

of arranging lines of type on a page.

The first is justified: all the lines are the same length and align both on the left and on the right.

The second is unjustified: the lines are of different lengths and

align on the left and are ragged on the right.

The third is a similar arrangement,

except now the lines align on the right and are ragged on the left.

The fourth possibility is centered: the lines are of unequal lengths with both

sides ragged. The fifth possibility is a random, or asymmetric,

arrangement with no predictable pattern in the placement of the lines,

limited only by the designer's imagination.

5 | Random settings offer an opportunity to create a more personal and distinctive design.

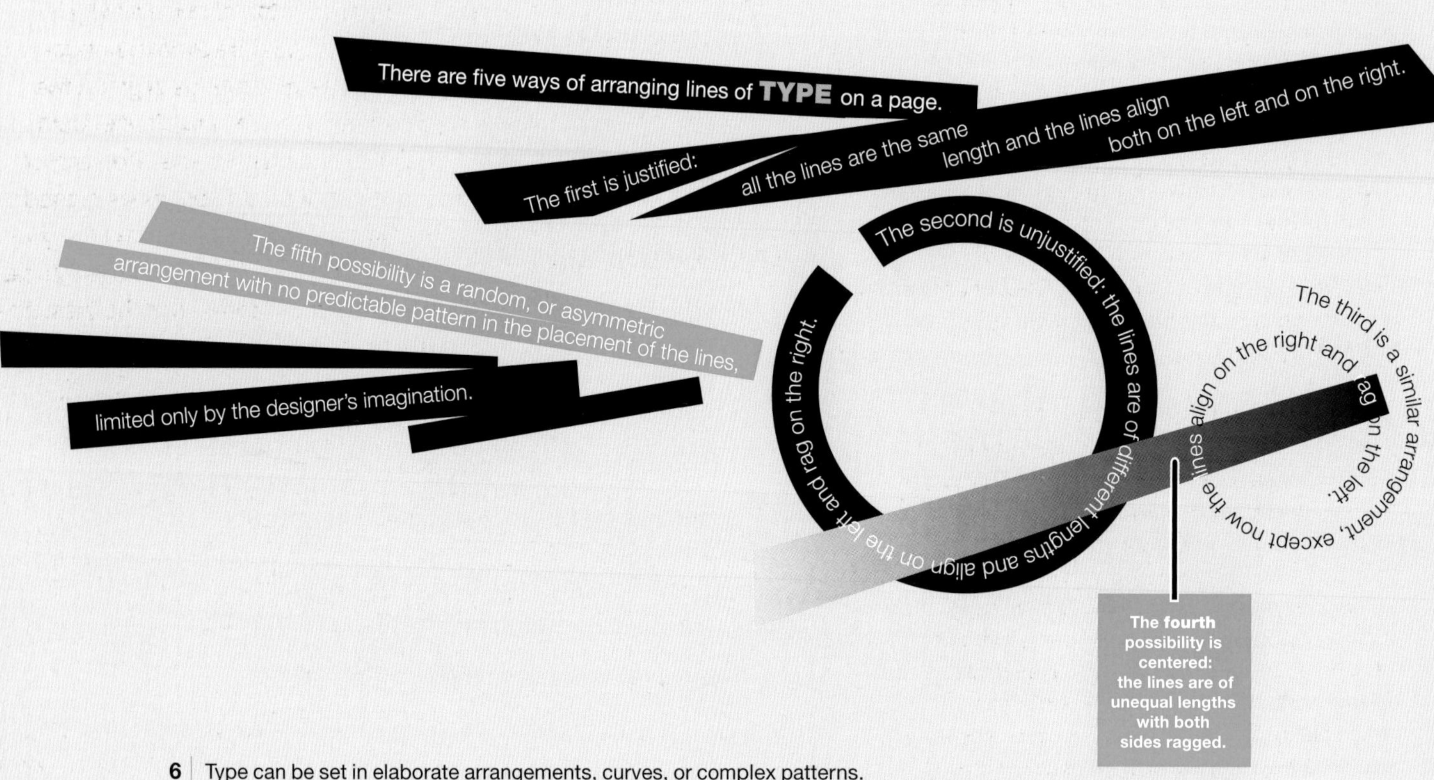

6 | Type can be set in elaborate arrangements, curves, or complex patterns.

Random, or Asymmetrical

This broad category of type arrangement is a dramatic departure from the other four, as random settings reflect no predictable pattern in length, placement, or arrangement of the lines (5). Thanks to their unusual arrangements, random settings can be visually exciting. Although not recommended for textbooks or lengthy reading matter, they provide a dramatic effect when type is used to attract attention. For this reason, random settings are widely used for posters, book jackets, flyers, advertisements, and short amounts of copy.

With random settings there are no rules to follow. Just set the lines so they look "right." A random arrangement allows for great flexibility and individuality, since no two designers will set the same lines in exactly the same manner. If handled carelessly, a random arrangement can be an unfortunate choice: too much type set randomly can be difficult to read and distract from the message. To avoid such problems, pay close attention to wordspacing, linespacing, and the overall arrangement of the elements. As with centered type, try to break the lines for sense.

In addition to the more conventional random arrangements, typesetting today is open to extreme experimentation, made possible by digital technology. This means unique typographic options can be created through trial and error, and immediate effects can be judged directly on the monitor. **Type no longer needs to be set in straight lines; it can be made to follow elaborate curves, spirals, and waves or to create complex patterns (6).** How well the type can be read is a question that has to be weighed carefully against the esthetic value created by special effects.

Runarounds and Contour Settings

Two more conventional special settings are referred to as runarounds and contour settings (7). A runaround, as the name suggests, is type that surrounds an image, a display initial, or even an empty space. The opposite is a contour setting, where the type takes on the shape of an object with a recognizable silhouette: a ball, vase, lightbulb, or geometric shape, for example. If readability is not a first priority, this setting can be employed. When planning either a runaround or a contour setting, always make sure there is an adequate amount of type to fit your layout. Try to keep your type evenly spaced. Holes and uneven spacing can be distracting and will minimize the effectiveness of the intended shape. ■

There are five ways of arranging lines of type on a page. The first is justified: all the lines are the same length and align both on the left and on the right. The second is unjustified: the lines are of different lengths and align on the left and are ragged on the right. The third is a similar arrangement, except now the lines align on the right and ragged on the left. The fourth possibility is centered: the lines are of unequal lengths with both sides ragged. The fifth possibility is a random, or asymmetric, arrangement with no predictable pattern in the placement of the lines, limited only by the designer's imagination.

There are five ways of arranging lines of type on a page. The first is justified: all the lines are the same length and align both on the left and on the right. The second is unjustified: the lines are of different lengths and align on the left and are ragged on the right. The third is a similar arrangement, except now the lines align on the right and are ragged on the left. The fourth possibility is centered: the lines are of unequal lengths with both sides ragged. The fifth possibility is a random, or asymmetric, arrangement with no predictable pattern in the placement of the lines, limited only by the designer's imagination.

7 | Runarounds and contour settings

Paragraph Indications

1-EM INDENT

3-EM INDENT

1-LINE SPACE

HANGING INDENT

NO INDENT

PARAGRAPH MARK

The reader must be able to distinguish where one paragraph ends and another begins. This is done in a number of ways.

The most common method of indicating a paragraph is to indent the opening line with a 1-em space, which is a square of the type size.

Indents larger than 1-em can also be used. This paragraph begins with a 3-em indent.

Paragraphs can also be separated by a half-line or a full-line space. Or a combination of indent and space may be used.

One unusual method is the hanging indent, where the first line of each paragraph begins to the left of the main body of text. This is commonly used in directories.

Another method is to use neither indent nor space. In this case the only indication that a new paragraph has begun is that the previous line falls short of the full measure. ❦ Still another possibility is to run the paragraphs together in a solid block of type and indicate the start of each paragraph with a typographic device such as a paragraph mark or a box.

1 | Popular ways of indicating paragraphs

■ Clear indications of paragraph changes must be provided for the reader. **There are many ways of indicating the start of a new paragraph (1).** The most common method is a 1-em indent. (As covered on page 22, an em is the square of the type size and therefore the indent is always in proportion to the type size.)

The text you are now reading is set with a 1-em indent, or 8.5 picas. When type is set to a wide measure, or a particular effect is desired, larger indents can be used, such as two ems or more. Non-traditional paragraph indents may be specified in picas, millimeters, or inches instead of ems.

Paragraphs can also be indicated through additional spacing — usually a half line or full line between paragraphs. Using full-line spaces between paragraphs has an advantage in that lines of type in adjacent columns will always align with each other, which will not happen if you use half-line spaces. It is also possible to combine line spaces and indents; variations of this style are quite common in contemporary magazines, books, and advertisements.

Another approach is no indentation, that is, to use neither an indent nor additional space between paragraphs. In this case the signal of a new paragraph depends solely on the length of the last line of the previous paragraph. The last line, however, must be shorter than the full measure. If a paragraph ends with a full or almost full line, the reader will be uncertain as to where one paragraph ends and another begins.

A more unusual method of starting a new paragraph is with a hanging indent. The first line of the paragraph is set to the full measure and subsequent lines are indented. This is commonly used for dictionaries and other reference sources.

Another possibility is the method used by early printers: all paragraphs were run together to form a solid block of type, and a typographic device indicated the start of each new paragraph. The traditional paragraph mark looks like this ¶, but any graphic device can be used. One of the most common devices is a solid square box or the traditional leaf or flourish, which looks like this: ❦.

While these solutions represent traditional methods of indicating paragraphs, today's technologies provide great opportunities to experiment. **Paragraphs can be indicated in countless ways (2).** Among the most common are setting type in unusual shapes, alternating typefaces, changing type sizes, inserting rules, introducing color, or by combining any of the above.

In all cases, designers must be sensitive to balance the impact of creativity against readability (3). ■

Johannes Gutenberg was born in Mainz, Germany, sometime around 1397. Little is known about his early years, but it is clear that he was the right man in the right place at the right time.

Gutenberg was the right man because of his familiarity with the craft of the goldsmith and the die maker. He was in the right place because Mainz was a cultural and commercial center. It was the right time because the Renaissance thirst for knowledge was creating a growing market for books that could not be satisfied with traditional handwritten manuscripts.

Handwritten manuscripts were made to order and were usually expensive. They were laboriously copied by scribes who had to either read from a manuscript or have it read to them while copying. This process not only was time-consuming but led to many errors, which had to be corrected. Adding to the expense was the scarcity and high cost of vellum and parchment. As a result, these handwritten manuscripts were limited to a select few: clergymen, scholars, and wealthy individuals.

A relatively inexpensive means of producing multiple copies of books seems to have been developed just a little before Gutenberg began his experiments with printing. This was the so-called block book, whose pages had illustrations and minimal text cut together on the same block. The carved blocks were inked, and images were transferred onto paper.

Gutenberg's genius was realizing that printing would be more efficient if, instead of using a single woodblock to print an entire page, the individual letters were cast as separate blocks and then assembled into pages. In this manner, pages could be corrected more rapidly, and after printing, the type could be cleaned and reused.

Johannes Gutenberg was born in Mainz, Germany, sometime around 1397. Little is known about his early years, but it is clear that he was the right man in the right place at the right time. **G**utenberg was the right man because of his familiarity with the craft of the goldsmith and the die maker. He was in the right place because Mainz was a cultural and commercial center. It was the right time because the Renaissance thirst for knowledge was creating a growing market for books that could not be satisfied with traditional handwritten manuscripts. **H**andwritten manuscripts were made to order and were usually expensive. They were laboriously copied by scribes who had to either read from a manuscript or have it read to them while copying. This process not only was time-consuming, but led to many errors, which had to be corrected. Adding to the expense was the scarcity and high cost of vellum and parchment. As a result, these handwritten manuscripts were limited to a select few: clergymen, scholars, and wealthy individuals. **A** relatively inexpensive means of producing multiple copies of books seems to have been developed just a little before Gutenberg began his experiments with printing. This was the so-called block book, whose pages had illustrations and minimal text cut together on the same block. The carved blocks were inked, and images were transferred onto paper. **G**utenberg's genius was realizing that printing would be more efficient if, instead of using a single woodblock to print an entire page, the individual letters were cast as separate blocks and then assembled into pages. In this manner, pages could be corrected more rapidly, and after printing, the type could be cleaned and reused.

2 | Paragraphs can be indicated in many ways besides indents and line spaces.

Johannes Gutenberg was born in Mainz, Germany, sometime around 1397. Little is known about his early years, but it is clear that he was the right man in the right place at the right time.

Gutenberg was the right man because of his familiarity with the craft of the goldsmith and the die maker. He was in the right place because Mainz was a cultural and commercial center. It was the right time because the Renaissance thirst for knowledge was creating a growing market for books that could not be satisfied with traditional handwritten manuscripts.

Handwritten manuscripts were made to order and were usually expensive. They were laboriously copied by scribes who had to either read from a manuscript or have it read to them while copying. This process not only was time-consuming, but led to many errors, which had to be corrected.

Adding to the expense was the scarcity and high cost of vellum and parchment. As a result, these handwritten manuscripts were limited to a select few: clergymen, scholars, and wealthy individuals.

A relatively inexpensive means of producing multiple copies of books seems to have been developed just a little before Gutenberg began his experiments with printing. This was the so-called block book, whose pages had illustrations and minimal text cut together on the same block. The carved blocks were inked, and images were transferred onto paper.

Gutenberg's genius was realizing that printing would be more efficient if, instead of using a single woodblock to print an entire page, the individual letters were cast as separate blocks and then assembled into pages. In this manner, pages could be corrected more rapidly, and after printing, the type could be cleaned and reused.

3 | Experimental solutions must take readability into account.

Creating Emphasis

Switching from roman to italic type is probably the most common way to draw attention to a particular word or phrase. And because italic is the same size and weight as roman, it does not disturb the overall appearance of the printed page. *Italic is a quiet way of attracting attention.*

1 | Italic: distinctive without being assertive

Caps are more assertive than italics; in fact, at times they may border on a command: BUY THIS PRODUCT NOW! Small caps offer an alternative. Like italics, small caps are UNASSERTIVE because they are small and there are no ascenders or descenders. In fact, they may get lost in the text unless set as CAPS AND SMALL CAPS.

2 | If caps are too assertive, try small caps.

Very few jobs are set without some word or phrase requiring emphasis, but which words are to be emphasized and to what degree? Too many words emphasized in too many ways can create an effect opposite from the one intended. The reader, instead of getting the message, will be confused or simply ignore the emphasis.

The number of words and their position within the copy may also affect the degree of emphasis required: a single word buried in the middle of the copy will need more emphasis than a lengthy phrase at the beginning of a paragraph.

Having determined the words to be emphasized, the designer must then decide upon the appropriate degree of emphasis. The following are a few of the more popular methods of creating emphasis. These possibilities range from subtle to assertive.

Roman with Italic

Most text is set in roman type, which means that the most common way to emphasize a word is by changing it from roman to italic (1). Italic type is the standard method of indicating such items as titles and foreign words. Because italic is the same size and weight as roman, it does not disturb the overall appearance of the printed page. Italic is a quiet way to attract attention. Be aware that sans serif italics are not always easy to distinguish from their roman counterpart.

Capitals or Small Caps

Another common type change is simply to switch from lowercase to all caps (2). Capitals are more assertive on the page than italics.

One of the advantages of using capitals is that they enable you to stay within the same font and point size. If you find the caps too assertive, consider setting them one size smaller than the text. Be certain that this reduced type size does not appear too light in juxtaposition to the regular type.

A more refined option is small caps, which can be substituted for capitals in instances where regular caps would be overly assertive and distracting. Because small caps are about the same height as the lowercase letters, they contribute to the uniformity of the page. If small caps lack the desired level of assertiveness, you may wish to combine regular caps with small caps, or letterspace the small caps to create emphasis. Be aware that very few fonts are available with true small caps and using caps of a smaller type size is not an acceptable substitute.

3

Mixing Type Sizes

A dramatic change in type size is commonly used for emphasis (3). While this design approach is often used for print ads, posters, book jackets, and other display applications, it can also be used in text settings by introducing a larger type size in the copy.

The appropriate size will depend on the degree of emphasis you wish to create and the given linespacing. If an increase in type size within the text is too great, the lines of type will overlap. Normally, increasing the type size is reserved for heads, chapter titles, callouts, folios, and related items that do not generally appear within the body of text.

Mixing Typestyles

An effective way to create strong emphasis is by staying within the same type size and changing the typestyle from regular to bold (4). Being a heavier version of the regular typeface, bold attracts more attention than either italics or caps. When used judiciously, bold type can be very effective. However, when dealing with lengthy copy, consider how the excessive blackness will affect the look of the setting and ultimately its readability.

Emphasis can also be achieved by using condensed or expanded typefaces from within the same family. This approach is generally limited to sans serif families in which a wider selection of typestyles is available.

There is a difference between "true" condensed and expanded typefaces and those created by stretching or compressing the letterforms. True condensed and expanded typefaces are individually designed as members of a specific type family.

Stretched or compressed typefaces lack the integrity of the original designs and legibility suffers. Where possible, always choose a true-drawn typeface that has been designed as a companion to the roman.

Mixing Typefaces

When mixing typefaces, choose two that present some contrast with each other (5). A marked difference will make the effect appear deliberate rather than accidental. For example, mixing Bodoni with Baskerville or Baskerville with Garamond may be too subtle and not provide sufficient contrast. And worse, this might even create the impression that you have mistakenly used the wrong font. A better combination might be a serif with a sans serif.

A dramatic type size change will always draw attention and is a very common design device used in advertising, especially with head-lines and blurbs. Be aware that there is a limit to the size increase within text—the larger type may overlap with the line above.

3 | Mixing type sizes

Next to italics, **bold type** is most widely used for emphasis. **It is difficult to ignore words set in bold type!** The use of condensed and expanded type for emphasis is usually limited to the sans serif families, such as Helvetica and Univers, in which a wide selection of typestyles is available.

4 | Mixing typestyles

When mixing type within a text setting, choose typefaces that present a contrast. Mixing Garamond with Baskerville is not as effective as mixing Garamond with **Helvetica**.

5 | Mixing typefaces

UNDER OVER STRIKE-THROUGH

6 | Underscore, overscore, and strike-through

Garamond	Old Style	1615
Baskerville	Transitional	1757
Bodoni	Modern	1788
Century	Slab Serif	1894
Helvetica	Sans Serif	1957

7 | Rules can help organize information.

□ 14-point type with open x-height box.

■ 14-point type with solid x-height box.

□ 14-point type with 14-point open box.

■ 14-point type with 14-point solid box.

□ 14-point type with oversized drop-shadow box.

14-point type with custom box.

14-point type with reverse box.

8 | Boxes can be customized for many purposes.

Underscoring

Underscoring is another way to create emphasis (6). In most cases the underscore falls just below the baseline and breaks for descenders. If you want the underscore to fall below the descenders, make sure there is enough linespacing to accommodate it.

Although less common than underscores, overscores and strike-throughs can also be used. While both can bring emphasis to a word or sentence, strike-throughs are more commonly used for making editorial corrections.

Rules

Rules can help to visually organize material and add character to a printed piece. **The weight of a rule, like linespacing, is specified in points and fractions of points (7).** Some rules are also referred to by name; for example, a 1/4-point rule is commonly referred to as a hairline rule. (See page 20.) Rules can also be created as a series of dots or dashes of varying weights. Always consider the amount of space you want above and below the rule. The length of the rule, like line length, can be specified in picas, as well as inches or centimeters.

Boxes

Boxes or squares can be generated in two basic styles: open (or outlined), and solid (or filled-in) boxes (8). Boxes have a number of typographic uses, the most common being for order forms and checklists. In this book a box is used at the beginning and end of each chapter.

Boxes can be created in any size. The traditional box is an em, the square of the type size: a 12-point box is 12 points square. When set, it aligns with the top of the ascender and the bottom of the descender. Therefore it will appear much larger than the text. If this is undesirable, you may prefer a box that is the square of the cap height. This is slightly smaller than the traditional box and can be set base-aligning. A further option is a box that matches the x-height and base-aligns, which attracts attention but does not overpower the text.

On the other hand, if you are setting a box for a practical purpose, such as checking off items, make sure it is large enough to fulfill its function.

Occasionally you may prefer to emphasize a word or phrase by drawing a custom box and framing the copy. The borders of these framed boxes can be specified in any weight or thickness and created in a wide range of styles.

Bullets

Bullets are characters that can be created in any size and used to emphasize items in a list (9). The size you choose is dictated in part by esthetics and in part by how strongly you want to emphasize a given item. The best position for a bullet is centered on the lowercase characters (x-height). If the bullet is fairly large, you may prefer to center it on the cap height.

When a hierarchy of information must to be presented in a bulleted list, a variety of sizes and shapes of bullets can be used. When doing so, it is often best to indent subordinate information in order to separate it better.

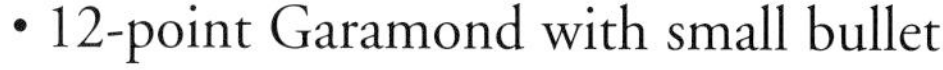

• 12-point Garamond with small bullet.

• 12-point Garamond with medium bullet.

● 12-point Garamond with large bullet.

9 | Bullets centered on lines of type

Position

One of the simplest methods of attracting attention is by positioning copy in a place or manner that is unexpected. For example, it is impossible to ignore graffiti scribbled on a wall or a poster. It may be disturbing but it attracts attention. **Because most type is set horizontally, simply setting the copy at an angle will set it apart (10).** This approach is usually restricted to small amounts of copy, such as heads, as no one wishes to read lengthy copy set in this manner.

10 | Positioning type in an unexpected way

Handwriting

Although this chapter is concerned primarily with the creative use of type, you should not dismiss handwriting as a means of creating emphasis, particularly for headlines and short statements (11). There is a quality to handwriting that is difficult to overlook. It may be its spontaneity, personal touch, or elegance. Whatever the reason, the informal character of handwritten script not only attracts attention but serves as a contrast to structured typography.

handwriting can be
an excellent means of
attracting attention.

11 | Although not type, handwriting can be effective.

Dingbats

Over the centuries, hundreds of typographic dingbats and ornaments have been designed for every imaginable purpose. (See page 154.) There are brackets, braces, flourishes, decorative borders, and countless other images that, when used appropriately, can be an effective way of attracting attention.

And who can ignore a pointing finger? ■

Grids

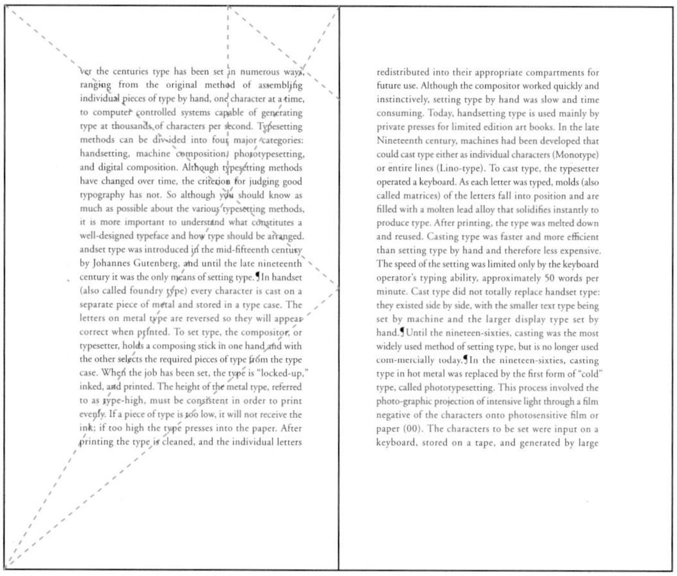

1 | Classic text proportions

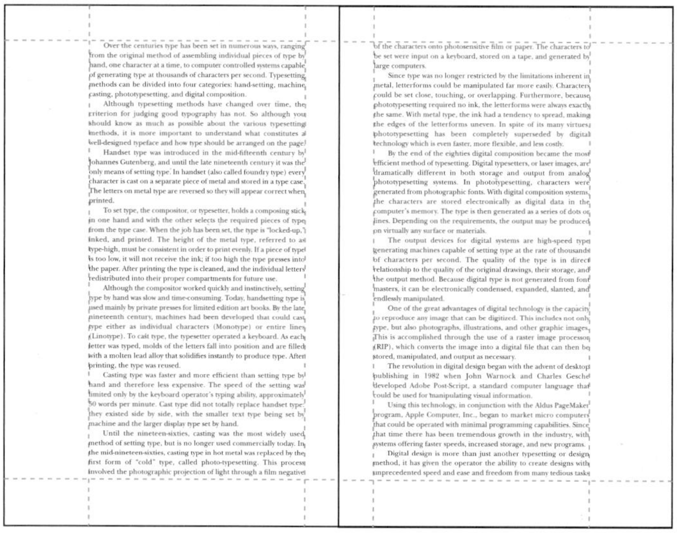

2 | Single-column grids require wider margins to avoid a line length that is too long for comfortable reading.

If you examine a well-designed publication, such as a book, magazine, or brochure, you will probably notice a strong sense of unity and logic throughout. To achieve this effect, the designer first creates a grid, which is a set of guidelines indicating horizontal and vertical divisions within the page. This grid is used as a guide for positioning the text, headlines, folios, captions, and illustrations. Although grids may seem restrictive, they allow for great innovation and bring a sense of unity to a publication. Even when using the same grid, no two designers will produce the same results.

Good designers use grids like recipes, following them only as long as they work. If some element of the design seems awkward when positioned within an otherwise well-designed grid, it is repositioned so that it looks correct visually — even if doing so "breaks" the format of the grid. However, if exceptions become too frequent, it may be time to reconsider the original grid.

Grids can range from the simple single-column to the more complex mutiple-column. In some cases, working without a grid is a possibility and can produce interesting results.

One-Column Grids

A one-column grid has a single column for both text and illustrations. With a single-column grid, the designer's main concern is selecting a suitable typeface and establishing a measure that is not too long.

A single-column grid allows white space to function as a quiet border, a format desirable for lengthy reading. **In classic text proportions, the outside margin is greater than the inside margin, and the top (head) margin is less than the bottom (foot) margin (1).** This lends balance to the page. Books such as novels and biographies are designed with variations on this format.

If a single column is too wide for comfortable reading, it is possible to reduce the column width slightly and reposition the column on the right or left side of the page (2). Although this offers a smaller text area, readability is enhanced and the page has a more open feeling.

Multiple-Column Grids

Multiple-column grids, like the one used for this book, allow for more flexibility and creative use of space (3). Most magazines as well as illustrated books are designed around multiple-column grids. Text and images may occupy one or more columns; illustrations may even run off the page (bleed).

Column widths may also vary: for instance, wide columns for text and narrow ones for captions and callouts. The grid for this book is five columns, usually two for text and three left for illustrations, which may not always sit on the grid.

Some grids designed for specific applications are very complex, having multiple columns that vary in width. Technical books, for example, may require a grid with special columns for data or charts as well several horizontal page divisions for organizing information.

Other grids may be designed with columns that can be shifted or overlapped to afford even greater design flexibility. Many publications have one grid format for editorial feature articles and another for classified ads or listings.

Working without a Grid

Perhaps the most challenging approach of all is to work without a grid. In this case, layouts are basically free-form, with each spread designed according to its own rules. With this method, the entire publication is held together by a common style or design concept. Cutting-edge publications often use this approach to achieve a free-form energy that can be dynamic and appealing.

To design several pages without the unifying properties of a grid may seem quite easy. But for any lengthy publication, the "no grid" approach can be very demanding on the designer as well as the reader. Students should begin by understanding the attributes of the grid before attempting to design without one.

Parts of a Page

There are a number of terms used by editors and designers to refer to all the elements that make up a printed page (4). Simple books usually contain body text, heads, and folios. More complex publications may contain many typographic details that provide additional information, such as running heads or running feet, callouts, or footnotes. Sometimes slightly different terms are used in different fields—a callout in a book is referred to as a deck in a magazine. Short passages that accompany a central story, called sidebars, are popular in newspapers today. ■

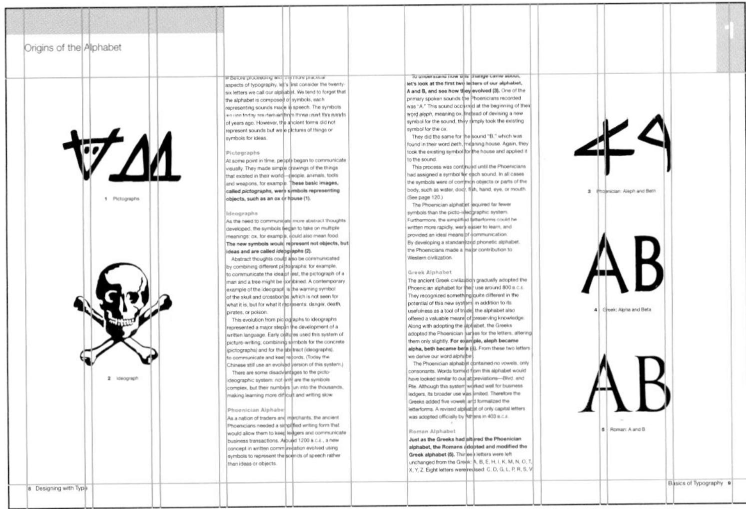

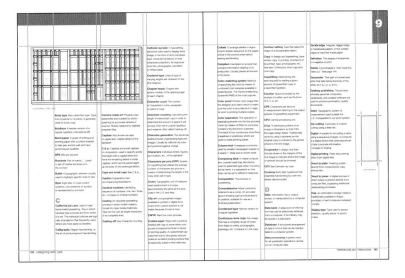

3 | Multiple-column grids allow for more flexibility and creative use of space.

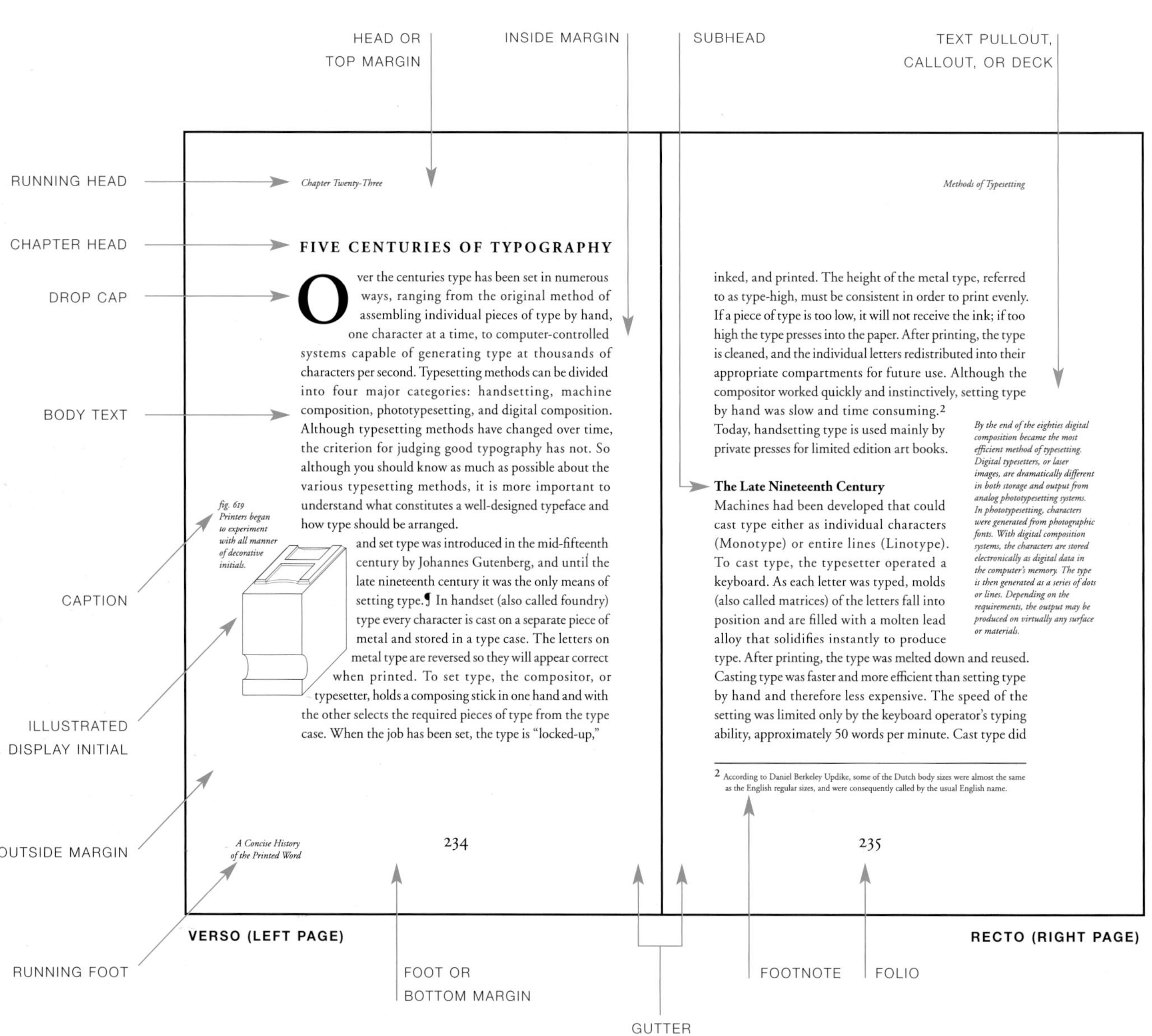

HEAD OR TOP MARGIN
INSIDE MARGIN
SUBHEAD
TEXT PULLOUT, CALLOUT, OR DECK
RUNNING HEAD
CHAPTER HEAD
DROP CAP
BODY TEXT
CAPTION
ILLUSTRATED DISPLAY INITIAL
OUTSIDE MARGIN
RUNNING FOOT
Chapter Twenty-Three
Methods of Typesetting
FIVE CENTURIES OF TYPOGRAPHY
Over the centuries type has been set in numerous ways, ranging from the original method of assembling individual pieces of type by hand, one character at a time, to computer-controlled systems capable of generating type at thousands of characters per second. Typesetting methods can be divided into four major categories: handsetting, machine composition, phototypesetting, and digital composition. Although typesetting methods have changed over time, the criterion for judging good typography has not. So although you should know as much as possible about the various typesetting methods, it is more important to understand what constitutes a well-designed typeface and how type should be arranged.
fig. 619 Printers began to experiment with all manner of decorative initials.
and set type was introduced in the mid-fifteenth century by Johannes Gutenberg, and until the late nineteenth century it was the only means of setting type.¶ In handset (also called foundry) type every character is cast on a separate piece of metal and stored in a type case. The letters on metal type are reversed so they will appear correct when printed. To set type, the compositor, or typesetter, holds a composing stick in one hand and with the other selects the required pieces of type from the type case. When the job has been set, the type is "locked-up,"
inked, and printed. The height of the metal type, referred to as type-high, must be consistent in order to print evenly. If a piece of type is too low, it will not receive the ink; if too high the type presses into the paper. After printing, the type is cleaned, and the individual letters redistributed into their appropriate compartments for future use. Although the compositor worked quickly and instinctively, setting type by hand was slow and time consuming.2 Today, handsetting type is used mainly by private presses for limited edition art books.
By the end of the eighties digital composition became the most efficient method of typesetting. Digital typesetters, or laser images, are dramatically different in both storage and output from analog phototypesetting systems. In phototypesetting, characters were generated from photographic fonts. With digital composition systems, the characters are stored electronically as digital data in the computer's memory. The type is then generated as a series of dots or lines. Depending on the requirements, the output may be produced on virtually any surface or materials.
The Late Nineteenth Century
Machines had been developed that could cast type either as individual characters (Monotype) or entire lines (Linotype). To cast type, the typesetter operated a keyboard. As each letter was typed, molds (also called matrices) of the letters fall into position and are filled with a molten lead alloy that solidifies instantly to produce type. After printing, the type was melted down and reused. Casting type was faster and more efficient than setting type by hand and therefore less expensive. The speed of the setting was limited only by the keyboard operator's typing ability, approximately 50 words per minute. Cast type did
2 According to Daniel Berkeley Updike, some of the Dutch body sizes were almost the same as the English regular sizes, and were consequently called by the usual English name.
A Concise History of the Printed Word
234
235
VERSO (LEFT PAGE)
RECTO (RIGHT PAGE)
FOOT OR BOTTOM MARGIN
FOOTNOTE
FOLIO
GUTTER

4 | Parts of a page

Designing with Display Type

With virtually unlimited display typefaces available, the designer has opportunities that did not exist a generation ago. New technologies allow for typographic expressions from the traditional to the most outlandish. In some cases display type may even serve strictly as a design element whose primary purpose is not conveying information but simply attracting attention or creating an interesting texture with letterforms.

Selecting Display Type

Many of the design principles appropriate for text type can be applied to display type. Since display type's primary purpose is to attract attention, however, you must consider additional factors as well.

First, consider the various ways you may be using display type. For example, the display type selected for a chapter title in a book serves a very different function from the type used in magazines, advertisements, and billboards. In the first instance, the reader is already involved in the book, and the display type merely signals a new chapter. In a magazine the display type generally reflects the spirit of an article. In an advertisement the display type is meant to attract the attention of readers, engage their interest in the copy, and entice them to buy a product while simultaneously competing with other ads. On a billboard the type must be read quickly while traveling in a moving vehicle.

Next, as with text type, consider your audience: is the reader a child buying a candy bar, a driver looking for a road sign, a scientist studying a reference book, or a consumer seeking information on cosmetics? All the above will influence your typeface selection and your final design.

Display type
does not have to be large
to attract attention.

Harmony or Contrast

When selecting a display type, consider also the relationship between it and the text type. Will the display type be from the same family as the text type, or will it be in contrast to it? For example, if the text is Bodoni, the display type could be a larger size of Bodoni. Or it could be a variation of Bodoni, such as Bodoni Bold, Bodoni Condensed, or Ultra Bodoni, which would create harmony between display type and text.

If you prefer contrast, select a typeface from a different family. To be effective, the contrast should be obvious—a bold sans serif display type with a roman serif text face, for example.

Not all combinations are successful. As a rule, two similar typefaces from different families may produce a weak result because of their lack of contrast. It would be ineffective to combine Garamond with Baskerville, for example, or Helvetica and Futura.

Expressive Display Type

Display types have personalities: they can create a wide range of expressions, from solemn to shocking. As you work with display type, you will become aware of these attributes. Roman typefaces, like ancient Roman inscriptions, are dignified, austere, and graceful. Egyptian and slab serif typefaces have a strong presence; they are forceful and assertive. Sans serif faces create a modern, businesslike quality, an efficient, no-nonsense feeling, while the moods created by script typefaces are as varied as the handwritings they simulate.

Study the words *Rome, circus,* and *steel.* They are set in three different display faces. **Decide which face you feel is the most appropriate for each word (1).** You will probably find that most people will agree with your choice.

Ornate Display Type

If the copy is a short or easily recognizable word or phrase, the typeface can be ornate and still communicate its meaning (2). Easily identified words are almost indestructible. For example, the word *sale* is recognizable regardless of the typeface. **On the other hand, lengthy or unfamiliar words in an ornate typeface may confuse the reader or go unread (3).**

Text Type as Display Type

Type used for display need not be 16 points or larger. A text-size type, by its position, color, or surrounding white space, may function successfully as display. The notion that the larger the type, the greater the success in attracting attention is not necessarily true. Bigger is not always better. ■

ROME CIRCUS STEEL

ROME CIRCUS STEEL

ROME CIRCUS STEEL

1 | Some words seem more appropriately set in one typeface than in another.

SALE SALE SALE

SALE SALE SALE

SALE SALE SALE

2 | Easily recognizable words can be set in any typeface.

3 | Unfamiliar words set in ornate typefaces can be confusing.

Arranging Display Type

DESIGNING WITH DISPLAY TYPE

ALL CAPS

designing with display type

ALL LOWERCASE

Designing With Display Type

CAP FIRST LETTER OF EVERY WORD

Designing with Display Type

CAP FIRST LETTER OF IMPORTANT WORDS (TITLE CASE)

Designing with display type

CAP FIRST LETTER OF FIRST WORD ONLY (SENTENCE CASE)

1 | First, determine which letters should be capitalized.

Having reviewed some of the factors dictating your choice of display types, now consider ways of setting and arranging the type. **First, let's begin with five basic settings of a single line of type, using the words *designing with display type* (1).** The basic choices are as follows:

1. All caps
2. All lowercase
3. Cap first letter of every word
4. Cap first letter of important words (title case)
5. Cap first letter of first word only (sentence case)

Don't be misled by what seems to be only a slight difference between the last three settings. The use of capitals in a word may seem insignificant, but remember that caps can change not only the way the word looks but also its impact. Consider, for example, the impact of your name written in lowercase letters. In typography even the most subtle changes in settings can produce very noticeable differences.

Once you have determined how you wish to set the type, now consider its arrangement. Suppose you have decided to work with all caps. Here are five possible ways to arrange the words:

1. Type set on one line
2. Flush left, ragged right
3. Flush right, ragged left
4. Centered
5. Random, or asymmetrical

Using the above five arrangements, you can see the wide range of possibilities available (2). Notice how the various settings differ in terms of readability and character. These examples are a mere inventory of basic ways to create a typographic effect and should serve simply as a point of departure. Your final selection will depend on your choice of typeface, the letters you choose to capitalize, and the unique needs of the specific project.

In spite of the many solutions possible, the majority of typographic problems are solved by one of the first two arrangements: type set on one line or as flush left, ragged right. These arrangements do not suggest a lack of imagination on the part of designers, they happen to be the easiest to read. ■

DESIGNING WITH DISPLAY TYPE

SET ON ONE LINE

DESIGNING WITH
DISPLAY TYPE

FLUSH LEFT, RAGGED RIGHT

DESIGNING
WITH
DISPLAY TYPE

DESIGNING
WITH
DISPLAY
TYPE

DESIGNING WITH
DISPLAY TYPE

FLUSH RIGHT, RAGGED LEFT

DESIGNING
WITH
DISPLAY TYPE

DESIGNING
WITH
DISPLAY
TYPE

DESIGNING WITH
DISPLAY TYPE

CENTERED

DESIGNING
WITH
DISPLAY TYPE

DESIGNING
WITH
DISPLAY
TYPE

DESIGNING WITH
DISPLAY TYPE

RANDOM, OR ASYMMETRICAL

DESIGNING
WITH
DISPLAY TYPE

DESIGNING
WITH
DISPLAY
TYPE

2 | Next, decide the most effective type arrangement.

Optical Considerations

1 | Less space is required between circular letters than vertical ones.

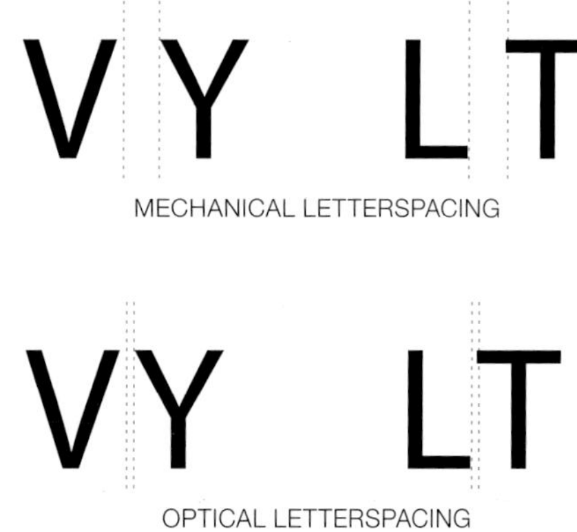

2 | Some combinations defy simple solutions.

■ Designers spend a great deal of time fine-tuning their designs by adding or removing space between letters and lines of type to achieve a desired effect. They understand that just because the space between letters, words, and lines of type is mechanically equal, it may not appear optically equal or visually balanced. When this occurs, adjustments must be made.

Letterspacing and Wordspacing

Since display type is generally large, any inconsistency in letterspacing or wordspacing is distracting and tends to hinder readability. This is seldom a problem with lowercase letters because they tend to set evenly, but words set in all caps often have inconsistent letterspacing. To correct this, you must open up some letter combinations and tighten others.

Most design programs have an automatic kerning feature to ensure that letters fit together properly. Despite the sophistication of these programs, you may still need to adjust some letters individually. Let your trained eye, not the computer, be the final judge. Here are some guidelines regarding specific letter combinations.

Between circular letters, such as two Os, less space is required than between straight letters, such as an I and an H (1). Angular letters and letters that have overhanging strokes, such as V, Y, L, A, and T, also require less space and, in some cases, extreme kerning (2).

Whether space is added or deleted, most adjustments will be subtle, but they will make a difference. Remember, adjusting the letterspacing also requires the wordspacing to be adjusted so that they are compatible.

Words set in all caps, such as heads or titles, are generally improved by letterspacing and optical adjustments. **Letterspacing lowercase letters, although less common, can also be effective (3).**

N A P O L E O N

n a p o l e o n

3 | Capital letters are more frequently letterspaced than lowercase letters.

Linespacing

Just as there are optical discrepancies with letterspacing and wordspacing, there may also be optical irregularities with linespacing (4). When display type is set in all caps, the linespacing appears equal because there are no ascenders and descenders.

With lowercase type, however, ascenders and descenders can play tricks on your eyes, making some of the lines appear closer together. In such cases, the space between certain lines may have to be increased or decreased mechanically until you feel the linespacing looks optically correct.

Alignment

When lines of display type are set flush left, the vertical alignment may seem irregular, especially when the first letter in each line is a cap. Letters having straight vertical strokes, such as B, E, F, H, I, M, N, P, and R, align perfectly, while irregular letters, such as A, C, J, O, T, V, W, and Y, may seem out of alignment even though the type is mechanically correct. **To achieve better alignment, move the letters slightly left or right until they appear optically correct (5).**

There are times when no amount of adjusting seems to work. For example, the cap T can be awkward; no matter what you do, it will not appear to align. If you align the vertical stroke, the crossbar juts into the margin. If you align the crossbar, the letter appears indented. Neither solution is satisfactory. You will need to experiment by visually adjusting the characters until the result looks acceptable.

Centering Type

When positioning a single line or a block of text on a page, adjustments must be made if you wish the type to appear to be centered. **A dot set in the center of a square may be located in the true center, but to look visually centered, the dot must be raised slightly above true center (6).**

The same principle applies to a line of type, or the crossbar on the cap H, or any image you want to center. There should always be fractionally more white space below the image than above. ■

TYPE SET IN
ALL CAPS CREATES
EQUAL LEADING,
but when type is set in
lowercase, the leading
may appear irregular.

4 | Linespacing may need adjusting.

IRREGULAR
CAP LETTERS,
SUCH AS A, C,
J, O, T, V, W,
AND Y, MUST
BE ALIGNED
OPTICALLY.

5 | Good vertical alignment can be challenging.

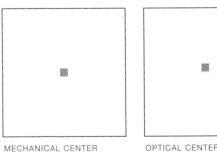

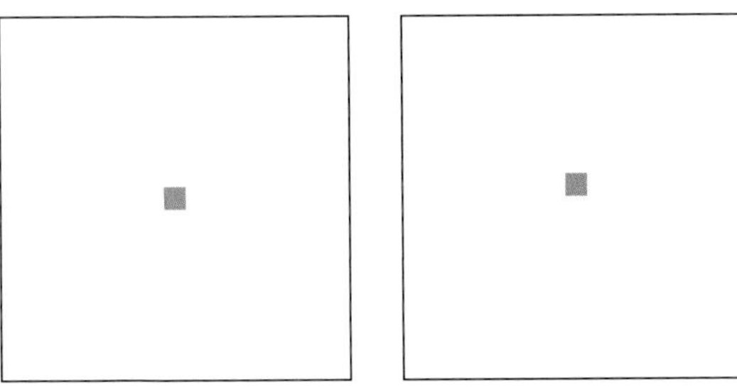

6 | Mechanical and optical centers differ.

Punctuation

"When punctuation marks are set outside the type measure, they are referred to as 'hung' punctuation. Hanging punctuation in the margin preserves the straight vertical edge created by flush lines of type. Small punctuation, such as commas, periods, hyphens, apostrophes, asterisks, and quotation marks, have less weight than full-size characters, and when set inside the measure they may create 'holes' in the flush alignment. This can be distracting, especially for small amounts of type in highly visible areas, such as ads."

1 | Hung punctuation

Ms. I.K. Scala, N.Y.C., N.Y.

Ms. I.K. Scala, N.Y.C., N.Y.

2 | Space after punctuation often need adjusting.

"A quote can be dramatized by setting the quotation marks larger than the type."

3 | Enlarged punctuation marks add drama.

How you handle punctuation, whether in display or text settings, can have a decided visual impact on your design and in some cases even affect readability. Here are some design considerations you should keep in mind when working with display type where punctuation is highly visible.

Hung Punctuation

Small punctuation marks (commas, periods, hyphens, apostrophes, asterisks, and quotation marks) have less weight than full-size characters and, when set inside the measure, may create visual indents in the flush vertical alignment. For this reason, you may wish to consider setting small punctuation marks outside the measure in order not to disturb the vertical type alignment. **When punctuation marks are set outside the type measure, they are referred to as "hung" punctuation (1).**

Larger punctuation marks (colons, semicolons, question marks, and exclamation points), which have the same visual weight as full-size characters, are set within the measure. The em-dash, because of its length, is also set within the measure.

Keep in mind that hanging punctuation is not usually an automatic feature available in many design programs. In these instances, the designer must manually create this refinement.

Space after Periods

Normally, a single wordspace is required after a period. This is fine for the end of a sentence but too generous when periods follow an abbreviation. **With display type, always use less-than-normal wordspacing when setting abbreviations (2).** In some cases, because of the configuration of the letters, abbreviations can be set with no wordspacing at all, as in U.S.A.

Enlarging Punctuation Marks

Punctuation marks can be used as a design element to emphasize a point (3). For example, a quote can be made more dramatic by setting the quotation marks in a larger type size than the quote itself, or an oversized question mark can be used to bring attention to a query. Exclamation marks also lend themselves to dramatization.

It is also possible, though less common, to reduce punctuation marks when there is either an unusual amount of punctuation or the copy is set in bold type. To create a better visual balance between the punctuation and the copy, consider setting the punctuation marks one or two sizes smaller than the display type.

Short and Long Dashes

Most typefaces have two standard dashes: the *em-dash* and the *en-dash*, also referred to as the *long dash* and the *short dash*. Some designers feel that the em-dash creates a hole in the text, so they use an en-dash or even a hyphen. But these dashes are editorially inappropriate.

It is better to customize the em-dash by compressing it approximately 25% and adding a small amount of extra space on either side (4). Remember that dashes have specific editorial uses. You may need to check with the copywriter or client before you decide to use customized dashes.

Many designers feel that the em-dash—being too long—creates a hole in the text. They prefer to use a shorter en-dash – with a small amount of additional space on either side of it.

4 | Some dashes may require adjusting.

Hyphens

Hyphens are designed to be centered on the x-height. This is ideal for lowercase letters but too low for words set in all caps. **When setting hyphenated words in all caps, center the hyphen on the cap height. The same applies when setting dashes and parentheses (5).**

When reviewing typeset copy, check for excessive or awkward hyphenation. In general, try to avoid hyphenation with unjustified type. For example, when type is set flush left, ragged right, the option exists to vary the line length, and therefore reduce the need for hyphenation.

In justified settings, where hyphenation is often necessary, try to avoid two consecutive lines in which hyphens occur. In all cases, three or more consecutive lines ending with a hyphen is considered bad typography. Also avoid hyphenating a proper name and always consult a dictionary if you are uncertain about a specific word break.

(Cap-height) (CAP-HEIGHT)

5 | Hyphens (and parentheses) with caps require adjusting.

Breaking Lines

When setting unjustified copy, study it carefully and decide where you want to break the lines. **The preferred treatment is to "break for sense," that is, so that words can easily be read while forming an interesting pattern on the page (6).**

To accomplish this, you may have to reconsider your design or request that the copy be altered. Obviously, the latter can be a problem when you are dealing with classic literature or other forms of copy that cannot be altered. In most cases, however, there is great deal of give and take between designers, copywriters, and editorial personnel. ■

NOTE | See page 156 for rules on punctuation.

Break copy
not only
for the shape,
but also
for content,
as a means
of improving
readability.

6 | Making copy easy to read and esthetically pleasing

Display Initials

D isplay initials offer the designer an effective method of embellishing a printed piece. Simply by adding a display initial, the designer can completely change the look, feeling, and character of a printed piece. Display initials fall into three basic categories: raised, inset, and hanging. Other methods of using display initials are variations on these.

1 | Raised initial

D isplay initials offer the designer an effective method of embellishing a printed piece. Simply by adding a display initial, the designer can completely change the look, feeling, and character of a printed piece. Display initials fall into three basic categories: raised, inset, and hanging. Other methods of using display initials are variations on these.

2 | Inset or inserted display initial

D isplay initials offer the designer an effective method of embellishing a printed piece. Simply by adding a display initial, the designer can completely change the look, feeling, and character of a printed piece. Display initials fall into three basic categories: raised, inset, and hanging. Other methods of using display initials are variations on these.

3 | Hanging display initial

■ Display initials (or initial caps) can be an effective typographic device to attract attention and direct the eye to the opening of a paragraph or section. A display initial may be raised, inset, or hung in the margin. Other methods of using display initials are probably variations on these three. In all instances, optical alignment plays an important part in a successful treatment.

Raised Initials

A raised initial base-aligns with the first line of text (1). The amount of indent is dictated by the width of the display initial and by your eye to achieve the desired effect. Although the initial is usually set to align with the text on the left, you may prefer to indent the initial so that it is positioned well inside the measure.

Consider also the space following the raised initial. Display letters that do not finish with a vertical stroke, such as T, V, and F, may create too much space between the display initial and the following letter. This can be corrected by tightening the space between the display initial and the text type to ensure the first word is unified.

Inset Initials

An inset, or drop, initial is set into the text (2). A number of lines must be indented equally to allow space for the initial. The exact number of lines and the amount of the indent are dictated by the width and depth of the initial. An inset initial looks best when it aligns at the top with the cap height of the first line of type and on the bottom with the baseline of another line of type.

There are many variations on inset initials. For example, with a cap A you may wish to set the first line of the text closer to the initial than the lines that follow. Or with a cap V you may prefer to have the type follow the contour of the letter rather than have the initial sitting in a rectangular white space.

Hanging Initials

The hung initial is probably the least common of the display initials (3). It is usually positioned in the left margin outside the measure and aligns with the first line of type, although the hung initial can be placed along the column wherever it seems to work best. The distance between the initial and the text can be determined mechanically or optically. ■

4

Modifying Type

Until now we have dealt with the more traditional and fundamental ways of setting and arranging text and display type.

Once you understand these basics, you should begin to explore the many fascinating typographic possibilities made possible with today's technologies,

Technology has always played a major role in the creative life of the designer. Over the centuries innovations in printing and typesetting have made it possible for designers to explore new typographic expression. With the improved printing presses and smoother papers of the eighteenth century, typefaces became more refined. In the early nineteenth century, wood type enabled designers to create large customized lettering. In the 1970s the intoduction of phototypesetting freed designers from the restrictions of metal type by ushering in an era of free-form typography.

However, no technological innovation of the past has provided more opportunities for creative experimentation in both typeface design and innovative layouts than digital technology.

Innovative Typefaces

Like many fine artists, graphic designers and typeface designers continually challenge tradition. In recent years many designers have questioned traditional type design and conventional standards of typographic excellence. They have demanded new standards to replace what they consider to be old typefaces and tired conventions.

Today, digital typography has placed typographic control directly in the hands of designers. Now, a computer is all that is required in order to experiment with layouts, manipulate type, or even design a new typeface.

From this innovation has come a dizzying array of new typefaces, the likes of which had never been seen before (1). Some are quirky, intentionally imperfect, and others are very personal. Many challenge the limits of legibility. Designers have seized upon these new tools and are generating a new and exciting approach to typography.

Amelia

Emigre Fifteen

FARFELL FELT TIP

Lunatix

Motion Light

Old Dreadful No 7

Pesto

POKER PARTY NAKED

RED FIVE

Schablone Label

1 | Some innovative display faces

designing
WITH TYPE

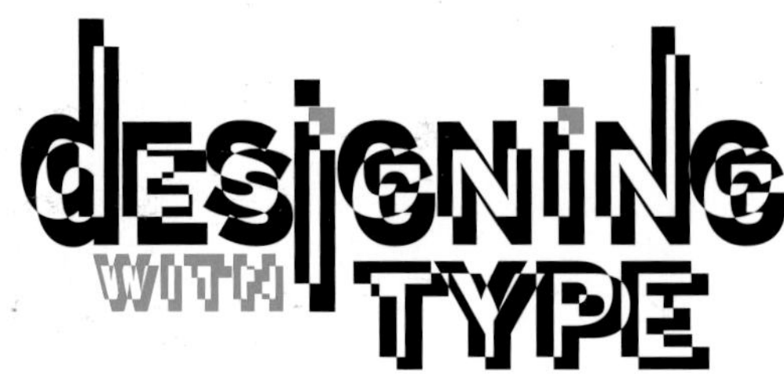

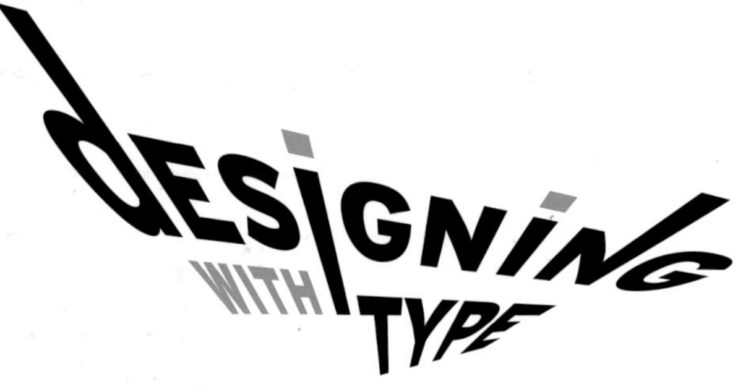

2 | Digitally manipulated type

Innovative Layouts

Most design applications have been created to provide graphic designers with total typographic control. Designers can change typefaces, sizes, styles, spacing, and output in seconds, all without the the need for outside services. With illustration and image-editing applications, designers can achieve special effects, distortions, and custom type manipulation. **Almost any design that can be imagined can be produced through the use of these applications (2).**

With this new wealth comes responsibility and the need for good judgment in selecting and setting the appropriate typeface for any given job. Designers can no longer rely upon the expertise of outside typesetting services and editorial input. Decisions that contribute to typographic excellence, such as spacing, kerning, hyphenation, and proper grammar have now become the designer's responsibility. (See *Punctuation* on page 156.)

Today it is a challenge for designers to avoid being seduced by technology. As sophisticated as computer applications may be, they are only tools for the creative mind. Truly successful designs begin with ideas and concepts. As you execute your designs on the computer, your knowledge of typography, combined with your trained eye and esthetic judgment, will provide the path to the most creative solution.

Not all assignments call for "cutting edge" design. Some designers have the luxury—and clients—that permit them to do experimental typography and still make a living. Other designers, catering to a more conservative clientele that prefers more traditional typography, may integrate new design motifs into their work to give it a contemporary look. ■

NOTE | What is original and dynamic today, will be yesterday's design tomorrow. New and innovative typography does not necessarily replace existing forms of typographic expression, but supplements them and thereby enriches the world of typography.

Learn to appreciate all forms of typography, determining for yourself what is appropriate for specific projects.

Color

Color is perhaps the most dramatic means of attracting attention and enhancing a design. Even a single word in a composition when printed in color will attract attention.

Color can also help to establish a mood. There is an emotion suggested by every color, whether it be fire-engine red, sky blue, or baby pink.

Some of the factors to consider besides selecting a "nice" color are type size, surrounding colors, background images, and whether the job is to be printed with inks (solid or process colors) or projected with light.

Understanding the advantages and limitations of each will enable you to work more effectively with color and type.

Spot Colors

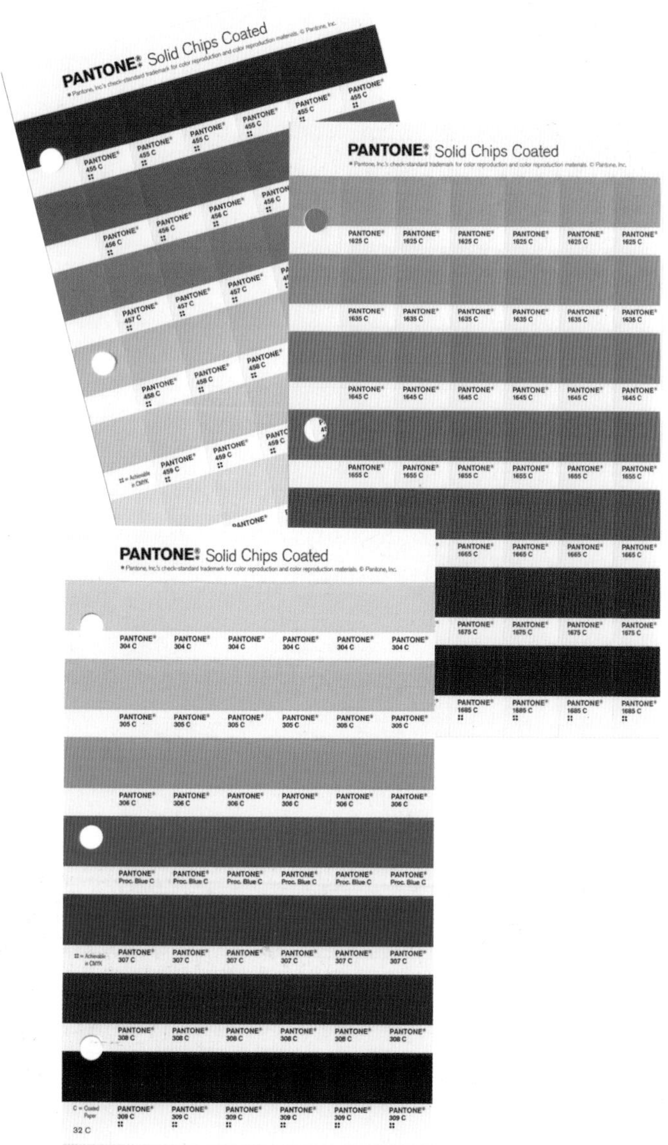

1 | Solid inks are indicated by a name or number code.

■ *Spot colors,* also known as *solid colors*, are individually blended printing inks whose variations run into the thousands, including a full range of metallics, fluorescents, and pastels. **Using a "swatchbook," the designer selects a numbered color that the printer will match (1).** Among the most popular color-matching systems is the Pantone Matching System, more commonly referred to as PMS.

Swatchbooks come in uncoated, coated, and matte-coated papers. It is important to select the ink color based on the paper's finish, as it will have a definite effect on how the color will look when printed. With uncoated papers, inks are absorbed into the fibers of the paper, making the colors appear duller. With coated papers (including matte-coated), the inks tend to sit on the surface of the paper and appear brighter.

Solid colors are commonly used in two- and three-color jobs, such as the cover of this book; the blue is Pantone 299 and the yellow is Pantone 108 and, of course, black is also considered an ink color.

Tints

A tint is a color printed less than its full density, thus making a lighter shade of the same color (2). This effect is created by *screening*, that is, by converting the solid image into a pattern of dots of varying sizes—the smaller the dots, the lighter the tint.

Traditionally, tints were produced in values of ten: with 10% being the lightest and 100% the solid color. Although any value can be specified nowadays, most designers tend to stay with the traditional values, or sometimes use increments of 5%.

Tints are a great asset when a project is limited to a single color and the effect of a broader range of color is desired. The appropriate tint will be determined by such factors as the readability, the effect you wish to create, and, of course, the size of the type — because if the type is too small, it will not be able to hold the dot pattern and will break up.

By reviewing the chart on the facing page, you can get a good idea of how different type sizes are affected by the value of the tint (3).

NOTE | What you see on the monitor will seldom match the printed piece. Always refer to an industry swatchbook such as a Solid Color Specifier or Tint Specifier for an accurate color reference.

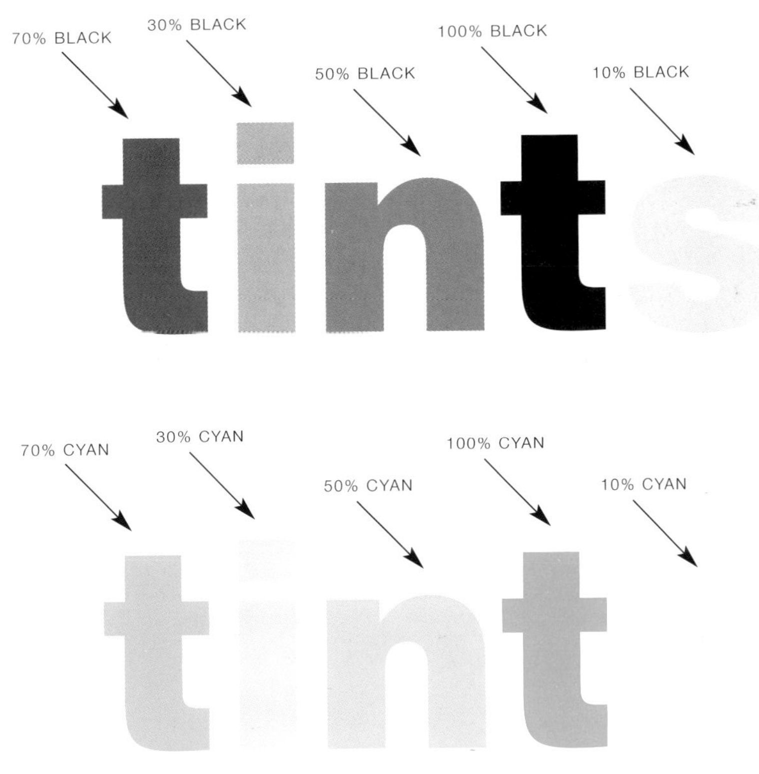

2 | Tints can be used to create the effect of additional colors.

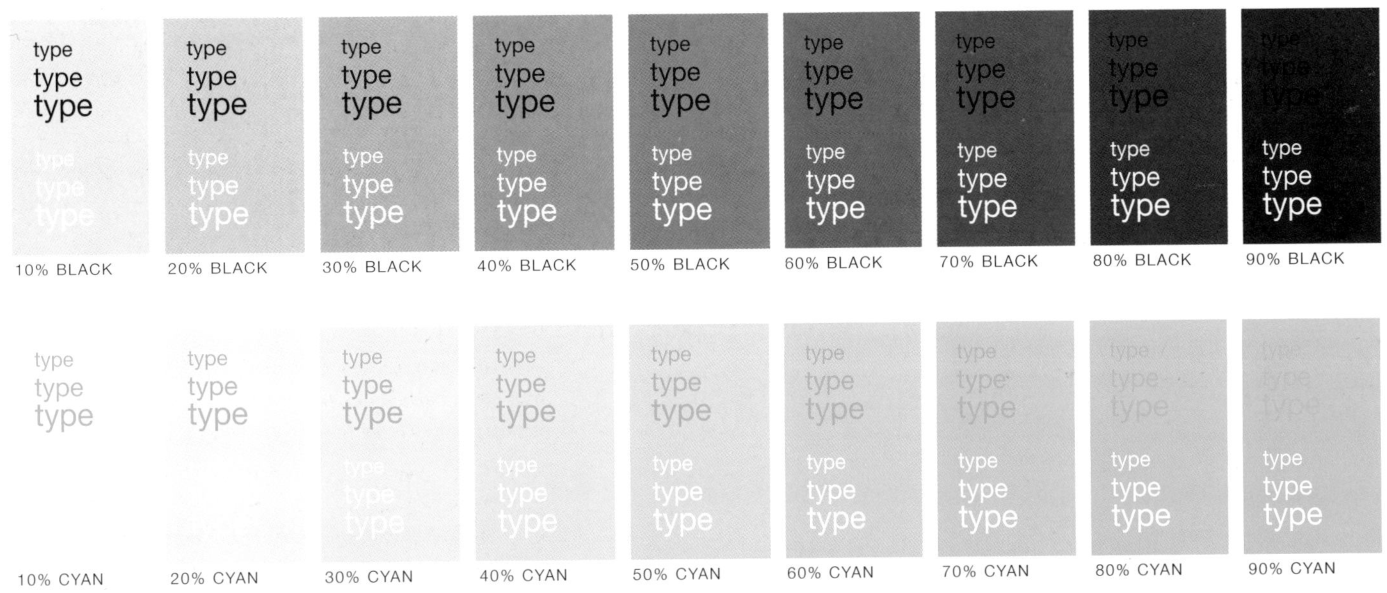

3 | Readability is affected by the typeface, type size, and tint.

Reversing

Reversing, also called *knocking out*, is when type is dropped out of a background color, tint, illustration, or photograph.

When reversing type, special considerations must be given to selecting the right typeface (4). Normally, when type is printed black on white, the black ink tends to spread, making the strokes heavier. This is called *ink squeeze*. When the type is reversed, the ink now spreads into the white areas, making the strokes narrower and in some extreme cases nonexistent.

Reversing type is a common means of creating emphasis. However, this effect has potential drawbacks. When reversed, text type has a tendency to sparkle and long passages may go unread. This precaution is not meant to suggest that you should avoid reverse type, but may serve as a warning against using small typefaces or typefaces having exceptionally fine strokes or serifs, such as Bodoni.

When reversing type,
consider the typeface carefully.
Avoid small type sizes or typefaces
having exceptionally fine strokes or serifs,
as they tend to fill in
when printed.

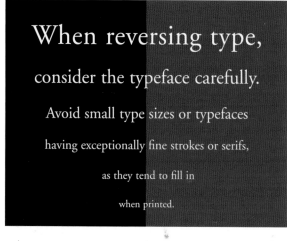

4 | Reversed type in various sizes and backgrounds

Overprinting

Overprinting, also called *surprinting,* is when one color is printed over another. **An example of this is when type is printed over a solid color or tint (5).**

With overprinting, ink squeeze can be an asset in most cases. When type is overprinted, the action of the ink squeeze makes the type appear slightly heavier. However, this may present a problem when printing very small type sizes, as the space between the letters and counters may fill in.

Consider the appropriate typeface and type size carefully when overprinting (or reversing) type on backgrounds that may be too dark or too busy. **This is especially the case with photographs where the background varies from one area to another (6).**

Typeface and type size should be considered when selecting a background color for reversing or overprinting type (7). ■

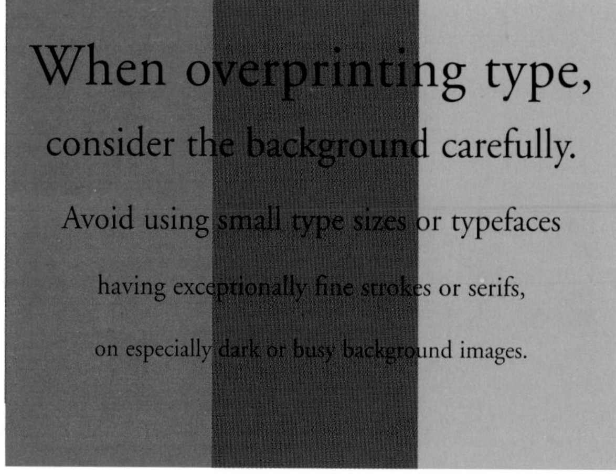

5 | Overprinted type in various sizes and backgrounds

NOTE | There will be times when neither reversing nor overprinting will be possible due to a background that is simply too busy. After trying and exhausting all the obvious solutions, such as increasing the type size and experimenting with various colors and locations, you may have to resort to a more practical solution. In this case, consider creating a quiet area of solid color on which you can either print or reverse the type.

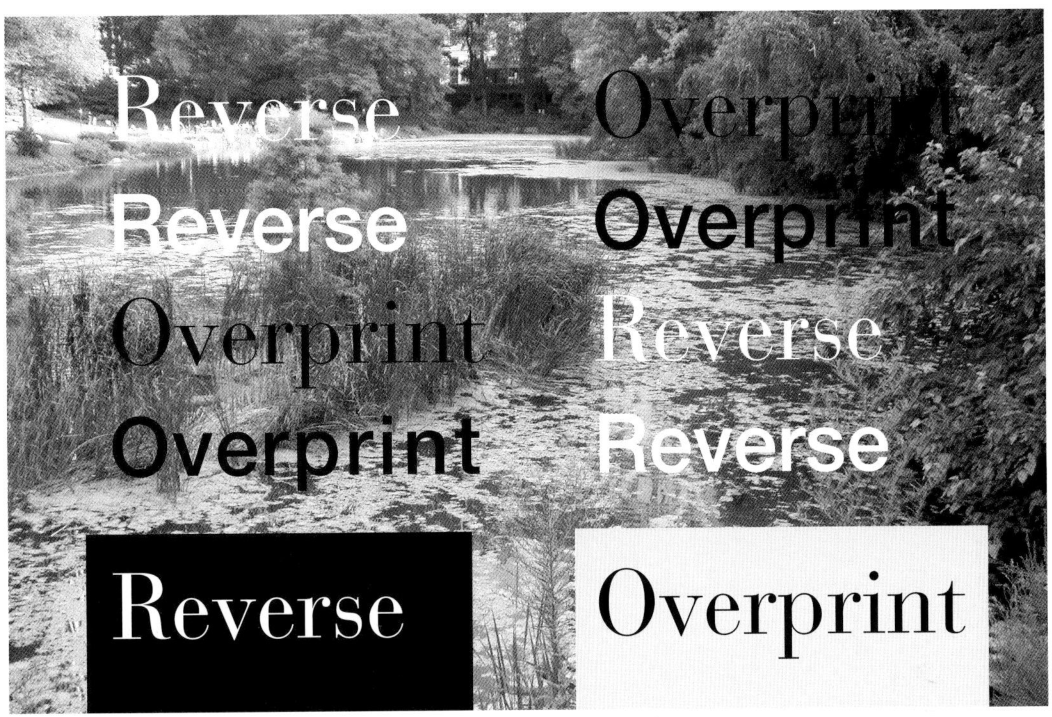

6 | Reversing and overprinting type can be problematic with busy backgrounds.

Garamond	Baskerville	Century	Bodoni	Helvetica
Garamond	Baskerville	Century	Bodoni	Helvetica
Garamond	Baskerville	Century	Bodoni	Helvetica
Garamond	Baskerville	Century	Bodoni	Helvetica
Garamond	Baskerville	Century	Bodoni	Helvetica
Garamond	Baskerville	Century	Bodoni	Helvetica

7 | Various typefaces and sizes reversed and overprinted

Process Colors

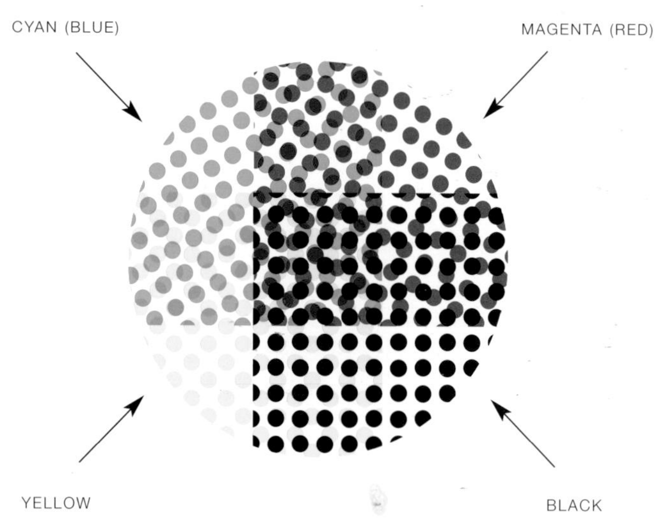

1 | Enlarged patterns of process color dots

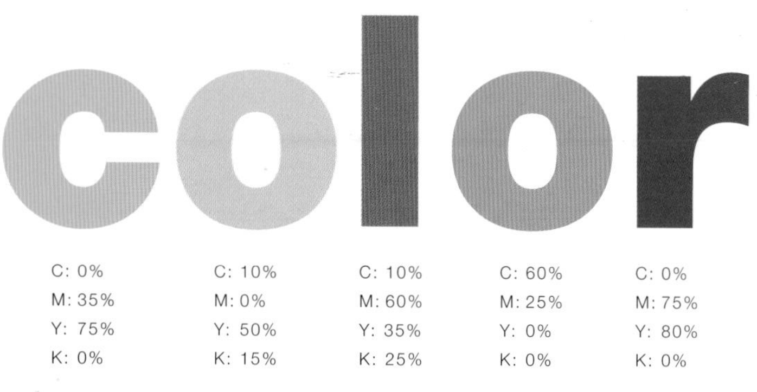

C: 0%	C: 10%	C: 10%	C: 60%	C: 0%
M: 35%	M: 0%	M: 60%	M: 25%	M: 75%
Y: 75%	Y: 50%	Y: 35%	Y: 0%	Y: 80%
K: 0%	K: 15%	K: 25%	K: 0%	K: 0%

2 | Colors are created by mixing cyan, magenta, yellow, and black inks.

Process colors are the four specific colors used by the printing industry (and digital printers) to reproduce full-color images, such as photographs and illustrations, and continuous-tone copy.

The process colors are cyan (blue), magenta (red), yellow, and black, indicated by CMYK. (The letter K is used to designate black.) By combining these four colors, the printer is able to re-create the illusion of the original full-color image.

The first step in reproducing full-color images is to make "color separations," that is, to break down the original image into the four process colors. This is accomplished through the use a scanner.

Once the art has been scanned, the four process colors appear as tints, which when combined in printing will approximate the full range of colors found in the original image (1).

It is interesting to note that the colors are created not by the overprinting of inks, but by the optical mixing of the four process colors by the viewer's eye. (This is similar to the principle of the pointillist painting technique by Impressionist painter Georges Seurat.) **When working with process inks, opportunities arise for creating unique colors by specifying combinations of solid colors and tints (screens) of two or more colors (2).**

Because process colors are created by mixing tints of four inks, if one or more colors are out of registration, the type will be blurred. It is important to carefully consider typeface, type size, and whether the type is being reversed or overprinted.

An additional problem arises when attempting to print type on a full-color photograph. Finding an area that is not too "busy" so the type can be read can be a challenge. **Study the illustration on the facing page to see how readability is affected by type size, color, and the nature of the background (3).** More delicate typefaces such as Bodoni suffer due to the hairline strokes and fine serifs, while the Helvetica remains readable.

This book was printed with process colors.

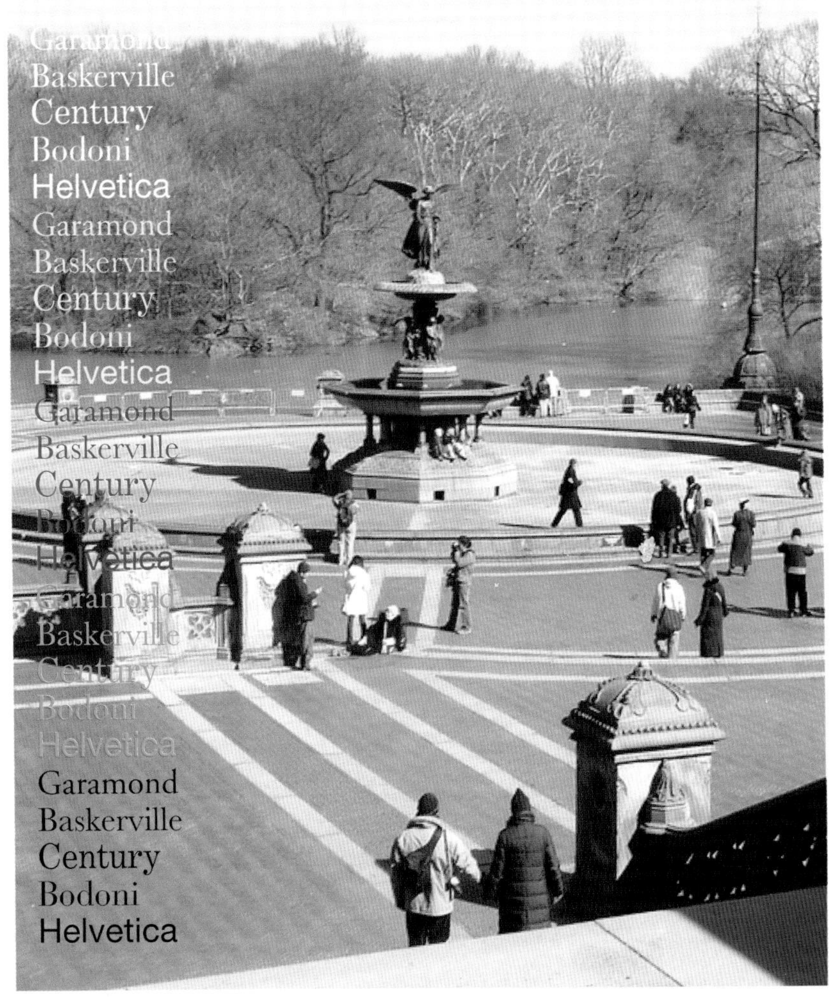

Garamond	Garamond	Garamond	Garamond	Garamond
Baskerville	Baskerville	Baskerville	Baskerville	Baskerville
Century	Century	Century	Century	Century
Bodoni	Bodoni	Bodoni	Bodoni	Bodoni
Helvetica	Helvetica	Helvetica	Helvetica	Helvetica

3 | Reversing and overprinting colored type can be problematic with busy images or colored backgrounds.

Projected Colors

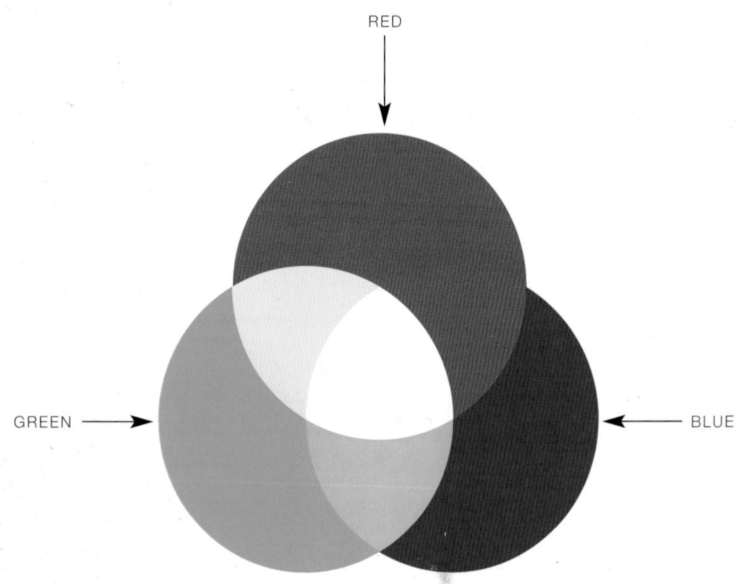

1 | Red, green, and blue light mix to create projected colors.

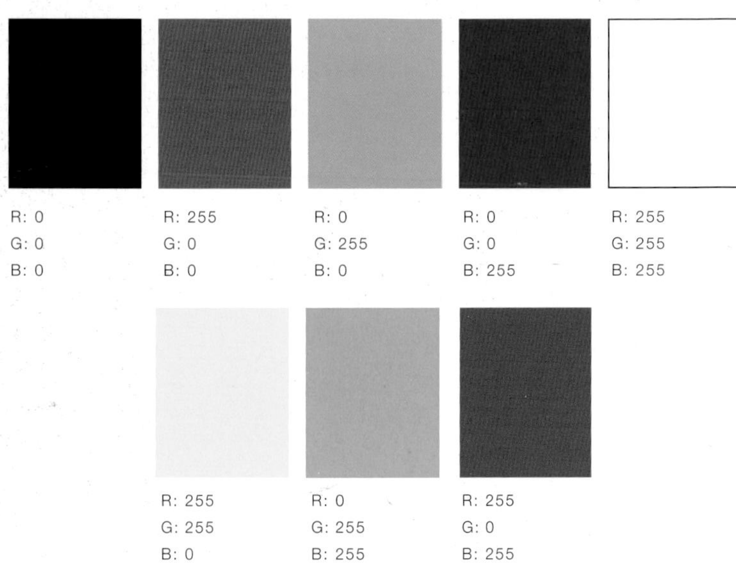

2 | Colors are created by varying the amount of red, green, and blue light.

Projected colors are rendered by light rather than pigments and are used with light-projection devices, such as computer monitors, televisions, and overhead projectors.

With projection devices, type is rendered as a pattern of pixels (tiny picture elements), that can be round, oval, square, or rectangular. The *resolution* of a projected image is the number of pixels per inch. The higher the resolution, the finer the image. The lower the resolution, the less detail is possible, causing letters to look rough around the edges.

Designing projection-based presentations has unique challenges. While dark type printed on light paper is comfortable to read, the opposite tends to be true with projected light: reading long passages on a brightly glowing light source can tire the reader. Also, due to limitations in resolution, text types used for projection tend to be larger than those commonly used for print.

Typeface design is also an important factor, as there is a difference between typefaces designed for print and for projection. Just as old style typefaces lacked fine detail due to primitive printing technology, early projection typefaces started out with little refinement. However, with improved technology, more refined typefaces are being designed specifically for the screen.

RGB Colors

To create colored type and images, light-projection devices use mixtures of red, green, and blue light, commonly referred to as RGB colors (1).

The level, or intensity, of each color is represented by a number ranging from 0 to 255 (2). When mixed in varying intensities, these three colors can create a palette of millions of colors.

NOTE | As the illustrations on this page represent projected colors of light, they cannot be accurately reproduced with printing inks.

Projects

A good design project must challenge students' creative abilities while expanding their typographic knowledge. These projects range from simple to complex—from the typographic enhancement of a single word to the design of an eight-page brochure. All projects can be completed within an intensive one-semester course.

Solutions to the projects should be creative yet practical. Overly experimental approaches at this early stage tend to subvert the goal of developing a strong fundamental understanding of typography.

For this reason, it is recommended that all projects be solved using the five classic typefaces upon which the program is built. Additional typefaces can be introduced at the instructor's discretion for display purposes.

Solving Design Problems

Graphic design involves a decision-making process. As you discuss the project with your instructor (or client), each new piece of information must be weighed, new directions must be explored, and decisions must be made. To make these decisions you must draw on everything you have: your design skills, your understanding of the project, the needs of the client, the intended audience, and the work of famous designers. The broader your knowledge, the more you have to draw on.

"I am convinced that intensive investigation of elementary typographic exercises is a prerequisite for the solution of complex typographic problems."

WOLFGANG WEINGART

Analyzing the Problem

Before you create a satisfactory design, you must first understand the problem to be solved. Otherwise you will spend your time simply moving shapes around while hoping to stumble on a pleasing design.

If you do not understand the problem, then ask questions: not how to do the design—that's your job—but questions concerning the purpose of the project. What is the message and who is the intended audience? Are there any limitations or preferences regarding typefaces, type sizes, or colors? Answers to these questions, and others like them, will help give you direction, and the design will begin to take shape.

Researching

If you have ever watched a professional house painter at work, you are probably aware that more time is spent preparing the house to be painted than actually painting it. In many way it's the same with design; gathering information often takes more time than the actual designing.

Sometimes successful research means finding the one perfect photograph, illustration, or idea that will solve a difficult design problem. Get into the habit of collecting reference books, annuals, and typographic specimens that appeal to you, until you have your own research library.

Get to know your libraries. Most art schools have good libraries with many excellent books and periodicals of direct interest to graphic designers. Also your local public library, no matter how small, can have useful material. Get to know your librarian; most work very hard at being helpful and finding the information you need.

Explore other outlets as well. Stock photography and illustration companies have extensive archives of imagery that can be searched based on given criteria.

And probably the most helpful resource of all is the Internet. Not only a useful researching tool, the Internet could be a valuable source of inspiration. Search engines compile information on a given subject from a wide array of sources.

Time spent researching is time well spent.

Making Decisions

There are many ways of solving design problems. Some designers like to think about the problem for days before putting pencil to paper or hitting the keys. Others look for inspiration in design publications, while still others prefer to begin the process immediately by creating thumbnail sketches or experimenting on the computer.

Regardless of the method you choose, try to start the design process as soon as possible. By all means experiment. Start by thinking and doing research, but once you arrive at the most promising idea, begin to develop it.

As you begin to resolve the design, study the results carefully, not simply from an esthetic perspective but for its effectiveness and readability. Did you accomplish what you set out to do? Does the design attract attention? Can the type be read comfortably? Are you getting the idea across? If not, can the design be saved or should you start over?

Try to avoid spending excessive amounts of time discussing or philosophizing about what you might do, since this is a highly developed form of procrastination and reflects uncertainly on how to proceed.

Making decisions is essential to getting the job done. Unfortunately, there is no magic formula for turning chronic procrastinators into dynamic decision-makers; as there are deadlines to meet you will just have to learn to make decisions and live with the results.

Achieving Better Solutions

The goal all designers strive for is finding the "elegant" solution: simple, original, visually exciting, and successful. It is also a design that can be reproduced within budget without compromising the quality. Even the best designers in the world can't consistently come up with ideal solutions, so don't expect it to happen every time.

One way to get better solutions is by getting into the habit of creating more than one design for every problem. This will not only add depth to your creativity but bolster your confidence as well. Besides, in the event that a particular design is rejected, you will always have something to fall back on.

It is worth noting that in school the instructor will accept whatever you do and grade you accordingly. In business the job is either accepted or it is not. The client is not going to grade your efforts.

Using Technology Wisely

Today it is a challenge for designers to avoid being seduced by technology. As sophisticated as computer applications may be, they are only tools for the creative mind. You should not expect the computer to provide the design solution.

Truly successful designs begin with ideas and concepts. As you execute your designs on the computer, your knowledge of typography, combined with your trained eye and esthetic judgment, will direct you to the most creative solution.

Twelve Projects

The following twelve projects are presented as an introduction to typography. The first nine are designed to build upon one another, first by experimenting with single words and sentences, and finally by designing a brochure. The final three can be given at any time during the semester.

The projects are also designed to encourage you to develop your computer skills. All formats and time allowances are merely suggestions and can be altered. ■

NOTE | For additional solutions to projects shown here and new projects contributed by major design schools from around the world, log onto www.designingwithtype.com/5. Students have been credited where possible.

"Ideas don't work
unless you do."

ANONYMOUS

Project | Five Classic Typefaces

Purpose

To introduce the five classic typefaces — Garamond, Baskerville, Bodoni, Century Expanded, and Helvetica — while encouraging perfection of basic computer skills. This project offers an opportunity to experiment with letterspacing, wordspacing, linespacing, and to learn how these choices affect readability.

Garamond

Baskerville

Bodoni

Century Expanded

Helvetica

Assignment

Although the copy and specifications are optional, the text describing the individual typefaces is shown here. (See pages 28, 34, 40, 46, and 52.) Using the appropriate copy for each of the typefaces, set the type following the specifications below. Printing out the results will allow you to better judge the settings than viewing them on the monitor.

DISPLAY TYPE FOR EACH OF THE FIVE TYPEFACES

Set display type in 72-point, solid, U/lc (uppercase and lowercase), and all caps. Type set in all caps will generally require adjustments in letterspacing to achieve even spacing throughout.

TEXT TYPE FOR EACH OF THE FIVE TYPEFACES

Set all text type 11-point x 20 picas, justified. Start by setting the type solid (11/11) and continue adding additional linespacing (leading) in 1-point increments (11/12, 11/13, etc.).

Compare the results for readability and color. Select the setting you deem best and experiment with different amounts of letterspacing and wordspacing (tracking). Study the results and begin to form practical and esthetic judgments.

Next, continue the investigation by varying the measure to see how the line length affects the color, readability, hyphenation, etc.

Part of this project can be done by comping with pencil and paper. (See *Traditional Skills* on pages 137 to 144.)

SET NAME

To help you better understand the individual personalities of the five typefaces, set your name in both all caps and uppercase and lowercase. Study the results and decide which you feel most closely reflects your personality.

FORMAT | Optional

TIME | 4 hours

Garamond
GARAMOND

Garamond is an Old Style typeface. Claude Garamond, who died in 1561, was originally credited with the design of this elegant French typeface; however, it has recently been discovered that this typeface was designed by Jean Jannon in 1615. Many of the present-day versions of this elegant typeface may be either Garamond or Jannon designs, although they are all called Garamond. This is a typical Old Style face, having very little contrast between the thicks and thins, heavily bracketed serifs, and oblique stress. The letterforms are open and round, making the face extremely readable. The capital letters are shorter than the ascenders of the lowercase letters.

Garamond is an Old Style typeface. Claude Garamond, who died in 1561, was originally credited with the design of this elegant French typeface; however, it has recently been discovered that this typeface was designed by Jean Jannon in 1615. Many of the present-day versions of this elegant typeface may be either Garamond or Jannon designs, although they are all called Garamond. This is a typical Old Style face, having very little contrast between the thicks and thins, heavily bracketed serifs, and oblique stress. The letterforms are open and round, making the face extremely readable. The capital letters are shorter than the ascenders of the lowercase letters.

Garamond is an Old Style typeface. Claude Garamond, who died in 1561, was originally credited with the design of this elegant French typeface; however, it has recently been discovered that this typeface was designed by Jean Jannon in 1615. Many of the present-day versions of this elegant typeface may be either Garamond or Jannon designs, although they are all called Garamond. This is a typical Old Style face, having very little contrast between the thicks and thins, heavily bracketed serifs, and oblique stress. The letterforms are open and round, making the face extremely readable. The capital letters are shorter than the ascenders of the lowercase letters.

Jane Doe
JANE DOE

Jane Doe
JANE DOE

Jane Doe
JANE DOE

Jane Doe
JANE DOE

Jane Doe
JANE DOE

Project | Type Arrangements

Purpose

To introduce the most common ways of arranging type on a page and to understand how that decision affects typographic communication.

Assignment

Using the specifications below, set the descriptive copy for the five classic typefaces. (See pages 28, 34, 40, 46, and 52.)

Begin by setting all type with normal letterspacing and wordspacing (tracking). Print out the results and examine them carefully for both esthetics and readability; you will want both. (See *Type Arrangements* on page 70.)

This project can also be comped with pencil and paper. (See *Comping* on page 140.)

Type arrangements on the facing page are all shown in the same typeface. Use the following specifcations.

JUSTIFIED
11/15 Garamond x 13 picas

FLUSH LEFT, RAGGED RIGHT
11/13 Baskerville x 20 picas

FLUSH RIGHT, RAGGED LEFT
12/16 Bodoni x 18 picas

CENTERED
10/16 Century Expanded x 24 picas

RANDOM
Helvetica set in any text size and leading, but the arrangement must be random, that is not justified; flush left, ragged right; flush right, ragged left; or centered.

FORMAT | Optional

TIME | 4 hours

RANDOM

Garamond is an Old Style typeface. Claude Garamond, who died in 1561, was originally credited with the design of this elegant French typeface; however, it has recently been discovered that this typeface was designed by Jean Jannon in 1615. Many of the present-day versions of this elegant typeface may be either Garamond or Jannon designs, although they are all called Garamond. This is a typical Old Style face, having very little contrast between the thicks and thins, heavily bracketed serifs, and oblique stress. The letterforms are open and round, making the face extremely readable. *The capital letters are shorter than the ascenders of the lowercase.*

JUSTIFIED

Garamond is an Old Style typeface.
Claude Garamond, who died in 1561,
was originally credited with the design of
this elegant French typeface; however, it has
recently been discovered that this typeface
was designed by Jean Jannon in 1615.
Many of the present-day versions of this
elegant typeface may be either Garamond
or Jannon designs, although they are all
called Garamond. This is a typical Old Style
face, having very little contrast between
the thicks and thins, heavily bracketed serifs,
and oblique stress. The letterforms are
open and round, making the face extremely
readable. *The capital letters are shorter than
the ascenders of the lowercase.*

FLUSHED LEFT, RAGGED RIGHT

Garamond is an Old Style typeface.
Claude Garamond, who died in 1561,
was originally credited with the design of
this elegant French typeface; however, it has
recently been discovered that this typeface
was designed by Jean Jannon in 1615.
Many of the present-day versions of this
elegant typeface may be either Garamond
or Jannon designs, although they are all
called Garamond. This is a typical Old Style
face, having very little contrast between
the thicks and thins, heavily bracketed serifs,
and oblique stress. The letterforms are
open and round, making the face extremely
readable. *The capital letters are shorter than
the ascenders of the lowercase.*

FLUSHED RIGHT, RAGGED LEFT

Garamond is an Old Style typeface.
Claude Garamond, who died in 1561,
was originally credited with the design
of this elegant French typeface;
however, it has recently been discovered
that this typeface was designed by
Jean Jannon in 1615.
Many of the present-day versions
of this elegant typeface
may be either Garamond or Jannon designs,
although they are all called Garamond.
This is a typical Old Style face,
having very little contrast between
the thicks and thins, heavily bracketed serifs,
and oblique stress.
The letterforms are open and round,
making the face extremely readable.
The capital letters are shorter than the ascenders of the lowercase letters.

CENTERED

Project | Typestyles

Purpose
To introduce alternative typestyles and show how they affect the appearance, readability, and length of the setting.

Assignment
Select a piece of copy or use the copy from one of the five classic typefaces. (See pages 28, 34, 40, 46, and 52.)

Set the paragraph (11/13 x 20 picas, flush left, ragged right) with the following typestyles: roman, italic, bold, all caps, and caps with small caps.

Study the results. Is one more readable than another? Note how the emphasis changes from quiet to assertive depending upon the typestyle. Notice also how the length of the setting varies and decide which typestyle would benefit by adding linespacing.

If the copy you select has dates, now is an excellent time to experiment with old style figures to see how well they integrate with the roman text.

FORMAT | Optional

TIME | 2 hours

Roman

Italic

Bold

ALL CAPS

Caps and Small Caps

ROMAN

A love of letters is the beginning of typographical wisdom. That is, the love of letters as literature and the love of letters as physical entities, having abstract beauty of their own, apart from the ideas they may express or the emotions they may evoke.

ITALIC

A love of letters is the beginning of typographical wisdom. That is, the love of letters as literature and the love of letters as physical entities, having abstract beauty of their own, apart from the ideas they may express or the emotions they may evoke.

BOLD

A love of letters is the beginning of typographical wisdom. That is, the love of letters as literature and the love of letters as physical entities, having abstract beauty of their own, apart from the ideas they may express or the emotions they may evoke.

ALL CAPS

A LOVE OF LETTERS IS THE BEGINNING OF TYPOGRAPHICAL WISDOM. THAT IS, THE LOVE OF LETTERS AS LITERATURE AND THE LOVE OF LETTERS AS PHYSICAL ENTITIES, HAVING ABSTRACT BEAUTY OF THEIR OWN, APART FROM THE IDEAS THEY MAY EXPRESS OR THE EMOTIONS THEY MAY EVOKE.

CAPS AND SMALL CAPS

A LOVE OF LETTERS IS THE BEGINNING OF TYPOGRAPHICAL WISDOM. THAT IS, THE LOVE OF LETTERS AS LITERATURE AND THE LOVE OF LETTERS AS PHYSICAL ENTITIES, HAVING ABSTRACT BEAUTY OF THEIR OWN, APART FROM THE IDEAS THEY MAY EXPRESS OR THE EMOTIONS THEY MAY EVOKE.

QUOTATION BY JOHN R. BIGGS

Project | Paragraph Indications

Purpose

To demonstrate a wide variety of ways to indicate paragraphs and to show how they affect the look and readability of the setting.

Assignment

Using a series of paragraphs, either of text of your own choosing or of the text from page 75, create variations that treat the delineation between paragraphs differently. Create five alternate ways of indicating new paragraphs, ranging from conservative to outrageous. (In the last case readability is not a criterion.) Study the results, weighing the trade-off between the traditional approaches and those that are more exploratory, and consider how the various solutions affect readability.

FORMAT | 10 x 10 inches (25 x 25 cm)

TIME | 4 hours

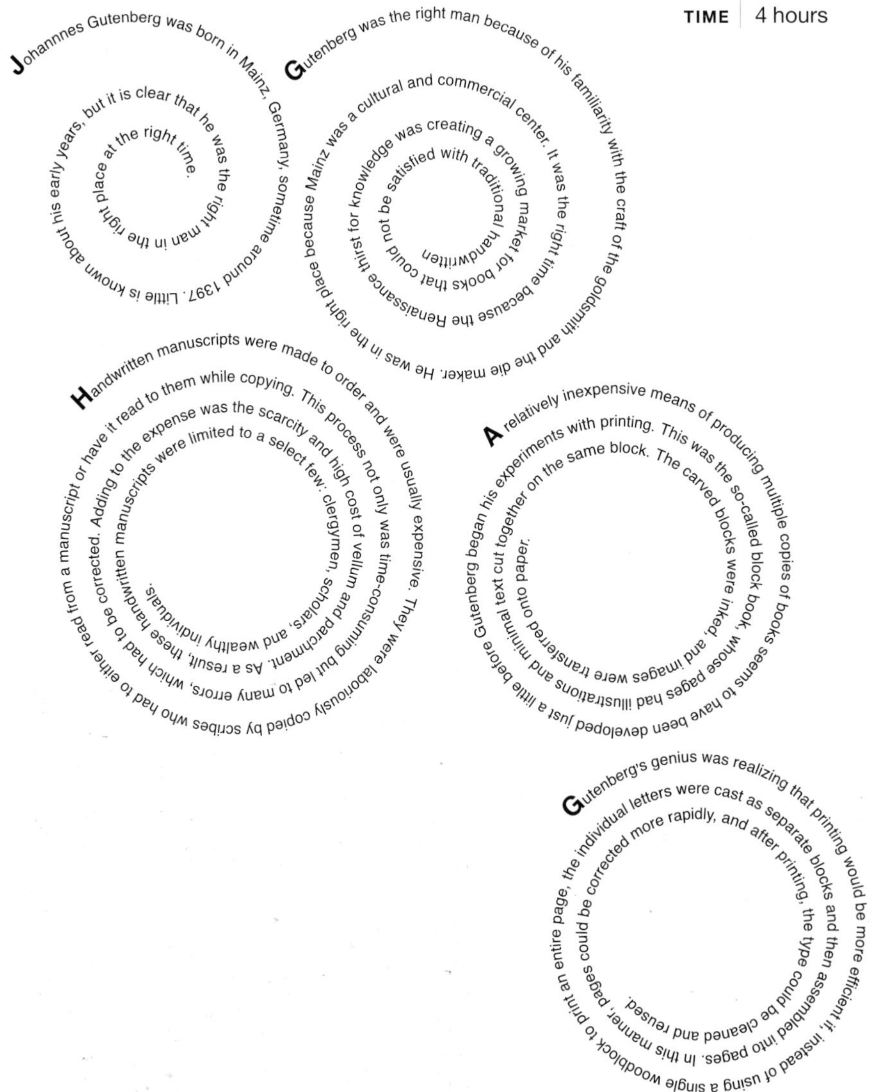

JOHANN Gutenberg was born in Mainz, Germany, some time around 1397. Little is known about his early years, but it is clear that he was the right man in the right place at the right time. Gutenberg was the right man because of his familiarity with the craft of the goldsmith and die maker. He was in the right place because Mainz was a cultural and commercial center. It was that right time because the Renaissance thirst for knowledge was creating a growing market for books that could not be satisfied with the traditional handwritten manuscripts. **HANDWRITTEN** manuscripts were made to order and were usually expensive. They were laboriously copied by scribes who had either to read from a manuscript or have it read to them while copying. This process was not only time-consuming, but led to many errors, which had to be corrected. **ADDING** to the expense was the scarcity and high cost of vellum and parchment. As a result, these handwritten manuscripts were limited to a select few: clergymen, scholars, and wealthy individuals. **A RELATIVELY** inexpensive means of producing multiple copies of books seems to have been developed just a little before Gutenberg began his experiments with printing. This was the so-called block book whose pages had illustrations and minimal text cut together on the same block. The carved blocks were inked, and images were transferred onto paper in multiples by rubbing or by the use of a screw press. Block books are believed to have been made for semiliterate, preaching friars who brought the word of God to the urban working class and the poor. **GUTENBERG'S** genius was realizing that printing would be more efficient if, instead of using a single woodblock to print an entire page, the individual letters were cast as separate blocks and then assembled into pages. In this manner, pages could be corrected more rapidly, and, after printing, the type could be cleaned and reused.

FRANCESCA AMOS

Printing in Germany

Johann Gutenberg was born in Mainz, Germany, some time around 1397. Little is known about his early years, but it is clear that he was the right man in the right place at the right time. Gutenberg was the right man because of his familiarity with the craft of the goldsmith and die maker. He was in the right place because Mainz was a cultural and commercial center. It was that right time because the Renaissance thirst for knowledge was creating a growing market for books that could not be satisfied with the traditional handwritten manuscripts.

Handwritten manuscripts were made to order and were usually expensive. They were laboriously copied by scribes who had either to read from a manuscript or have it read to them while copying. This process was not only time-consuming, but led to many errors, which had to be corrected.

Adding to the expense was the scarcity and high cost of vellum and parchment. As a result, these handwritten manuscripts were limited to a select few: clergymen, scholars, and wealthy individuals.

A relatively inexpensive means of producing multiple copies of books seems to have been developed just a little before Gutenberg began his experiments with printing. This was the so-called block book whose pages had illustrations and minimal text cut together on the same block. The carved blocks were inked, and images were transferred onto paper in multiples by rubbing or by the use of a screw press. Block books are believed to have been made for semiliterate, preaching friars who brought the word of God to the urban working class and the poor.

Gutenberg's genius was realizing that printing would be more efficient if, instead of using a single woodblock to print an entire page, the individual letters were cast as separate blocks and then assembled into pages. In this manner, pages could be corrected more rapidly, and, after printing, the type could be cleaned and reused.

ALICE WETTERLUND

Printing in Germany

Johann Gutenberg was born in Mainz, Germany, some time around 1397. Little is known about his early years, but it is clear that he was the right man in the right place at the right time.

Gutenberg was the right man because of his familiarity with the craft of the goldsmith and the diemaker. He was in the right place because Mainz was a cultural and commercial center. It was the right time because the Renaissance thirst for knowledge was creating a growing market for books that could not be satisfied with the traditional handwritten manuscripts.

Handwritten manuscripts were made to order and were usually expensive. They were laboriously copied by scribes who had either to read from a manuscript or have it read to them while copying. This process was not only time-consuming, but led to many errors, which had corrected. Adding to the expense was the scarcity and high cost of vellum and parchment. As a result, handwritten manuscripts were limited to a select few: clergymen, scholars, and wealthy individuals.

A relatively inexpensive means of producing multiple copies of books seems to have been developed just a little before Gutenberg began his experiments with printing. This was the so called block book whose pages had illustrations and minimal text cut together on the same block. The carved blocks were inked, and images were transferred onto paper in multiples by rubbing or by the use of the screw press. Block books were believed to have been made for semiliterate, preaching friars who brought the word of God to the urban working class and the poor.

Gutenberg's genius was realizing that printing would be more efficient if, instead of using a single woodblock to print an entire page, the individual letters were cast as separate blocks and then assembled into pages. In this manner, pages could be made up faster, errors could be corrected more rapidly, and, after printing, the type could be cleaned and reused.

KAROLINA LACH

Johann Gutenberg was born in Mainz, Germany, sometime around 1397. Little is known about his early years, but it is clear that he was the right man in the right place at the right time. Gutenberg was the right man because of his familiarity with the craft of the goldsmith and die maker. He was in the right place because Mainz was a cultural and commercial center. Adding to the expense was the scarcity and

It was the right time because the Renaissance high cost of vellum and parchment. As a result,
Handwritten manuscripts were made to order and
thirst for knowledge was creating a growing these handwritten manuscripts were limited to
were usually expensive. They were laboriously
market for books that could not be satisfied a select few: clergymen, scholars, and wealthy
copied by scribes who had either to read from a
with the traditional handwritten manuscripts. individuals.
manuscript or have it read to them while copying.

A relatively inexpensive means of producing multiple copies of Gutenberg's genius was realizing that printing would be more
This process was not only time-consuming, but
books seems to have been developed just a little before Gutenberg efficient if, instead of using a single woodblock to print an entire
led to many errors, which had to be corrected.
began his experiments with printing. This was the so-called block page, the individual letters were cast as separate blocks and
book whose pages had illustrations and minimal text cut together then assembled into pages. In this manner, pages could be
on the same block. The carved blocks were inked, and images were corrected more rapidly, and, after printing, the
transferred onto paper in multiples by rubbing or by the use of a cleaned and reused.
screw press. Block books are believed to have been made for
semiliterate, preaching friars who brought the word of God to the
urban working class and the poor.

JOSEPH DURICKAS

Johann Gutenberg was born in Mainz, Germany, some time around 1397. Little is known about his early years, but it is clear that he was the right man in the right place at the right time. Gutenberg was the right man because of his familiarity with the craft of the goldsmith and die maker. He was in the right place because Mainz was a cultural and commercial center. It was that right time because the Renaissance thirst for knowledge was creating a growing market for books that could not be satisfied with the traditional handwritten manuscripts.

Handwritten manuscripts were made to order and were usually expensive. They were laboriously copied by scribes who had either to read from a manuscript or have it read to them while copying. This process was not only time-consuming, but led to many errors, which had to be corrected.

Printing in GERMANY

Adding to the expense was the scarcity and high cost of vellum and parchment. As a result, these handwritten manuscripts were limited to a select few: clergymen, scholars, and wealthy individuals.

A relatively inexpensive means of producing multiple copies of books seems to have been developed just a little before Gutenberg began his experiments with printing. This was the so-called block book whose pages had illustrations and minimal text cut together on the same block. The carved blocks were inked, and images were transferred onto paper in multiples by rubbing or by the use of a screw press. Block books are believed to have been made for semiliterate, preaching friars who brought the word of God to the urban working class and the poor.

Gutenberg's genius was realizing that printing would be more efficient if, instead of using a single woodblock to print an entire page, the individual letters were cast as separate blocks and then assembled into pages. In this manner, pages could be corrected more rapidly, and, after printing, the type could be cleaned and reused.

OSCAR HENRIQUEZ

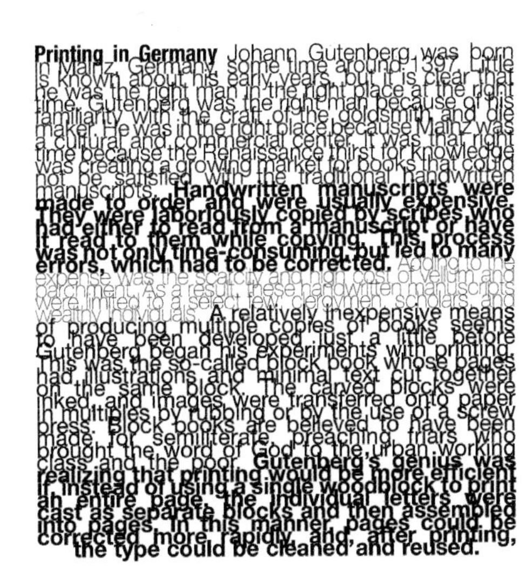

MATTHEW STEINBERG

Project | Expressive Words

Purpose
To typographically enhance the meaning of a single word.

Assignment
Select five words and explore their expressive quality by manipulating the letterforms. To achieve the desired effect, avoid simply repeating the words or creating an illustration from the letterforms. The best solutions not only enhance the word's meaning but are clever and esthetically pleasing. Sometimes an unexpected effect can be achieved when the typographic solution contradicts the meaning of the word, setting the word *big* with small type, for example.

As this exercise requires manipulating typefaces, styles, sizes, and positions, it is an excellent project for developing computer skills.

FORMAT | Optional

TIME | 3 hours

E

X

L

P

O

S

I

O

N

INBRED

KAREN PENTLAND

DIETING

SUSAN CHEUNG

echoechoecho

SHELLY YODICE

hiccup

IRINA KRIKSUNOVA

TITANIC

ROLAND KURZITZA

disoriented

OSCAR HENRIQUEZ

Project | Visually Enhanced Quotation

Purpose

To demonstrate how a simple quotation, song, or poem can be typographically enhanced.

Assignment

Select a favorite quotation, song, or poem and find a way to express the sentiment typographically. The use of photographs or illustrations is optional. Although this project is more apt to be created on the computer, the examples shown here were set by hand in metal type and printed on a Vandercook proofing press.

Chose your quotation carefully. The results of this project will be judged not only by your design, but also on the quotation you have chosen.

For complete texts of illustrated quotations, visit www.designingwithtype.com/5.

FORMAT | 10 x 10 inches (25 x 25 cm)

TIME | 10 hours

H Y S T E R I A

As she laughed I was aware of becoming involved in her laughter and being part of it, until her teeth were only accidental stars with a talent for squaddrill. I was drawn in by short gasps, inhaled at each momentary recovery, lost finally in the dark caverns of her throat, bruised by the ripple of unseen muscles. An elderly waiter with trembling hands was hurriedly spreading a pink and white checked cloth over the rusty green iron table, saying: "If the lady and gentleman wish to take their tea in the garden, if the lady and gentleman wish to take their tea in the garden . . ." I decided that if the shaking of her breasts could be stopped, some of the fragments of the afternoon might be collected. I concentrated my attention with careful subtlety to this end.

T. S. E L I O T

EILEEN O'NEILL

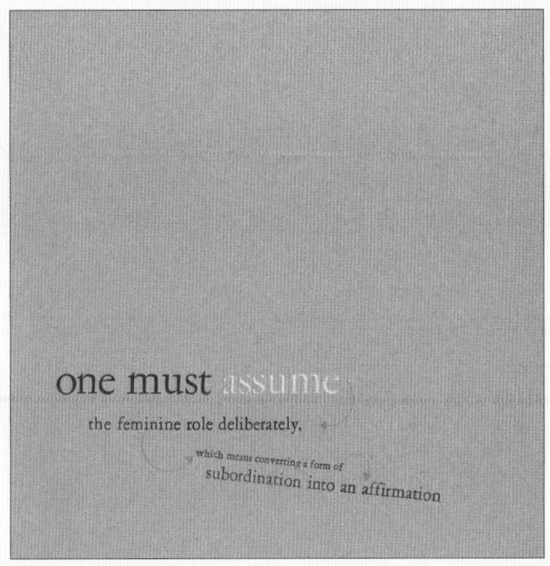

one must assume
the feminine role deliberately,
which means converting a form of
subordination into an affirmation

MICAELA PIREATO

In the winter river,
a whole sheet of newspaper,
soaked through, floating.

UNKNOWN

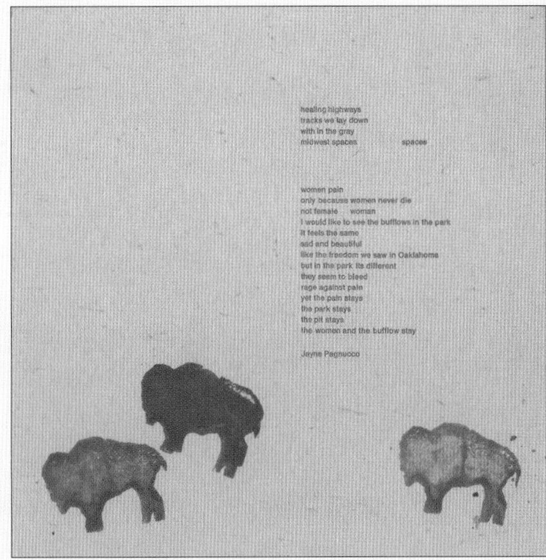

SUSAN EHLID

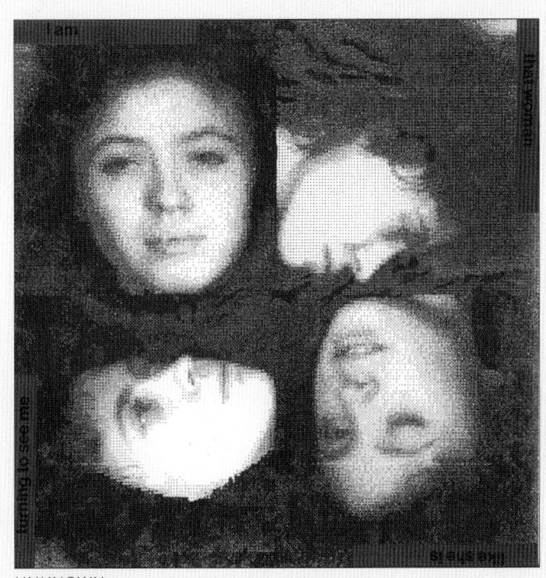

UNKNOWN

On my wall hangs a Japenese carving,
The mask of an evil demon decorated
with gold lacquer
Sympathetically I observe
the swollen veins of the forehead,
indicating
what a strain it is to be evil.
bertolt brecht

E. KAHU

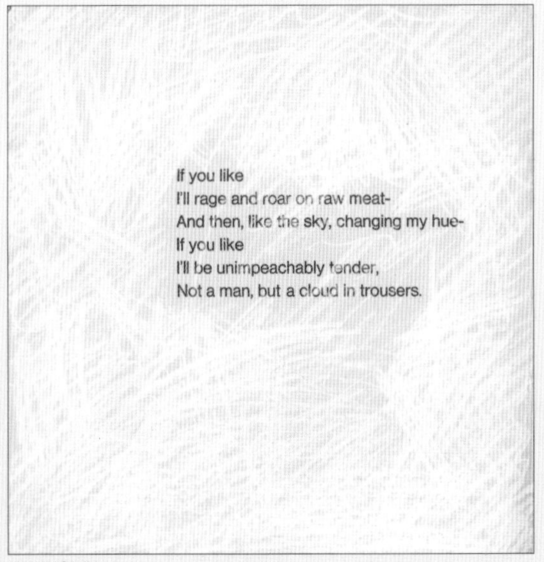

If you like
I'll rage and roar on raw meat-
And then, like the sky, changing my hue-
If you like
I'll be unimpeachably tender,
Not a man, but a cloud in trousers.

UNKNOWN

Everything great in the world comes from neurotics.-Marcel Proust

UNKNOWN

Indeed the only truly serious questions are ones that even a child can formulate.
Milan Kundera

AGNIESZKA GASPARSKA

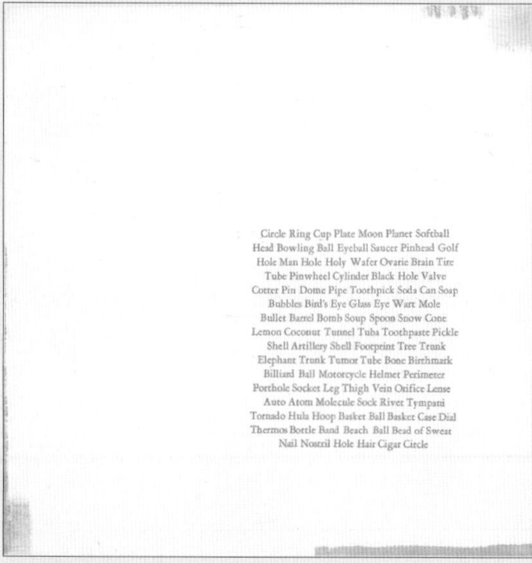

Circle Ring Cup Plate Moon Planet Softball
Head Bowling Ball Eyeball Saucer Pinhead Golf
Hole Man Hole Holy Wafer Ovarie Brain Tire
Tube Pinwheel Cylinder Black Hole Valve
Cotter Pin Dome Pipe Toothpick Soda Can Soap
Bubbles Bird's Eye Glass Eye Wart Mole
Bullet Barrel Bomb Soup Spoon Snow Cone
Lemon Coconut Tunnel Tuba Toothpaste Pickle
Shell Artillery Shell Footprint Tree Trunk
Elephant Trunk Tumor Tube Bone Birthmark
Billiard Ball Motorcycle Helmet Perimeter
Porthole Socket Leg Thigh Vein Orifice Lense
Auto Atom Molecule Sock Rivet Tympani
Tornado Hula Hoop Basket Ball Basket Case Dial
Thermos Bottle Band Beach Ball Bead of Sweat
Nail Nostril Hole Hair Cigar Circle

UNKNOWN

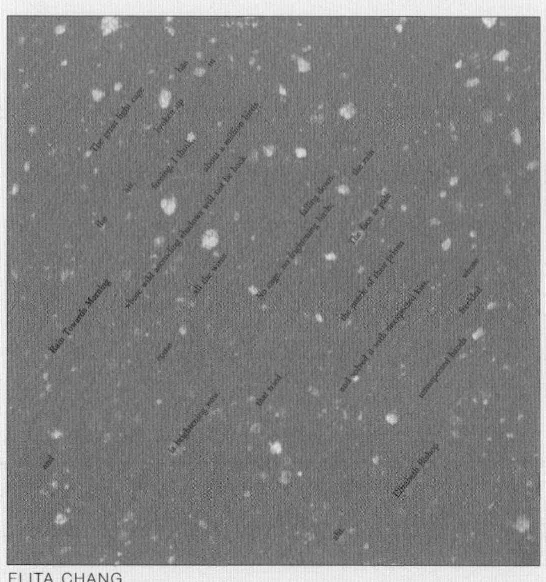

ELITA CHANG

MICHAEL VAN PATTEN

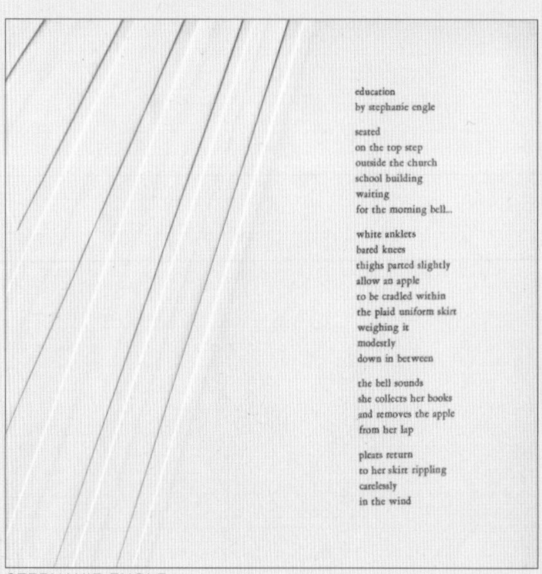

education
by stephanie engle
seated
on the top step
outside the church
school building
waiting
for the morning bell...
white anklets
bared knees
thighs parted slightly
allow an apple
to be cradled within
the plaid uniform skirt
weighing it
modestly
down in between
the bell sounds
she collects her books
and removes the apple
from her lap
pleats return
to her skirt rippling
carelessly
in the wind

STEPHANIE ENGLE

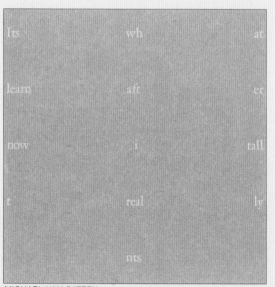

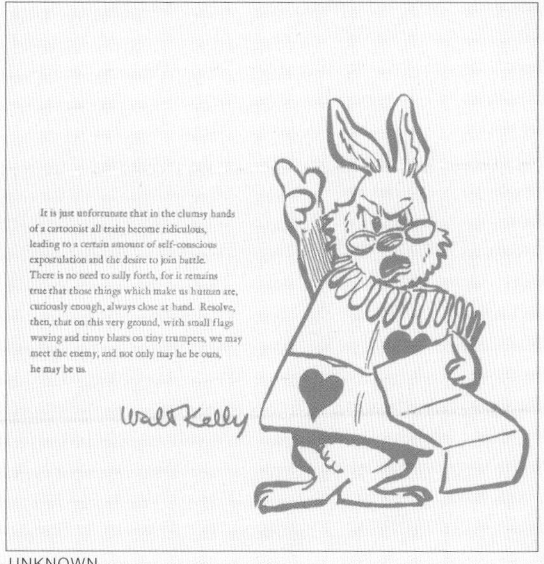

It is just unfortunate that in the clumsy hands of a cartoonist all traits become ridiculous, leading to a certain amount of self-conscious expostulation and the desire to join battle. There is no need to sally forth, for it remains true that those things which make us human are, curiously enough, always close at hand. Resolve, then, that on this very ground, with small flags waving and tinny blasts on tiny trumpets, we may meet the enemy, and not only may he be ours, he may be us.
Walt Kelly

UNKNOWN

the death of the goldfish
who used to make love at
ninety kilometers an hour

has given

Christian

UNKNOWN

Love is a grave mental disease. Plato

DENISE PORTHUN

Every word that is
si taht drow yreve.
uttered evokes the
eht sekove deretu
idea of its opposite.
etisoppo sti fo aedi

Goethe

UNKNOWN

Everyman dies,
When the Autumn-fall comes
We all see our lives,
Take one from our sums.
The leaves all die,
And fall to the ground.
Will I be here,
The next time around?

W. MURRAY

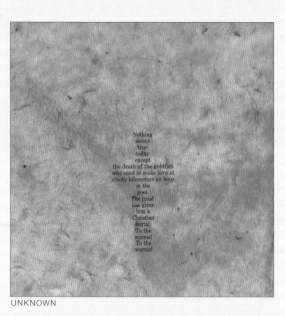

THE METAMORPHOSIS
As Gregor Samsa awoke one morning from uneasy dreams he found himself transformed in his bed into a gigantic insect. He was lying on his hard, as it were armored-plated, back and when he lifted his head a little he could see his dome-like brown belly divided into stiff arched segments on top of which the bed quilt could hardly keep in position and was about to slide off completly. His numerous legs, which were pitifully thin compared to the rest of his bulk, waved helplessly before his eyes.

UNKNOWN

Project | Early Letterform

Purpose

To provide a comprehensive overview of the design process, from copywriting to producing a final design. This project also encourages explorations of multiple solutions to a given project.

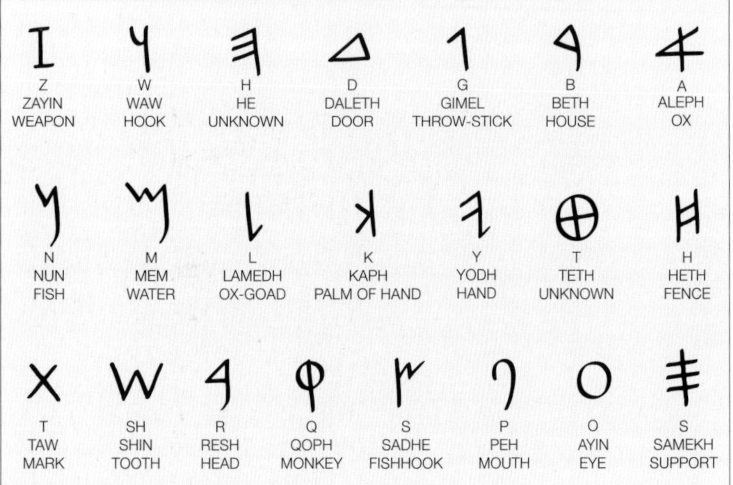

Phoenician alphabet

Greek alphabet

Assignment

First, the copywriting. Select a letter from the Phoenician or Greek alphabet, research the letter, and write approximately 100 words. Your text should highlight the meaning or illustrate some aspect of the symbol. Write it to be interesting, clever, funny, poetic, inspiring, etc. If you don't find your text interesting, the viewer won't either. This is an excellent opportunity to introduce proofreaders' marks by giving the copy to a professional editor for proofreading.

Next, the designing. This can either be a two-color or a full-color project. Either way, create three designs, each distinctively different. All compositions must contain three elements: symbol, display type, and text type. All design elements should be two-dimensional.

SYMBOL

In the first comp, make the symbol the most prominent element. Prominent does not necessarily mean the largest element. Consider other ways to create emphasis.

DISPLAY TYPE

In the second comp, make the display type the most prominent element.

TEXT TYPE

In the third comp, make the text type the most prominent element.

Although the goal is to create three distinct designs with different emphasis, it is possible that some of the better designs will be ambiguous as to which element dominates.

In all cases consider the white space (open areas) as an equally important part of your design.

Use any of the five classic typeface families of type: Garamond, Baskerville, Bodoni, Century Expanded, or Helvetica. You may use a different typeface for each solution.

FORMAT | 10 x 10 inches (25 x 25 cm)

TIME | 3 weeks

OSCAR HENRIQUEZ

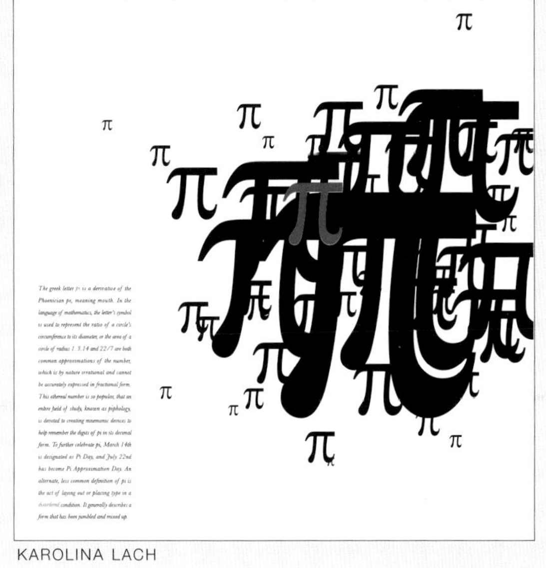

KAROLINA LACH

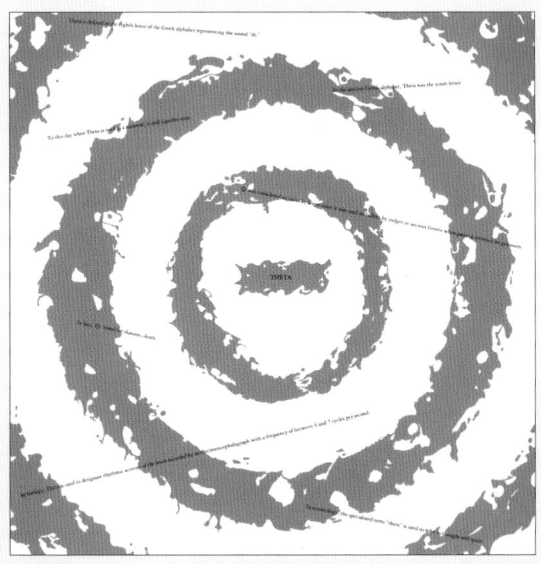

KAREN NGAI

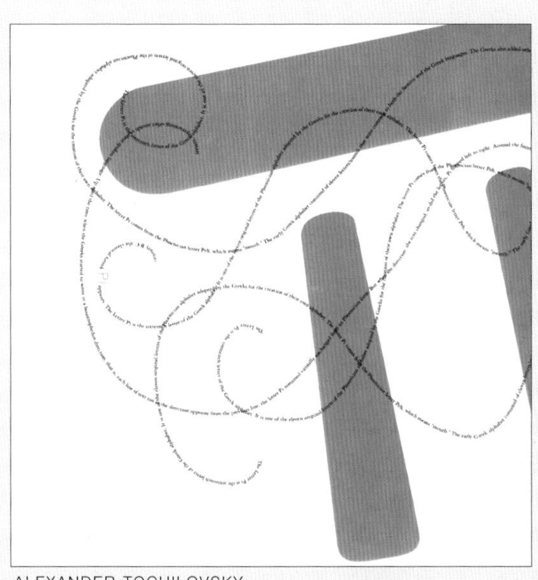

ALEXANDER TOCHILOVSKY

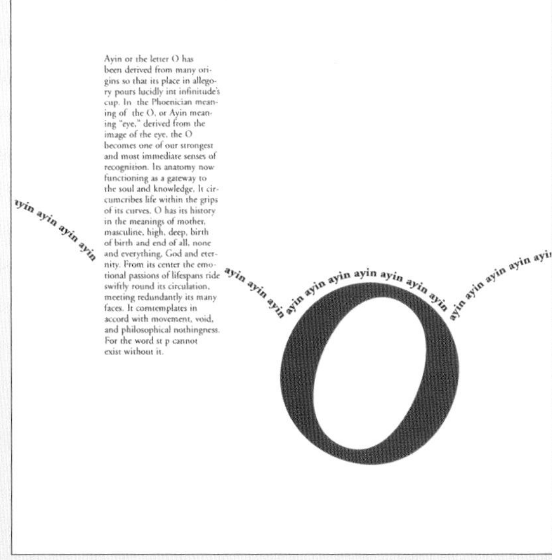

WILLIAM VILLALONGO

JENNIFER CRUPI

sig
a
A Simple Sigma Synopsis
Σ spelled S I G M A is the eighteenth letter of the Greek alphabet. Sigma symbolizes the sound "S" as in SUN. Sigma is the Phoenician Shin (W) standing sideways. Sigma also signifies certain stars situated somewhere in the vast solar system. Statistically, Sigma symbolizes standard deviations. In mathematics, Sigma is a symbol suggesting summation.

UNKNOWN

b e t h :
Born unto the Phoenicians around 1600 B.C., Beth meaning house was the second letter in their alphabet. Beth bides its time, bearing the burden of being benched second to Aleph. Still bummed in second place today, B also bewilders by flipping over and being able to balance on its head, which becomes its base. Whatever the case may be, this brings broader notions to its bouncy bearings. So why not bequeath a bow whenever you have this letter before you and ask yourself while bending: To B or not to B?

UNKNOWN

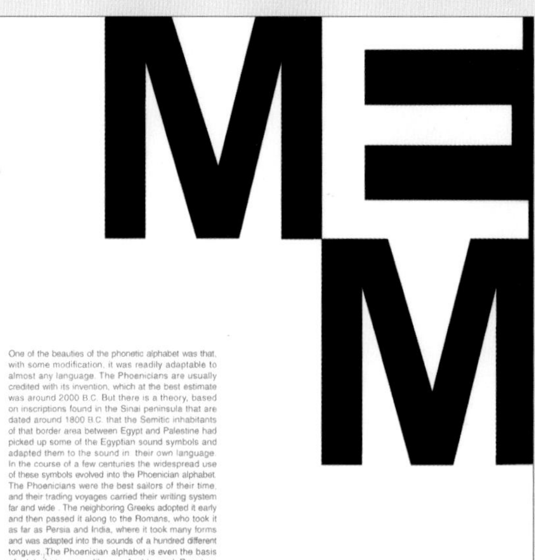

One of the beauties of the phonetic alphabet was that, with some modification, it was readily adaptable to almost any language. The Phoenicians are usually credited with its invention, which at the best estimate was around 2000 B.C. But there is a theory, based on inscriptions found in the Sinai peninsula that are dated around 1800 B.C. that the Semitic inhabitants of that border area between Egypt and Palestine had picked up some of the Egyptian sound symbols and adapted them to the sound in their own language. In the course of a few centuries the widespread use of these symbols evolved into the Phoenician alphabet. The Phoenicians were the best sailors of their time, and their trading voyages carried their writing system far and wide. The neighboring Greeks adopted it early and then passed it along to the Romans, who took it as far as Persia and India, where it took many forms and was adapted into the sounds of a hundred different tongues. The Phoenician alphabet is even the basis of alphabets as unlike as Arabic and Russian.

GLEB YENTUS

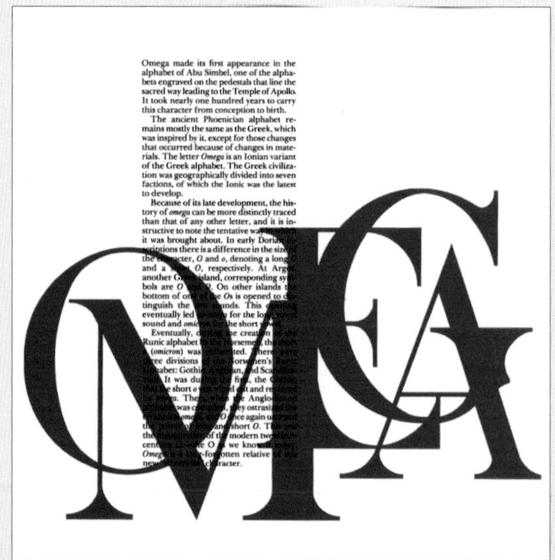

Omega made its first appearance in the alphabet of Abu Simbel, one of the alphabets engraved on the pedestals that line the sacred way leading to the Temple of Apollo. It took nearly one hundred years to carry this character from conception to birth.
The ancient Phoenician alphabet remains mostly the same as the Greek, which was inspired by it, except for those changes that occurred because of changes in materials. The letter Omega is an Ionian variant of the Greek alphabet. The Greek civilization was geographically divided into seven factions, of which the Ionic was the latest to develop.
Because of its late development, the history of omega can be more distinctly traced than that of any other letter, and it is instructive to note the tentative

UNKNOWN

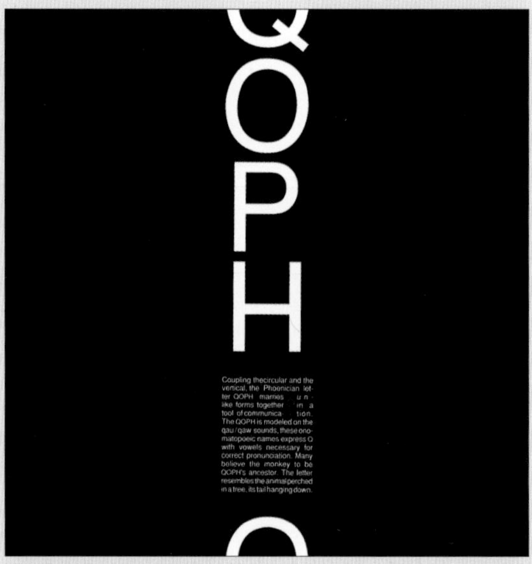

QOPH
Coupling thecircular and the vertical, the Phoenician letter QOPH marries unlike forms together in a tool of communication. The QOPH is modeled on the qau/qaw sounds, these onomatopoeic names express Q with vowels necessary for correct pronunciation. Many believe the monkey to be QOPH's ancestor. The letter resembles the animal perched in a tree, its tail hanging down.

JULIE YEE

Heth is who I am. The Phoenicians are my originators, the conceivers of my birth, yet my form has existed since the beginning of time. For I am merely a mingling of four lines. They call me "fence," but I define myself simply as parallels that intersect, my stability established in the four points that hold me together. A fence I may seem, but I'm internally more like a ladder, ladder on which to climb higher and higher beyond any fence that plots to contain me. Freedom is what I seek. But I was captured by the Greeks and was stamped down forever. To this day I am known as H, stable and straight. That is just my fate.

YOUNG-MI CHA

Hello, I am *Sameth*, and in the form presented here I am a letter in the Phoenician alphabet. My shape and name have changed so drastically over the long centuries that you probably wouldn't know what letter I am today. My beginnings originate with the Egyptians, when in their hieroglyphic alphabet I was a picture of a sword. During years of change, my image lost some of its ornate qualities until in the Hieratic alphabet I became just a simplified symbol of a sword. I looked like a long, horizontal stroke intersected on one side by two short strokes. It was then that I received my name *Sameth*. When the Phoenicians took me over, they kept my old name, yet they added one more horizontal stroke and turned me 90° so now I am standing up instead of lying down. I guess in the form that I appear here I could pass for a letter in some Oriental alphabet. But that is not the end of my story, and you are probably wondering if I am still around and in use in the 20th century? Well, during my takover by the Greeks I do not change my form much, yet they rename me. My name is now *xi*. Then the Romans, while adapting me into their alphabet, change my shape into something that looks like the letter X. So I am still around, not as an S, which might be a pretty good guess, but as the third from the last letter in the alphabet used in writing this. A letter most often used to represent mysterious and unknown factors, numbers, people, etc.... X. Hello, I am *Sameth*, and in the form presented here I am a letter in the Phoenician alphabet. My shape and name have changed so drastically over the long centuries that you probably wouldn't know what letter I am today. My beginnings originate with the Egyptians, when in their hieroglyphic alphabet I was a picture of a sword. During years of change, my image lost some of its ornate qualities until in the Hieratic alphabet I became just a simplified symbol of a sword. I looked like a long, horizontal stroke intersected on one side by two short strokes. It was then that I received my name *Sameth*. When the Phoenicians ook me over, they kept my old name, yet they added one more horizontal stroke and turned me 90° so now I am standing up instead of lying down. I guess in the form that I appear here I could pass for a letter in some Oriental alphabet. But that is not the end of my story, and you are probably wondering if I am still around and in use in the 20th century? Well, during my takover by the Greeks I do not change my form much, yet they rename me. My name is now *xi*. Then the Romans, while adapting me into their alphabet, change my shape into something that looks like the letter X. So I am still around, not as an S, which might be a pretty good guess, but as the third from the last letter in the alphabet used in writing this. A letter most often used to represent mysterious and unknown factors, numbers, people, etc.... X. Hello, I am *Sameth*, and in the form presented here I am a letter in the Phoenician alphabet. My shape and name have changed so drastically over the long centuries that you probably wouldn't know what letter I am today. My beginnings originate with the Egyptians, when in their hieroglyphic alphabet SAMETH was a picture of a sword. During years of change, my image lost some of its ornate qualities until in the Hieratic alphabet I became just a simplified symbol of a sword. I looked like a long, horizontal stroke intersected on one side by two short strokes. It was then that I received my name *Sameth*. When the Phoenicians took me over, they kept my old name, yet they added one more horizontal stroke and turned me 90° so now I am standing up instead of lying down. I guess in the form that I appear here I could pass for a letter in some Oriental alphabet. But that is not the end of my story, and you are probably wondering if I am still around and in use in the 20th century? Well, during my takover by the Greeks I do not change my form much, yet they rename me.

UNKNOWN

Qoph is the seventeenth letter in
the alphabet. In its earliest days, it
most likely represented an eye of a
needle. The Phoenicians used this
to form their own Q, which was
slightly different in appearance from
ours. In their Q, the diagonal stroke
was vertical, extending to the top of
the loop. However, compared with
other letters, the Q has remained
relatively unchanged throughout
history. As for the sound, in the
Semitic language, the letter was
pronounced gutturally. In Greek,
the letter was virtually discarded.
However, the Calcedonians made
good use of Q and passed it on to
the Etruscans, who in turn, passed

ANN KIM

ALPHA

MY NAME IS ALPHA, THE VERY FIRST LETTER IN THE GREEK ALPHABET, JUST AS I REMAIN TODAY. NO ONE REALLY KNOWS HOW I CAME TO BE WHO I AM. THE CURRENT LEGEND, AS TOLD IN A PASSAGE FROM THERODOTUS, SAYS THAT CADMUS INTRODUCED MY COUSINS IN THE PHOENICIAN ALPHABET INTO GREECE, BUT NO CERTAIN DATE IS KNOWN AT WHICH THE MYTHICAL CADMUS DID SO. HOWEVER, I DO KNOW THAT I AM CAREFULLY ARRANGED AND COMPOSED IN A PLEASING WAY. SOME SAY I'M PERFECT. I AM FORMED FROM A CIRCLE AND A SQUARE, THE SUM OF WHICH AMOUNTS TO 52, WHENCE IS DERIVED THE PERFECT NUMBER 10. I AM VERY POPULAR. EVERYONE KNOWS AND LOVES ME. MOST LIKELY, I WAS THE FIRST LETTER YOU LEARNED IN SCHOOL. I AM ONE OF THE ONLY LETTERS YOU CAN USE ALONE. ALSO THE SOUND I MAKE IS KNOWN TO ALL, ESPECIALLY CANADIANS A ' HA

ALPHA

LAURA ASHBY

CHI

When one stops to **consider** the wealth of me**an**ings the greek letter chi h**as amas** sed over the ce**n**turies, it is not surprising that **it origin**ally meant "**ch**asm," or "chaos." Chasm, being an **abyss**, and chao**s, b**eing the original yawning abyss of **Greek l**egend **fr**om which everything and everyone en**tered i**nto **th**is universe of logic and order. Further**more, as a** n interesting example of greek logic, right a**long wi** th this secular view of creation, chi also came **to stan** d for Christ. After years of personal bewilderm**ent and** wonder, it is finally obvious to me how the **ab**b**reviatio** n "Xmas" came into being. Chi also sta**n**ds for **the cru**cifix, or cross, as well as for Christ. H**o**wever, in **recent** times chi has come to not only the **ho**ly cross, bu**t any cr** oss. Take for example a pede**str**ian Xing. Th**erefore,** if you "keep your fingers cro**ss**ed," it is a prayer **for goo**d luck. However, if you k**ee**p your fingers crosse**d whil** e telling a lie, you are **sa**ved from an eternity **in hell.**

UNKNOWN

ay in

o

The Phoenicians developed a system for recording language that was easy for the common citizen to learn. They were the first to destroy the monopoly priests and scribes had on the written language and bring it down into the hands of the people. The Phoenicians invented symbols to represent concepts rather than objects. One example is the ankh, which was the symbol of life as well as death. Many Phoenician concepts embodied paradoxical ideas. Cyclical patterns pervaded everyday Phoenician life and ideology. Fruit begot seed and seed begot fruit. It was every farmer's sacred lesson. Ayin is the Phoenician symbol for "no sound," or mute. Being circular, it has no beginning or end, only continuity. It is merely a space between events in a phrase. Its essence is negative, but its function is plain in the formulation of sound. It itself embodies the idea of nothing becoming something and something nothing.

JANET TWOGOOD

Mem. The Phoenician 𐤌, or *mem*, was derived from an earlier sign representing waves of water. It is curious how this came to be. Thousands of years ago a lonely Phoenician scholar stood along the shoreline staring at the ocean. As he looked at the waves he had the urge to record the motion of the water. He drew a symbol for waves on his crude clay tablet, which he much admired. Excited about his incredible new design, he ran to show it to all his friends. Now this contemplative Phoenician was very different and not always understood by his common friends. Upon seeing his marvelous new creation, they stared at it quite baffled. They saw no resemblance between this scribble 𐤌 and the churning of the sea. Their only comments were a pensive "*Mmm*" and "*Em*, I see." From there grew the legend of *mem*. Not quite what the scholarly Phoenician had in mind, but at least *mem* 𐤌 caught on. 𐤌

UNKNOWN

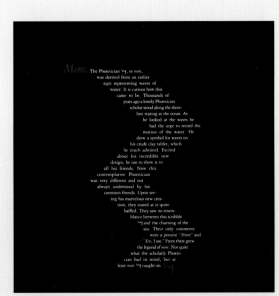

Project | Grids

Purpose

To introduce the use of the grid in publication design and the many typographic decisions that must be made regarding the parts of a page.

This project also puts into practice lessons learned from previous projects.

Assignment

For this project, a grid should be specified and the necessary materials provided so that the designer can focus on solving the design problems rather than on researching and gathering material for the project. This can be further enhanced by limiting the design to black and white to keep the focus on typography.

Using the assigned text and illustrations, design a double-page spread on a multiple-column grid of assigned proportions. The design should include text type, display type, heads, subheads, folios, illustrations, and captions. (See *Parts of a Page* on page 82 for additional information.)

FORMAT | Each page: 10 x 10 inches (25 x 25 cm)

TIME | 6 to 8 hours

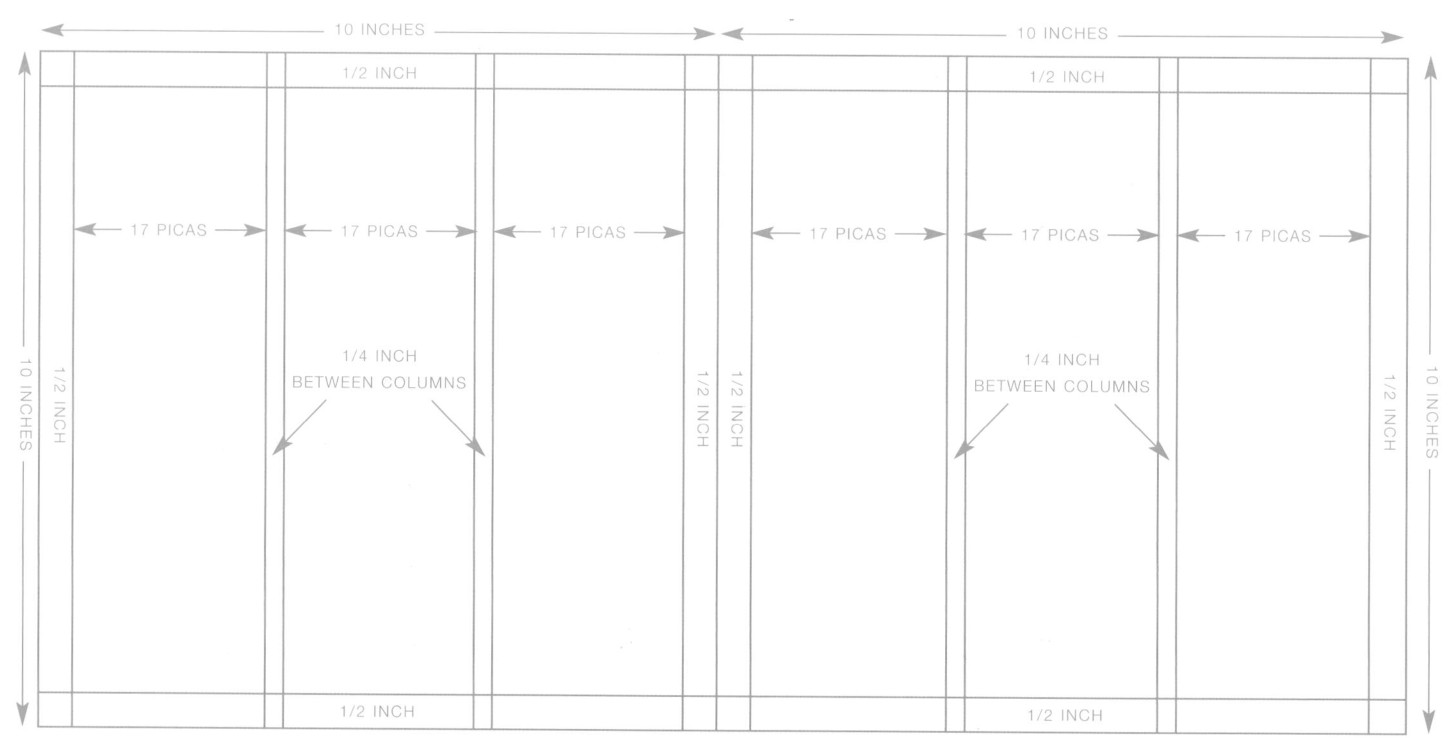

Graphic Arts

The most significant event of the century—and one that dramatically affected the course of history—was Johann Gutenberg's invention of printing from individual pieces of cast type. The success of Gutenberg's press was phenomenal. It is estimated that by the end of the century more than a thousand printing shops were operating in more than two hundred centers, and that 40,000 editions, or 10 to 20 million books, had been printed—a total that represents more books than had ever been produced before Gutenberg's time.

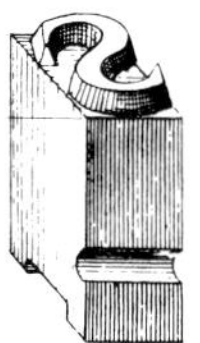

piece of metal type

Printing in Germany

Johann Gutenberg was born in Mainz, Germany, some time around 1397. Little is know about his early years, but it is clear that he was the right man, in the right place at the right time. Gutenberg was the right man because of his familiarity with the craft of the goldsmith and the diemaker. He was in the right place because Mainz was a cultural and commercial center. It was the right time because the Renaissance thirst for knowledge was creating a growing market for books that could not be satisfied with the traditional handwritten manuscripts.

2

Above: Type shown actual size
Left: casting type by hand

3

Graphic Arts

The most significant event of the century—and one that dramatically affected the course of history—was Johann Gutenberg's invention of printing from individual pieces of cast type. The success of Gutenberg's press was phenomenal. It is estimated that by the end of the century more than a thousand printing shops were operating in more than two hundred centers, and that 40,000 editions, or 10 to 20 million books, had been printed—a total that represents more books than had ever been produced before Gutenberg's time.

PRINTING IN GERMANY

Johann Gutenberg was born in Mainz, Germany, some time around 1397. Little is know about his early years, but it is clear that he was the right man, in the right place at the right time

Gutenberg was the right man because of his familiarity with the craft of the goldsmith and the diemaker. He was in the right place because Mainz was a cultural and commercial center. It was the right time because the Renaissance thirst for knowledge was creating a growing market for books that could not be satisfied with the traditional handwritten manuscripts.

Handwritten manuscripts were made to order and were usually expensive. They were laboriously copied by scribes who had either to read from a manuscript or have it read to them while copying. This process was not only time-consuming, but led to many errors, which had corrected. Adding to the expense was the scarcity and high cost of vellum and parchment. As a result, handwritten manuscripts were limited to a select few: clergymen, scholars, and wealthy individuals.

A relatively inexpensive means of producing multiple copies of books seems to have been developed just a little before Gutenberg began his experiments with printing. This was the so called block book whose pages had illustrations and minimal text cut together on the same block. The carved blocks were inked, and images were transferred onto paper in multiples by rubbing or by the use of the screw press. Block books were believed to have been made for semiliterate, preaching friars who brought the word of God to the urban working class and the poor.

City of Mainz

INSIGHT AND INNOVATION

Gutenberg's genius was realizing that printing would be more efficient if, instead of using a single woodblock to print an entire page, the individual letters were cast as separate blocks and then assembled into pages. In this manner, pages could be made up faster, errors could be corrected more rapidly, and, after printing, the type could be cleaned and reused.

CONTINUING A LEGACY

After Fust and Schoeffer took over Gutenberg's shop, the first book they printed and published was the *Mainz Psalter* of 1457. This psalter was notable for a number of reasons: it was the first book with a *colophon* showing the printer's name, location, date of publication, and printer's mark or device. It was also the first book in which the display initials were printed in color rather than painted by hand. The partners printed a number of important books, two of which were the Latin Bible of 1462 and a Cicero of 1465.

While on a book-selling trip to Paris in 1466, Fust died of the plague. After Fust's death, Schoeffer continued publishing until his own death in 1502.

2

3

Project | Brochure

Purpose
To carry a consistent design theme throughout the brochure, working with text type, display type, heads, subheads, captions, folios, and a grid.

Assignment
First, select a topic that is of interest to you and one for which you have access to a plentiful supply of quality images and text.

Next, research and compile images and text for the design of your brochure. Sources can be varied: magazines, books, flyers, the Internet, etc.
The better your source materials are, the easier it will be to design your project. A wide variety of images, such as photographs, illustrations, diagrams, and graphics, offers greater design opportunities.

For copy, either write your own or use dummy type. Regardless of your choice, you should write accurate heads, subheads, captions, and folios.

The final brochure design should include all the typographic elements: text type, display type, heads, subheads, captions, folios, and a grid. One of the five classic typefaces is recommended for the text and captions; display type is optional.

The final brochure should be eight or more pages, including the front and back covers.

FORMAT | Each page: 10 x 10 inches (25 x 25 cm)

TIME | 8 to 12 hours

Frank Gehry
Designer: Oscar Henriquez

Text: 10/11 Helvetica x 17 picas
Arrangement: Flush left, ragged right
Heads: Citizen
Captions: Citizen

BACK AND FRONT COVER

2

American Centre
Paris (1988-94)

the man

Gehry was 18 when the family uprooted, leaving the familiarity of Toronto for sprawling Los Angeles. The move, Gehry later acknowledged, was an enormous upheaval that left him at once overwhelmed and fascinated by his new environment. Confused and unsure of himself, Gehry eventually enrolled at the University of Southern California to study, not architecture, but fine art.

The discovery of architecture took a while. One of Gehry's classes at USC was a ceramics course taught by Glenn Lukens. Lukens took an interest in Gehry and invited himround to his house to meet Raphael Soriano, the architect whome he had commissioned to design his new place. The meeting, Gehry says, left him "lit up".

"I had just come from Canada and I didn't know anything and it was a bad time. My father had lost everything. I was really on the floor with lack of self-esteem. Not knowing what I wanted to do when I was 17 or 18 I had started working as a truck driver and I was fascinated with people who did know what to do. I was looking for a model, I guess," he recalled in discussion with Kurt Forster.

The effect of the meeting with Soriano was obvious to Lukens, who suggested to Gehry that he might enjoy studying architecture. Gehry started night classes in the architecture department. "I did really well," he says. "It was the first connection to something. They skipped me to the second year. It was a big deal." And yet, even so, Gehry had not quite found himself. He was constantly pushing at the system and testing its limits, dreaming up joing projects with the art department that, given the throughly traditional nature of the university, where invariably rejected.

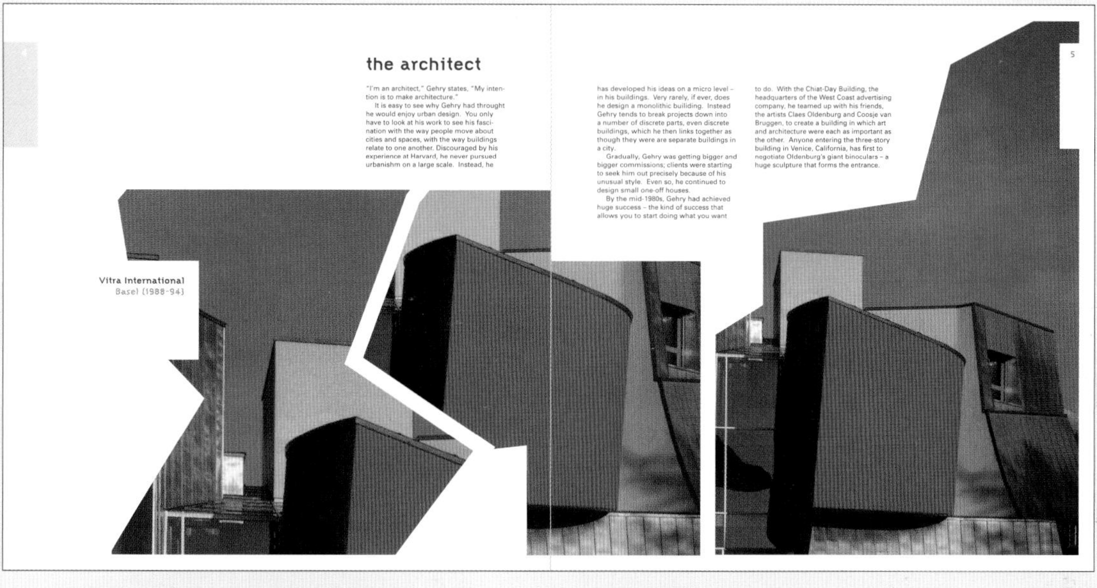

the architect

"I'm an architect," Gehry states, "My intention is to make architecture."

It is easy to see why Gehry had throught he would enjoy urban design. You only have to look at his work to see his fascination with the way people move about cities and spaces, with the way buildings relate to one another. Discouraged by his experience at Harvard, he never pursued urbanishm on a large scale. Instead, he has developed his ideas on a micro level – in his buildings. Very rarely, if ever, does he design a monolithic builiding. Instead Gehry tends to break projects down into a number of discrete parts, even discrete buildings, which he then links together as though they were are separate buildings in a city.

Gradually, Gehry was getting bigger and bigger commissions; clients were starting to seek him out precisely because of his unusual style. Even so, he continued to design small one-off houses.

By the mid-1980s, Gehry had achieved huge success – the kind of success that allows you to start doing what you want to do. With the Chiat-Day Building, the headquarters of the West Coast advertising company, he teamed up with his friends, the artists Claes Oldenburg and Coosje van Bruggen, to create a building in which art and architecture were each as important as the other. Anyone entering the three-story building in Venice, California, has first to negotiate Oldenburg's giant binoculars – a huge sculpture that forms the entrance.

5

Vitra International
Basel (1988-94)

6

Nationale Nederlanden
Prague (1992-1996)

the buildings

There are few buildings that people will corss the world to see. The Taj Mahal, the Pyramids, the Parthenon, maybe. Frank Gehry's Guggenheim Museum in Bilbao is one such. In the two years following its opening in 1997, more than two million visitors poured into the northern Spanish city whose principle – some would say only – attraction is the museum. Featured in countless newspapers, colour supplements and fashion magazines, Gehry's astonishing building has put Bilbao on the global map – so much so that the city's airport is having to expand to keep u pwith the demand – and has confirmed Gehry's position as the world's most famous living architect.

"The museum in Bilbao leads to a new era in building," said British architect Norman Foster at the time of the Guggenheims' opening. Gehry's friend, the sculptor Richard Serra, has claimed that "Frank represents a break with all contemporary architecture. His is not an architecture that arises from an older order. He is the first reality to break with the orthodoxy of the right angle."

The building has turned Gehry into an international celebrity. He is the architect that cities and organizations now want. Af Frank Gehry building is considered something that adds huge cachet to a place or a brand. Over the years, institutions as conservative as banks have commissioned him – he designed the Nationale_Nederlanden Building in Prague (see left), as have cities reinventing themselves for the 21st century – he is finishing a headquarters building in Pariser Platz in Berlin (1994-2000)

Korea
Designer: Elizabeth Lee

Text: 10/16 Baskerville x 17 picas
Arrangement: Flush left, ragged right
Heads: 24-point Baskerville, caps
Subheads: 10-point Baskerville, letterspaced
Captions: 8-point Baskerville italic

BACK AND FRONT COVER

MUGUNGHWA

the national flower

Mugunghwa is also known as the Rose of Sharon. The Mugunghwa symbolizes the strong and simple spirit of the Korean people which has endured the nation's long and often difficult history. According to records, Koreans have treasured the Rose of Sharon as a heavenly flower since ancient times. In fact, the Silla Kingdom called itself Mugunghwa Country. As the Rose of Sharon has been an important part of the Korean culture for centuries, it was only natural that the government adopted it as the national flower after Korea was liberated from Japanese rule.

botanical name

hibiscus syriacus L.

distribution

China, Northern India, Japan, and Korea

top left: A picture of the Korean Mugunghwa
above: Hangul taken from an old Korean newspaper

HANGUL

the korean alphabet

Koreans have developed and use a unique alphabet called Hangeul. It is considered to be one of the most efficient alphabets and has garnered unanimous praise from language experts for its scientific design and excellence.

the creator

Hangeul was created under King Sejong during the Joseon Dynasty. In 1446, the first Korean alphabet was proclaimed under the name Hunminjeongeum, which meant "the Correct Sounds for the Instruction of the People."

hangul today

Illiteracy is virtually nonexistent in Korea. This is another fact that attests to the easy learnability of Hangeul. It is not uncommon for a foreigner to gain a working knowledge of Hangeul after one or two hours of intensive studying. In addition, because of its scientific design, Hangeul lends itself to easy mechanization. In this age of computers, many people now are able to incorporate computers into their lives without difficulties, thanks to a large number of programs written in Hangeul.

2

top: a family dressed in the traditional hanbok.

HANBOK

raditional korean dress

The hanbok is characterized by its simple lines and the fact that it has no pockets. The women's hanbok comprises a wrap-around skirt and a bolero-like jacket. It is often called chimajeogori, chima being the Korean word for skirt and jeogori the word for jacket. The men's hanbok consists of a short jacket and pants, called baji, that are roomy and bound at the ankles. Both ensembles may be topped by a long coat of a similar cut called durumagi.

hanboks today

The traditional-style hanbok worn today are patterned after the ones worn during the Confucian-oriented Joseon Dynasty (1392-1910). Yangban, a hereditary aristocratic class based on scholarship and official position rather than on wealth, wore brightly colored hanbok of plain and patterned silk in cold weather and of closely woven ramie cloth or other high-grade, light-weight materials in warm weather. The commoners wore faded, worn-out colors.

3

TAEKWONDO

korean martial arts

Taekwondo is an officially acknowledged international sport that originated in Korea and is today practiced worldwide. Taekwondo uses the whole body, particularly the hands and feet. It not only strengthens one's physique, but also cultivates character via physical and mental training. Coupled with techniques of discipline, taekwondo is a self-defense martial art.

history

The evidence of taekwondo's existence as a systemized defense operation using the body's instinctive reflexes can be traced back to ceremonial games that were performed during religious events in the era of the ancient tribal states. During religious ceremonies such as Yeonggo and Dongmaeng (a sort of thanksgiving ceremony), and Mucheon (Dance to Heaven), ancient Koreans performed a unique exercise for physical training. This exercise was the original inception of taekwondo.

below: a man in a basic punch stance.

POTTERY

traditional koreaan pottery

Korea boasts an unexcelled cultural tradition of pottery. Deep-rooted in the nation's long history, Korean ceramics are world-renowned. In turn, ceramics have greatly influenced the lifestyle of the Korean people.

Pottery includes earthenware, ceramic ware, stoneware, and porcelain. Historical studies suggest that man first started making earthenware in approximately 10,000 to 6,000 B.C. The oldest kind of Korean earthenware found thus far dates back to 6,000 to 5,000 B.C.

history

Korea's earliest earthenware was made by firing clay at a temperature of 600 to 800 degrees centigrade or sometime even 1,000 degrees centigrade. The oldest earthenware included those that were just dried without firing. This type of earthenware was only made for a certain period of time. Later on, as man's ingenuity increased, not only was the way of kneading clay improved, but kilns also began to be built that could withstand the heat needed for firing.

above: examples of Korean pottery

5

MT. SEORAKSAN

tourist attration

Ask a Korean to name the most beautiful place in Korea and that person will no doubt say Mt. Seoraksan. It is arguably the area most beloved by Koreans.

With its high craggy peaks, boulder-strewn streams of crystal clear water, large waterfalls, unusual rock formations, and forests of pine and hardwood, it is certainly one of the most beautiful places Korea has to offer, any time of year.

climate

In Korea spring, summer, autumn and winter have climatic conditions that clearly distinguish them from each other, and no where is this more visible than Mt. Seoraksan. In spring, its slopes become a riot of various shades of pink, purple, white and yellow with the flowering of azaleas, rhododendrons, dogwoods and forsythia. In summer, it is lush with vegetation of every shade of green imaginable and its valleys are filled with the sound of rushing streams and thundering waterfalls. In autumn, it is a kaleidoscope of brilliant colors as nature changes the foliage to various shades of red, yellow and gold. In winter, it becomes white from its peaks down to its hills and its streams and waterfalls are hushed and still, all is serene.

above: a great overview of Mt. Seoraksan

6

Falling Pumpkin Eating Tweedled Green Eggs
Designer: Charlie Lora

Text: 12/14 Garamond x 10 picas
Arrangement: Flush left, ragged right
Heads: 34-point Garamond bold italic, reversed
Subheads: 26-point Garamond
Captions: 8-point Garamond italic

BACK AND FRONT COVER

pumpkin
Peter, Peter, pumkin-eater,
Had a wife, and couldn't keep her
He put her in a pumpkin-shell,
And there he kept her very well.
Peter, Peter Pumpkin Eater
the truth of rhymes?
6
7

Tweedledum, Tweedledee
a crazy couple
Tweduldum and Tweedledee
Resolved to have a battle,
For Tweedledum said Tweedledee
had spoiled his nice new rattle.
Just then flew by a monstrous crow
As big as a tar-barrel,
Which frightened both the heroes so
they quite forgot their quarrel.
9

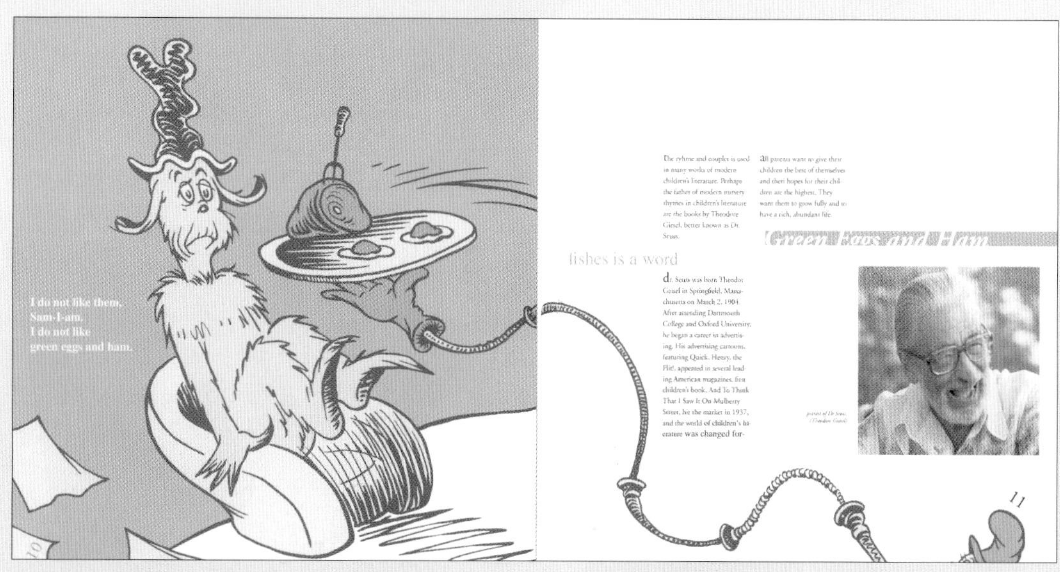
I do not like them,
Sam-I-am.
I do not like
green eggs and ham.
Green Eggs and Ham
fishes is a word
10
11

Project | Experimental Typography

Purpose
To stretch the imagination by creating a free-form design.

Assignment
Without preplanning, randomly cut a number of 3-inch squares from a newspaper, magazine, or other printed material. Select one that offers design possibilities. Enlarge the image to a 6-inch square.

Next, while retaining the character and proportions of the original, create a new variation by rewriting the copy or changing the typefaces and illustrations.

FORMAT | 6 x 6 inches (15 x 15 cm)

TIME | 3 hours

JILL MCCALLUM

STACY FRENETTE

MARK ZBOROVSKY

KLAUDIYA VINITSKY

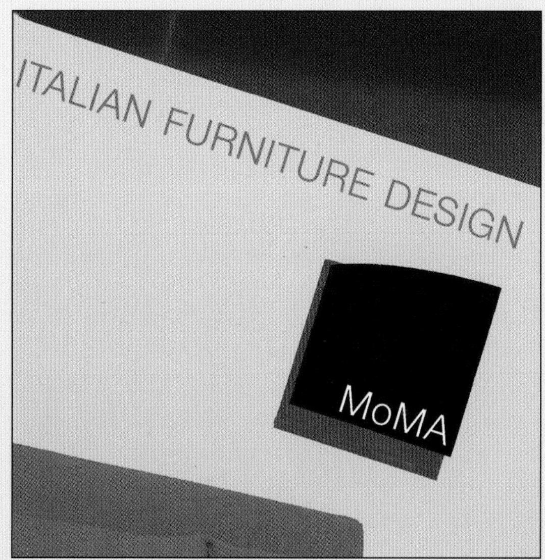

JOANNE D'ESPOSITO

MICHAEL MARK

Project | Ransom Note

Purpose
To explore the design potential in found typography. This project provides an opportunity to discover and combine interesting letterforms (including images is optional) to compose a creative collage.

Assignment
Cut type specimens from newspapers, magazines, or other printed material. Create a dramatic typographic effect by composing a short ransom note stating your actions, demands, and ultimatums.

It should be evident that the note has been created by a graphic designer. In other words, it has a design or esthetic rationale and is not just a random selection of type. You may also incorporate images into the design.

Having created a suitable design, you could extend this project to take a word or sentence from the ransom note and, with the addition of appropriate type, create a book jacket, CD cover, or poster, as shown below.

FORMAT | 10 x 10 inches (25 x 25 cm)

TIME | 4 hours

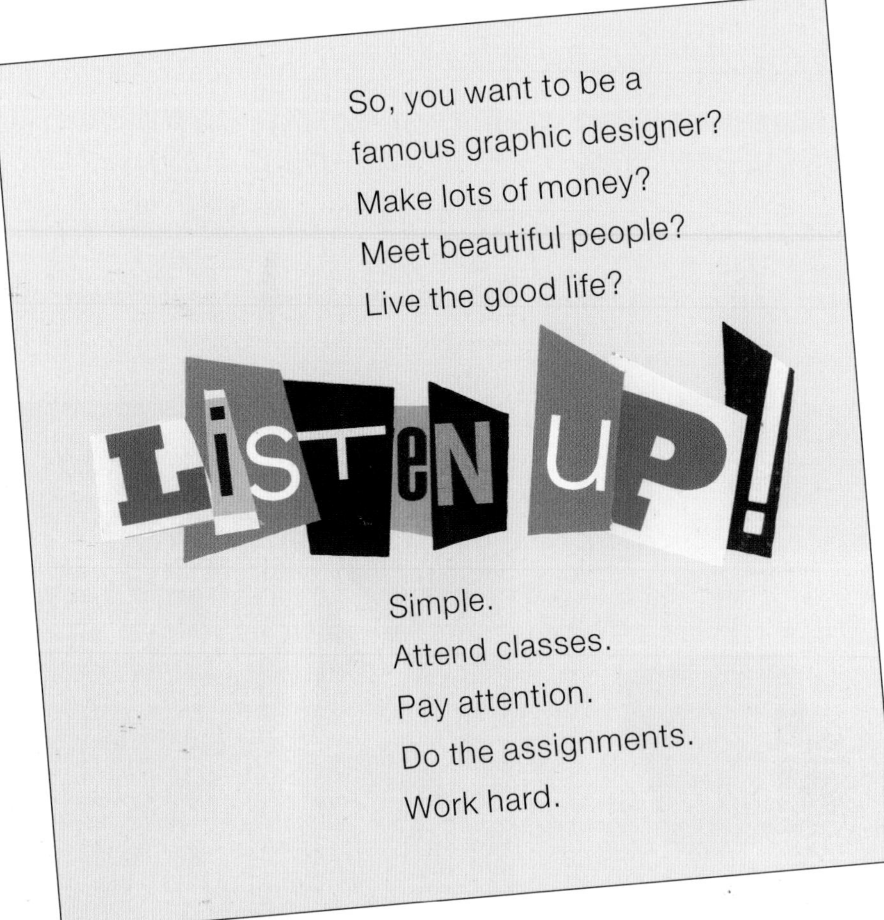

So, you want to be a
famous graphic designer?
Make lots of money?
Meet beautiful people?
Live the good life?
LiSTeN UP!
Simple.
Attend classes.
Pay attention.
Do the assignments.
Work hard.

6

OSCAR HENRIQUEZ

UNKNOWN

UNKNOWN

UNKNOWN

UNKNOWN

UNKNOWN

Project | Logo

Purpose
To explore the typographic possibilities of individual letters in the creation of a logo.

Assignment
Designing a logo as a company's identity is a lengthy and often complex process. However, it can also be an interesting and educational exercise.

Select two or three letters with which to create five different designs. Consider the effectiveness of each.

Although choice of typefaces is optional, it is suggested that you start with the five classic faces, mixing faces, weights, styles, sizes, etc.

Your designs should be in black and white, but you may wish to experiment with color to study the effect that it can have on the logo design.

The chosen letters should represent something, such as a service or a product. You may even wish to use your own initials. For example, the letters shown here, DWT, were taken from the title of this book, *Designing with Type,* and therefore the ideal logo should suggest something about typography.

FORMAT | Optional

TIME | 3 hours

left to right: ZANDER VAUBEL
JAMES MARK
ELIZABETH LEE
GUY LOUIS
VICTORIA KRASNY
SYLVAN MIGDAL

Traditional Skills

At one time, before computers, copyfitting, character counting, comping, and specifying type were fundamental skills practiced by every graphic designer. These were the traditional methods of appraising a design before incurring typesetting expenses.

Today's technologies have certainly reduced the need for these traditionally indispensable skills. Although seldom used today, comping requires little time to learn and is an excellent way to become familiar with the structure and "anatomy" of individual typefaces and arranging type on a page.

Copyfitting

■ Copyfitting begins when the designer is given an assignment along with the typewritten copy, called *hard copy*, to be set in type. Once a concept is decided upon, the next step is to make sure the type fits the allotted space. This process is called *copyfitting.* If the type fits, the designer creates a *comprehensive,* or *comp,* of the design with pencil and paper for approval.

Let's follow the process step by step, beginning with a single paragraph of typewritten copy. In this case we will use the descriptive copy for Garamond from page 28.

Designing with Type; elite typewriter.

ELITE: 12 CHARACTERS PER INCH

Designing with Type; pica typewriter.

PICA: 10 CHARACTERS PER INCH

1 | Two of the most popular typewriters: elite and pica

Character Counting

As a simple exercise we would like to fit the typewritten copy on the facing page into a space 20 picas wide, depth unknown. To establish the depth we must copyfit. This begins by determining the total number of characters in the paragraph.

It would take an endless amount of time to count each character individually in a manuscript. Fortunately there is a simpler method to arrive at a working character count.

The traditional typewriter produces hard copy in two popular formats: 10 pitch, referred to as *pica (not to be confused with the typographic term!)*; and 12 pitch, referred to as *elite*. **The 10 pitch produces rather large characters at the rate of 10 per inch. The 12 pitch produces smaller characters at the rate of 12 per inch (1).**

As the copy on the facing page was typed on a pica typewriter, we know there are 10 characters to the inch. Therefore, at 5 inches there are 50 characters. There are 13 full lines with 50 characters each for a subtotal of 650 characters. If extreme accuracy is not important, you may work with the subtotal.

However, for a more accurate count, you must now add the characters that exceed 5 inches and subtract the characters that fall short of 5 inches for a net of minus 18 characters. **Subtract 18 from the subtotal of 650 for an accurate count of 632 characters (2).**

Next, we must specify the type: 12-point Garamond with 3 points of linespacing (12/15) by 20 picas, set justified. **To determine how much space the typewritten copy (632 characters) will occupy when set we go to a characters-per-pica chart (3).** As our line length, or measure, is 20 picas, go to the 20 and read the figure below: 50 characters. Therefore, a 20-pica line of 12-point Garamond will contain approximately 50 characters.

Next, divide the total number of characters 632 by 50 and the result is 12 full lines plus 32 characters left over for an additional partial line, or a total of 13 lines.

We are now ready to prepare a comp of 13 lines of 12/15 Garamond by 20 picas justified. ■

NOTE | No matter how accurate the character count, the final setting will vary slightly depending upon factors such as letterspacing, wordspacing, and hyphenation.

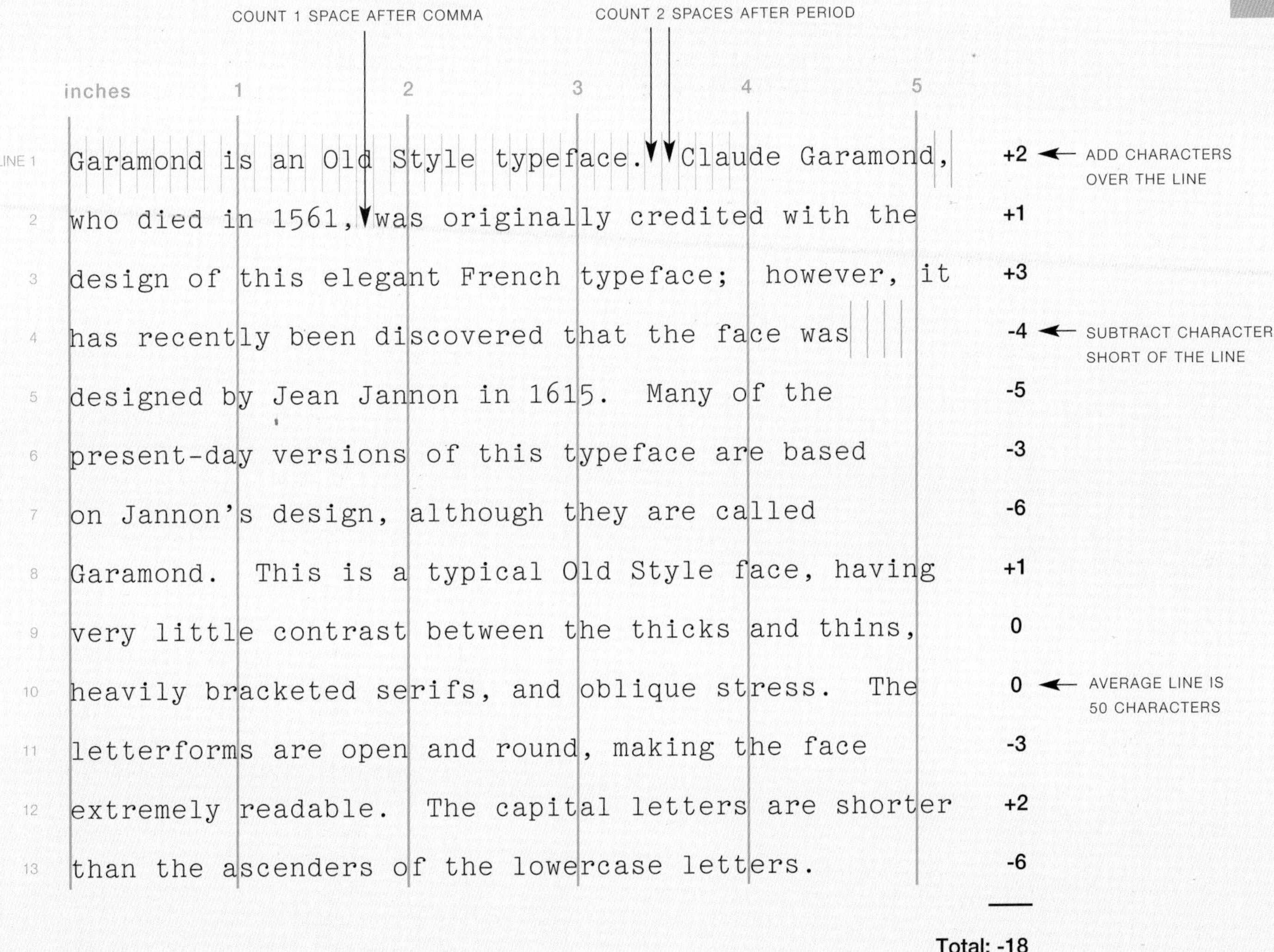

COUNT 1 SPACE AFTER COMMA
COUNT 2 SPACES AFTER PERIOD
inches 1 2 3 4 5
LINE 1 Garamond is an Old Style typeface. Claude Garamond, +2 ADD CHARACTERS OVER THE LINE
2 who died in 1561, was originally credited with the +1
3 design of this elegant French typeface; however, it +3
4 has recently been discovered that the face was -4 SUBTRACT CHARACTERS SHORT OF THE LINE
5 designed by Jean Jannon in 1615. Many of the -5
6 present-day versions of this typeface are based -3
7 on Jannon's design, although they are called -6
8 Garamond. This is a typical Old Style face, having +1
9 very little contrast between the thicks and thins, 0
10 heavily bracketed serifs, and oblique stress. The 0 AVERAGE LINE IS 50 CHARACTERS
11 letterforms are open and round, making the face -3
12 extremely readable. The capital letters are shorter +2
13 than the ascenders of the lowercase letters. -6
Total: -18

10 characters per inch x **5** inches per line = **50** characters per line

50 characters per line x **13** lines = **650** characters

650 characters – **18** characters = **632** characters

2 | A traditional method of counting characters

20-PICA MEASURE

RECOMMENDED LINE LENGTHS IN BOLD

LINE LENGTH IN PICAS	1	2	3	4	5	6	7	8	9	10	11	12	13	**14**	**15**	**16**	**17**	**18**	**19**	20	**21**	**22**	**23**	**24**	**25**	**26**	**27**	**28**	29	30	31	32	33	34	35	36
CHARACTERS PER LINE	3	6	8	10	13	15	18	20	23	25	28	30	33	**35**	**37**	**40**	**42**	**45**	**47**	50	**52**	**55**	**57**	**60**	**62**	**65**	**67**	**70**	72	75	77	80	82	85	87	90

3 | Charts showing the number of characters per pica were available in all type specimen books.

Comping

■ Before a design can be properly assessed, an accurate layout must be created showing the type and illustrations in position. These layouts are generally made with pencil and paper and are called comprehensives, or simply comps for short. The act of creating a comp is called *comping.*

1 | Two parallel lines are drawn to represent the x-height.

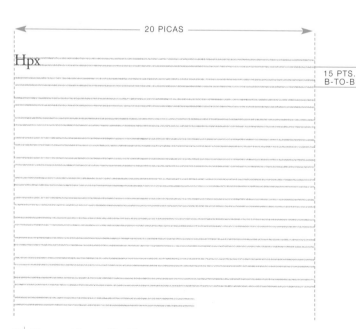

Comping Text Type

When comping text type, you need only suggest the lines of type, not render each individual word. **This is accomplished by drawing two parallel lines for every line of type; the bottom line is the baseline and the top line is the meanline (1).** The distance between the lines should match the x-height of the specific typeface, in our case 12-point Garamond.

Draw a box 20 picas wide and leave the bottom open. Next, using a type gauge, draw a dot every 15 points down the left side. These dots represent the baseline-to-baseline measurement of what will be 12/15 Garamond, as specified on the previous page.

To establish the x-height, go to the type specimen for 12-point Garamond on page 31. Lining a piece of paper alongside the type, indicate the x-height with two small dots.

Next, using the original baseline dots as a guide, transfer the x-height to your comp so that you have a series of multiple dots down the left side. Using a T-square, draw in 13 pairs of parallel lines.

Keep all the lines the same weight to create the uniform appearance of printed type. **You now have a comp of 12-point Garamond by 20 picas with 3 points of linespacing (2). When set, the number of lines should match your comp (3).**

NOTE | Remember to keep the last line of the paragraph short so that your comp resembles an actual setting.

20 PICAS

Hpx

15 PTS.
B-TO-B

2 | Comped lines of text type

12/15 GARAMOND X 20 PICAS

Garamond is an Old Style typeface. Claude Garamond, who died in 1561, was originally credited with the design of this elegant French typeface; however, it has recently been discovered that this typeface was designed by Jean Jannon in 1615. Many of the present-day versions of this elegant typeface may be either Garamond or Jannon designs, although they are all called Garamond. This is a typical Old Style face, having very little contrast between the thicks and thins, heavily bracketed serifs, and oblique stress. The letterforms are open and round, making the face extremely readable. The capital letters are shorter than the ascenders of the lowercase letters.

3 | Actual setting

Comping Display Type

When comping display type you must carefully trace each letter so the copy is readable and the typeface recognizable (4). We will use 72-point Helvetica to comp the word *Typography* both in uppercase and lowercase and all caps. (As there is no 72-point Helvetica in this book, you can print a complete alphabet from the computer.)

First, lightly draw a baseline on the tracing paper. Next, lay the tracing paper over the letter to be traced, making sure the baselines are properly aligned. Using a sharp pencil trace the outline of each letter.

As you trace the letters, consider the letterspacing carefully. Try to keep the spacing between letters visually even. Rounded letters, such as O, C, or G should fall slightly below the baseline in order to appear optically aligned.

When the outline is finished, use a softer pencil to fill in each letter with a uniform density (5). Be aware that the type, when set, will appear blacker and more assertive than your comp. However, there is no need to finish the comp in ink; pencil is adequate. Inking the letterforms tends to exaggerate any imperfections.

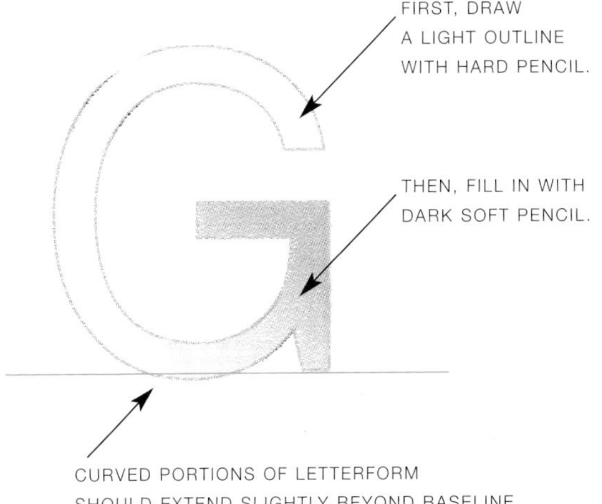

FIRST, DRAW
A LIGHT OUTLINE
WITH HARD PENCIL.
THEN, FILL IN WITH
DARK SOFT PENCIL.
CURVED PORTIONS OF LETTERFORM
SHOULD EXTEND SLIGHTLY BEYOND BASELINE.

4 | Trace each letter carefully and fill in.

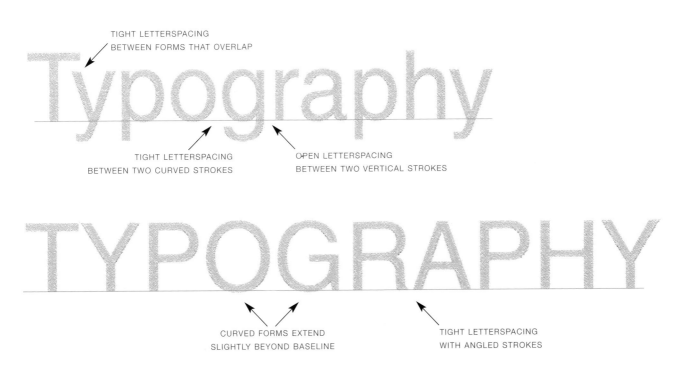

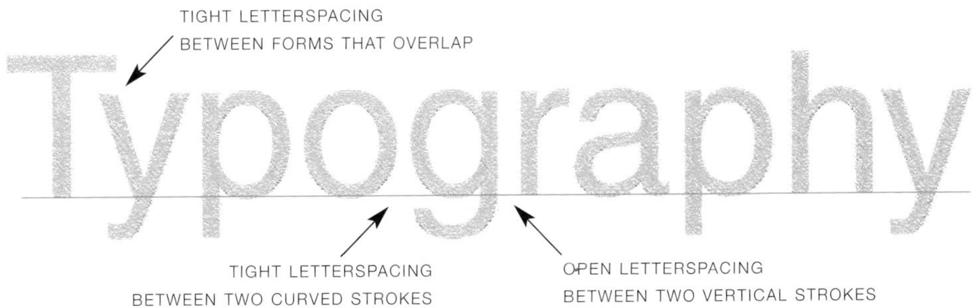

TIGHT LETTERSPACING
BETWEEN FORMS THAT OVERLAP

TIGHT LETTERSPACING
BETWEEN TWO CURVED STROKES
OPEN LETTERSPACING
BETWEEN TWO VERTICAL STROKES

CURVED FORMS EXTEND
SLIGHTLY BEYOND BASELINE
TIGHT LETTERSPACING
WITH ANGLED STROKES

5 | When set, the type will appear blacker and more assertive than your comp.

Copy Preparation

■ Although most copy today is transmitted as a digital file, there may be occasions when you will be required to work with typewritten copy. Either way, you must prepare the copy properly to avoid errors.

Typewritten Copy

It is good practice to discuss copy preparation with the client before beginning the job. In general, copy should be delivered as a double-spaced manuscript on standard 8 1/2 x 11–inch bond paper, with a generous margin on the left for design and/or editorial notations. Each page should contain approximately the same number of lines and should be numbered consecutively, with the job title indicated on each page as well.

SET IN 9/12 HELVETICA x 16½ PICAS FL LFT/ RG RT.

Preparing copy for the typesetter is a crucial procedure. Copy should be typed on standard 8 1/2 x 11 bond paper with a 10- or 12-pitch typewriter. A good column width is about 6 inches, which gives the page a generous margin. The lines should be double-spaced, each having approximately the same number of characters. Every page should contain the same number of lines. Corrections should be made neatly in pencil or ink. Make sure all pages are numbered consecutively in case the sheets get separated. Also make sure the job title appears on every page to prevent the copy from being mixed up with another job.

( ) CLOSE UP

INDENT 1-EM □ Write your own instructions, using the standard set of proofreaders' marks shown on page 144. Remember, typesetters are terribly literal: they will follow only the instructions you give them; you cannot expect them to make design decisions.

1 | Instructions must be precise and legible.

Specifying Type

If you are preparing copy for typesetting, you must accurately indicate the instructions. **They should be precise and legible and grouped in the left-hand margin of the manuscript, using a minimum number of words (1).**

When specifying type, always give the precise name as it appears on the computer or in a type specimen book. Include the manufacturer's name or font foundry in your instructions; for example, for Garamond, specify Adobe Garamond or Monotype Garamond. In addition, note the weight and style of the type, such as Monotype Garamond Bold.

It is also a good practice to include an accurate comp of your design with type specifications in order to give the typesetter or service bureau an idea of how you intend the final piece to look.

Proofs

Once the job has been set, you will receive a "first proof" (2). Check it carefully against your layout to make certain there are no errors; check the typeface, the linespacing, and the pica measure. The copy should also be proofread for spelling or grammatical errors.

Very few jobs are typeset without requiring some corrections and/or modifications. This entails additional work and charges. Changes can be divided into two categories: AAs and PEs. AAs, or "author's alterations," represent changes or corrections made by the designer or client, who will be responsible for any additional costs. PEs, or "printer's errors," represent errors and/or omissions on the part of the typesetter, service bureau, or print vendor. The costs involved in correcting such errors should be absorbed by the vendor.

When corrections or changes have been clearly indicated, the proof is returned to the typesetter. **After the corrections have been made, the final proofs are sent to you for approval (3).**

Proofreaders' Marks

The symbols used to communicate editorial and design instructions to the professional typesetter are called proofreaders' marks (4). These symbols, shown on page 144, are used by everyone associated with copy or typesetting: copywriters, editors, designers, typesetters, and proofreaders. You will notice there are two distinct sets of marks: one is written in the margin and the other indicated directly on the type. Although you may use only a dozen or so of the proofreaders' marks, it helps if you are familiar with all of them. ■

7

Preparing copy for the typesetter is a crucial procedure. Copy should be typed on staandard 8 1/2 x 11 bond paper with a 10- or 12-pitch typewriter. A good column width is about 6 inches, which gives the page a generous margin. The lines should be double-spaced, each having approximately the same number of characters. Every page should contain the same number of lines. Corrections should be made neatly in pen cil or ink. Make sure all pages are numbered consecutively in case the sheets get separated. Also make sure the job title appears on every page to prevent the copy from being mixed up with another job.

Write your own instructions, using the standard set of proofreaders' marks shown on page 144. Remember, typesetters are terribly literal: they will follow only the instructions you give them; you cannot expect to make design decisions.

2 | First proof with corrections indicated

Preparing copy for the typesetter is a crucial procedure. Copy should be typed on standard 8 1/2 x 11 bond paper with a 10- or 12-pitch typewriter. A good column width is about 6 inches, which gives the page a generous margin. The lines should be double-spaced, each having approximately the same number of characters. Every page should contain the same number of lines. Corrections should be made neatly in pencil or ink. Make sure all pages are numbered consecutively in case the sheets get separated. Also make sure the job title appears on every page to prevent the copy from being mixed up with another job. Write your own instructions, using the standard set of proofreaders' marks shown on page 144. Remember, typesetters are terribly literal: they will follow only the instructions you give them; *you cannot expect them to make design decisions.*

3 | Final proof for approval

EXPLANATION	MARK	EXAMPLE
Set in italic.	ital	I am the voice of today.
Set in roman.	rom	I am the *voice* of today.
Set in small caps.	sc	I am the voice of today.
Set in caps.	caps	I am the voice of today.
Set in boldface.	BF	I am the voice of today.
Set in lowercase.	lc	I am the VOICE of today.
Insert period.	⊙	I am the voice of today
Insert comma.	,	I am the voice of today
Insert space.	#	I am the voiceof today.
Insert word.	the/	I am voice of today.
Insert hyphen.	=	I am the voice of twenty one days.
Insert em-dash.	1/m	I am the voice of today and tomorrow.
Insert en-dash.	1/n	I am the voice of the 1980-1990 generation.
Insert parentheses.	(/)	I am the voice of today and tomorrow.
Insert colon.	:	I am the voice of today
Insert semicolon.	;	I am the voice of today
Insert question mark.	SET ?	I am the voice of today
Insert quotation marks.	"/"	I am the voice of today.
Delete or take out.	ϑ	I am the voice of of today.
Delete and close up.	ϑ	I am the vooice of today.
Make space between words equal.	eq #	I am the voice of today.
Spell out words in circle.	sp	I am the voice of the U.S.
Let it stand.	stet	I am the voice of today.
Query by editor.	"/" ?	I am the voice of today.
Transpose words or letters.	tr	I am voice the of today.
Close up.	⁀	I am the vo ice of today.
Move to left.	[	I am the voice of today.
Move to right.	]	I am the voice of today.
Center type.	ctr.	I am the voice of today.
Start new paragraph.	¶	¶ I am the voice of today.
Indent 1-em space.	□	□ I am the voice of today.
Indent 2-em space.	□□	□□ I am the voice of today.
No paragraph; run in.	run-in	...was yesterday. I am the voice of today.

4 | Proofreaders' marks are an efficient way of communicating instructions.

Type Specimens

There are hundreds of typefaces available and many are of questionable value. To help identify some of the better typefaces, additional type specimens have been added to the familiar classifications of Old Style, Transitional, Modern, Egyptian/Slab Serif, and Sans Serif. Typefaces from additional major type classifications have also been added: Decorative/Novelty, Script, Black Letter, and Ornaments/Icons/Flourishes.

Classifications

■ This section supplements the classic typefaces provided in Part Two. These specimens will give you some idea of the wide range of typefaces available.

There are typefaces in the familiar classifications of Old Style, Transitional, Modern, Egyptian/Slab Serif, and Sans Serif. Still others belong to major classifications that have not yet been represented: Decorative/Novelty, Script, Black Letter, and Ornaments/Icons/Flourishes. Some typefaces fall between categories, sharing characteristics of two or more categories.

Each setting shows the title of this book along with complete alphabets of uppercase and lowercase characters, and figures.

Many of the faces presented here function equally well for text and display purposes, while some are practical only as display.

Names of the type specimens' foundries are listed below along with their abbreviations.

Adobe (A)

Bitstream (BT)

Emigre Graphics

The Font Bureau (FB)

The Font Company (FC)

Fontshop (FF)

Image Club Graphics (ICG)

International Typeface Corporation (ITC)

Lanston Type Company (LTC)

Letraset (LET)

Linotype Library (LT)

Martin Majoor

Microsoft (MS)

Monotype Imaging or AGFA Monotype (MT)

The following is a brief description of the various typographic classifications.

OLD STYLE | Serif typefaces based on the earliest examples of printing. Letterforms show minimal thick and thin contrast between strokes, as well as obvious bracketed serifs.

TRANSITIONAL | Typestyles with more refined serifs and clearly drawn thick and thin main strokes. Historically, this classification was the bridge between Old Style and Modern typefaces.

MODERN | Typestyles characterized by strong contrast between thick and thin strokes, fine serifs with minimal bracketing, and strong vertical stress. Modern typefaces are usually modified for text settings to prevent the text from "sparkling." To achieve this, the contrast is reduced by lightening the thick strokes.

EGYPTIAN/SLAB SERIF | Typefaces characterized by thick, dominating serifs. Sometimes these serifs are equivalent to the thickness of the main strokes. Brackets are minimal or nonexistent. (This classification is also called *square serif.*)

SANS SERIF | A basic type classification primarily of twentieth-century origin, characterized by a lack of serifs. Sans serif typefaces usually have minimal variance between thick and thin strokes. Once considered ugly, sans serif typefaces were called "grotesques," a term still used in Great Britain.

DECORATIVE/NOVELTY | A wide range of custom and specialty typefaces, almost exclusively used for display purposes. This classification is a catch-all for faces that may defy categorization.

SCRIPT | Typestyles based on handwriting and calligraphy, especially the formal cursives of eighteenth- and nineteenth-century England. Modern scripts might also include brushstroke and sign-painter's writing.

BLACK LETTER | Typefaces based on mostly fourteenth- and fifteenth-century manuscripts. Letterforms are dense and compressed, with bold horizontal strokes. Also referred to as Gothic, Old English, or Broken.

ORNAMENTS/ICONS/FLOURISHES | These elements, like display initials, offer the designer an opportunity to embellish a printed piece. Some of these typographic devices can be used singly or repeated to create a border or overall pattern. An obvious way of attracting attention is through the use of typographic ornaments. ■

Old Style

ALDINE | BT

Designing with Type
ABCDEFGHIJKLMNOPQRSTUVWXYZ&
abcdefghijklmnopqrstuvwxyz1234567890

BEMBO | A

Designing with Type
ABCDEFGHIJKLMNOPQRSTUVWXYZ&
abcdefghijklmnopqrstuvwxyz1234567890

CASLON 540 | BT

Designing with Type
ABCDEFGHIJKLMNOPQRSTUVWXYZ&
abcdefghijklmnopqrstuvwxyz1234567890

DANTE | MT

Designing with Type
ABCDEFGHIJKLMNOPQRSTUVWXYZ&
abcdefghijklmnopqrstuvwxyz1234567890

GALLIARD | BT

Designing with Type
ABCDEFGHIJKLMNOPQRSTUVWXYZ&
abcdefghijklmnopqrstuvwxyz1234567890

PALATINO | LT

Designing with Type
ABCDEFGHIJKLMNOPQRSTUVWXYZ&
abcdefghijklmnopqrstuvwxyz1234567890

PLANTIN | A

Designing with Type
ABCDEFGHIJKLMNOPQRSTUVWXYZ&
abcdefghijklmnopqrstuvwxyz1234567890

SABON | A

Designing with Type
ABCDEFGHIJKLMNOPQRSTUVWXYZ&
abcdefghijklmnopqrstuvwxyz1234567890

Transitional

BULMER | BT

Designing with Type
ABCDEFGHIJKLMNOPQRSTUVWXYZ&
abcdefghijklmnopqrstuvwxyz1234567890

COCHIN | LT

Designing with Type
ABCDEFGHIJKLMNOPQRSTUVWXYZ&
abcdefghijklmnopqrstuvwxyz1234567890

FAIRFIELD | A

Designing with Type
ABCDEFGHIJKLMNOPQRSTVWXYZ&
abcdefghijklmnopqrstuvwxyz1234567890

JANSON TEXT | A

Designing with Type
ABCDEFGHIJKLMNOPQRSTUVWXYZ&
abcdefghijklmnopqrstuvwxyz1234567890

MRS EAVES | EMIGRE

Designing with Type
ABCDEFGHIJKLMNOPQRSTUVWXYZ&
abcdefghijklmnopqrstuvwxyz1234567890

USHERWOOD | ITC

Designing with Type
ABCDEFGHIJKLMNOPQRSTUVWXYZ&
abcdefghijklmnopqrstuvwxyz1234567890

VELJOVIC BOOK | ITC

Designing with Type
ABCDEFGHIJKLMNOPQRSTUVWXYZ&
abcdefghijklmnopqrstuvwxyz1234567890

ZAPF INTERNATIONAL | BT

Designing with Type
ABCDEFGHIJKLMNOPQRSTUVWXYZ&
abcdefghijklmnopqrstuvwxyz1234567890

Modern

BERNHARD MODERN | BT

Designing with Type
ABCDEFGHIJKLMNOPQRSTUVWXYZ&
abcdefghijklmnopqrstuvwxyz1234567890

DIDOT | LT

Designing with Type
ABCDEFGHIJKLMNOPQRSTUVWXYZ&
abcdefghijklmnopqrstuvwxyz1234567890

FENICE | BT

Designing with Type
ABCDEFGHIJKLMNOPQRSTUVWXYZ&
abcdefghijklmnopqrstuvwxyz1234567890

FILOSOPHIA | EMIGRE

Designing with Type
ABCDEFGHIJKLMNOPQRSTUVWXYZ&
abcdefghijklmnopqrstuvwxyz1234567890

MODERN 880 | BT

Designing with Type
ABCDEFGHIJKLMNOPQRSTUVWXYZ&
abcdefghijklmnopqrstuvwxyz1234567890

MODERN WIDE | MT

Designing with Type
ABCDEFGHIJKLMNOPQRSTUVWXYZ&
abcdefghijklmnopqrstuvwxyz1234567890

TORINO | FC

Designing with Type
ABCDEFGHIJKLMNOPQRSTUVWXYZ&
abcdefghijklmnopqrstuvxyz1234567890

WALDBAUM | A

Designing with Type
ABCDEFGHIJKLMNOPQRSTUVWXYZ&
abcdefghijklmnopqrstuvwxyz1234567890

Egyptian | Slab Serif

CITY | A
Designing with Type
ABCDEFGHIJKLMNOPQRSTUVWXYZ&
abcdefghijklmnopqrstuvwxyz1234567890

EGYPTIAN 710 | BT
Designing with Type
ABCDEFGHIJKLMNOPQRSTUVWXYZ&
abcdefghijklmnopqrstuvwxyz1234567890

GLYPHA | A
Designing with Type
ABCDEFGHIJKLMNOPQRSTUVWXYZ&
abcdefghijklmnopqrstuvwxyz1234567890

LUBALIN GRAPH | BT
Designing with Type
ABCDEFGHIJKLMNOPQRSTUVWXYZ&
abcdefghijklmnopqrstuvwxyz1234567890

QUADRAAT | FF
Designing with Type
ABCDEFGHIJKLMNOPQRSTUVWXYZ&
abcdefghijklmnopqrstuvwxyz 1234567890

SERIFA | BT
Designing with Type
ABCDEFGHIJKLMNOPQRSTUVWXYZ&
abcdefghijklmnopqrstuvwxyz1234567890

STYMIE | BT
Designing with Type
ABCDEFGHIJKLMNOPQRSTUVWXYZ&
abcdefghijklmnopqrstuvwxyz1234567890

SWIFT | LT
Designing with Type
ABCDEFGHIJKLMNOPQRSTUVWXYZ&
abcdefghijklmnopqrstuvwxyz1234567890

Sans Serif

AKZIDENZ GROTESK | BT

Designing with Type
ABCDEFGHIJKLMNOPQRSTUVWXYZ&
abcdefghijklmnopqrstuvwxyz1234567890

FRANKLIN GOTHIC | BT

Designing with Type
ABCDEFGHIJKLMNOPQRSTUVWXYZ&
abcdefghijklmnopqrstuvwxyz1234567890

FRUTIGER | A

Designing with Type
ABCDEFGHIJKLMNOPQRSTUVWXYZ&
abcdefghijklmnopqrstuvwxyz1234567890

FUTURA | A

Designing with Type
ABCDEFGHIJKLMNOPQRSTUVWXYZ&
abcdefghijklmnopqrstuvwxyz1234567890

GILL SANS | MT

Designing with Type
ABCDEFGHIJKLMNOPQRSTUVWXYZ&
abcdefghijklmnopqrstuvwxyz1234567890

META | FF

Designing with Type
ABCDEFGHIJKLMNOPQRSTUVWXYZ&
abcdefghijklmnopqrstuvwxyz1234567890

SCALA SANS | MAJOOR

Designing with Type
ABCDEFGHIJKLMNOPQRSTUVWXYZ&
abcdefghijklmnopqrstuvwxyz1234567890

UNIVERS | A

Designing with Type
ABCDEFGHIJKLMNOPQRSTUVWXYZ&
abcdefghijklmnopqrstuvwxyz1234567890

Decorative | Novelty

ADLIB | BT

Designing with Type
ABCDEFGHIJKLMNOPQRSTUVWXYZ&
abcdefghijklmnopqrstuvwxyz1234567890

CRITTER | A

DESIGNING WITH TYPE
ABCDEFGHIJKLMNOPQRST
UVWXYZ

FALSTAFF FESTIVAL | MT

DESIGNING WITH TYPE
ABCDEFGHIJKLMNOPQRSTUVWXYZ&
1234567890

FRANCES UNCIAL | LET

designing with type
abcdefghijklmnopqrstuvwxyz&1234567890

INDUSTRIA | A

Designing with Type
ABCDEFGHIJKLMNOPQRSTUVWXYZ& abcdefghijklmnopqrstuvwxyz1234567890

JAZZ | LET

Designing with Type
ABCDEFGHIJKLMNOPQRSTUVWXYZ&
abcdefghijklmnopqrstuvwxyz1234567890

REMEDY | EMIGRE

Designing with Type
ABCDEFGHIJKLMNOPQRSTUVWXYZ&
abcdefghijklmnopqrstuvwxyz1234567890

RUBINO SERIF | ICG

Designing with Type
ABCDEFGHIJKLMNOPQRSTUVWXYZ&
abcdefghijklmnopqrstuvwxyz1234567890

Script and Black Letter

BICKHAM SCRIPT | A

Designing with Type

ABCDEFGHIJKLMNOPQRSTUVWXYZ&

abcdefghijklmnopqrstuvwxyz1234567890

GRAVURA | A

Designing with Type

ABCDEFGHIJKLMNOPQRSTU

VWXYZ&abcdefghijklmnopqrstuvwxyz1234567890

SNELL ROUNDHAND | A

Designing with Type

ABCDEFGHIJKLMNOPQRSTUVWXYZ&

abcdefghijklmnopqrstuvwxyz1234567890

BLACKLETTER | BT

Designing with Type

ABCDEFGHIJKLMNOPQRSTUVWXYZ&

abcdefghijklmnopqrstuvwxyz1234567890

BLACKMOOR | LET

Designing with Type

ABCDEFGHIJKLMNOPQRSTUVWXYZ&

abcdefghijklmnopqrstuvwxyz1234567890

FETTE FRAKTUR | A

Designing with Type

ABCDEFGHIJKLMNOPQRSTUVWXYZ&

abcdefghijklmnopqrstuvwxyz1234567890

GOUDY TEXT | A

Designing with Type

ABCDEFGHIJKLMNOPQRSTUVWXYZ

&abcdefghijklmnopqrstuvwxyz1234567890

Ornaments | Icons | Flourishes

BOTANICAL | MT

FLEURONS | LANSTON TYPE

HOT METAL BORDERS | LINOTYPE

POETICA | ADOBE

WEBDINGS | MICROSOFT

WOODTYPE ORNAMENTS | A

ZAPF DINGBATS | BT

References and Resources

Until now we have been concerned mainly with understanding the basics of typography and learning how to design with type. This part introduces historical data and reference material that should be of interest to any serious graphic designer.

Among the items included is a brief history of typesetting methods over the centuries. This is followed by an extended glossary of important graphic design terms, a bibliography, and finally the index. In addition, as graphic designers have become their own typographers, we have included a section on the rules of proper punctuation.

Punctuation

The finest typography in the world is useless if the message cannot be understood. Before specifying type, review the copy to see if it makes sense and if there is an overall consistency of punctuation and style. This is especially important when dealing with display type or any highly visible copy such as heads, captions, lists, and tabular matter. However, do not change punctuation without first discussing it with the copywriter or editor. Although there are specific rules of punctuation, it is sometimes possible to have more than one acceptable solution. For example, there are "house styles" as well as differences between American and British usage. This means that the preferred punctuation of one client may not be the same as that of another. Here are the common punctuation marks and their uses. This represents a mere outline, and it is recommended that every designer acquire a copy of an accepted book on style such as *The Chicago Manual of Style* (University of Chicago Press) or *Words into Type* (Appleton-Century-Crofts).

{?.,&:;}

PERIOD | The period marks the end of a sentence. It is also used with abbreviations, such as Mr., Ms., U.S.A., etc. The period may sometimes be omitted in display type, after heads, and at the end of short captions. The period is always placed inside the closing quotation mark, whether it is part of the quoted matter or not.

> The designer said, "We need the type right away."

COLON | The colon is used after a word, phrase, or sentence to introduce a list, series, direct quote, or further amplification. It replaces the phrases "that is" and "for example." A colon is also used in expressions of time and in the salutation of a letter. When the colon is used as punctuation within a sentence, the clause following the colon starts with a lowercase letter. However, if the colon introduces a series of complete sentences, each sentence should start with a cap. Also, lists, tabular matter, and directional indications (left, right) following a colon may be capped. A colon is placed outside the closing quotation mark unless it is part of the quoted matter.

> Serif: the short stroke that projects from the ends of the main strokes. There are three measurements with which the designer should be familiar: points, picas, and units.
>
> The author asks: "Has digital typesetting created a new typography?"
>
> The name of a typeface may differ: Helvetica is also called Oaro, Helios, Geneva, or Vega.
>
> Dear Sirs: The time is 10:30 A.M.

SEMICOLON | The semicolon represents a pause greater than that marked by a comma and less than that marked by a period. Its most common use is to separate complete and closely related clauses. It is also used to separate items in a list that have internal comma punctuation. A semicolon is placed outside the closing quotation mark unless it is part of the quoted matter.

> The difference between one typeface and another is often subtle; it may be no more than a slight difference in the shape of the serif.
>
> Each typeface has a name for identification: it may be that of the designer, Baskerville; or of a country, Helvetica; or it may be simply a name, Futura.

COMMA | The comma signifies a pause while reading. It separates independent clauses, words in a series, items in a list, and figures. It also introduces a direct quote. The comma, like the period, is always placed inside the closing quotation mark.

> Here are some samples: The job is running late, and the designer needs the type right away.
>
> A point is a small, fixed amount of space.
>
> Picas, points, and units can be confusing.
>
> The test was May 1, 2006.
>
> The designer said, "Just keep on trying," and we could feel the tension in the air.

QUESTION MARK | The question mark is used after any sentence or phrase that asks a direct question. It should not be used after an indirect question ("I wonder if my computer will crash today.") or a question that embodies a request not requiring an answer ("Will you please be seated."). A question mark is placed outside the closing quotation mark unless it is part of the quoted matter.

> What is a typeface?

EXCLAMATION POINT | The exclamation point indicates strong feeling, surprise, or irony and is used to achieve emphasis. It is placed outside the closing quotation mark unless it is part of the quoted matter.

> A typeface refers to a specific design of an alphabet—and there are thousands!

QUOTATION MARKS | Quotation marks may be single (' ') or double (" "). In modern American usage, single quotes are used only when setting off a quote within a quote. For all other purposes double quotes are used. Quotation marks are used to set off direct quotes; excerpted text; titles of poems, stories, and articles; and to draw attention to a word or phrase.
When quoting excerpted text that is longer than one paragraph, each paragraph opens with a quotation mark but only the final paragraph closes with one.

No quotation marks are necessary if excerpted text is set indented or in a smaller type size. Commas and periods are always set inside the closing quotation mark. All other punctuation is set inside if it is part of the quote, outside if not.

Sans serif is French for "without serif."

HYPHEN | The hyphen is used to join compound words and to indicate a word break at the end of a line. It is also used to separate prefixes and suffixes from the root word.

The type you are now reading is 8-point Helvetica.

The job prints out in typewriter-like characters.

EN-DASH | The en-dash is slightly longer than the hyphen. It takes the place of the word "to." It is also used to hyphenate compounds in which one is already hyphenated.

The number of characters in a font is usually 86–120.

It is an open-source–based browser.

EM-DASH | The em-dash is the mark commonly meant by the term "dash." It indicates an abrupt break in thought or speech, and it may be used instead of commas or parentheses to set off a parenthetical clause. An em-dash is marked for the typesetter like this:

This book offers the designer—and nondesigner—a complete guide to phototypesetting.

To set lines of type equal in length—or justified—the space between words must be adjusted.

2-EM-DASH | The two-em-dash is used after an initial letter to represent a proper noun. It is marked for the typesetter like this:

Helvetica was designed by Mr. M⸺ in 1957.

3-EM-DASH | The three-em-dash is used to avoid repetition in bibliographies when there is more than one book by the same author. After the initial listing, the author's name is indicated by a three-em-dash. It is marked for the typesetter like this:

Craig, James. *Designing with Type*
⸻. *Phototypesetting: A Design Manual*
⸻. *Production for the Graphic Designer*

PARENTHESES | Parentheses are used to enclose matter that is not essential to the meaning of the sentence. They may also be used to enclose "asides" by the author as well as references in the text.

Some typestyles are created by varying the weight (thickness of stroke).

BRACKETS | Brackets are used to indicate parentheses within parentheses. They are also used to enclose editorial interpolations (comments, queries, explanations, corrections, or directions inserted into the text).

(See *Designing with Type* [5th ed.].)

A complete, graphically illustrated guide to phototypesetting [sic].

ELLIPSIS POINTS | Ellipsis points (or ellipses) are three periods set in a row. They indicate suspended thought, an omission in excerpted text, and in fiction, a pause in speech or thought. When omitting copy from an incomplete sentence, there should be a space before the final word and the first ellipsis point. When omitting copy after a complete sentence, the final word should be immediately followed by four points, the first of which is the period that ends the sentence.

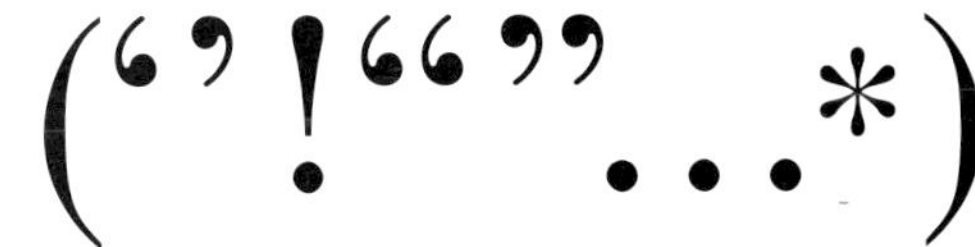

"A font is a complete alphabet of one size of one typeface.... The number of characters in a font varies, depending on..."

SLASH | A slash (also called a slant) between words indicates that the reader may choose between them. A slash may also be used in presenting numbers and tabular material, and in setting built-up fractions.

You can mix roman with italic and/or boldface.

BRACES | Braces are used to join two or more lines of type. They come in a range of sizes to accommodate any number of lines.

Garamond }
Bembo } Old Style typefaces
Poliphilus }
Blado }

ASTERISK | An asterisk after a word or sentence indicates that further information, or a reference, may be found in a footnote.* They are placed after all punctuation except an em-dash and a closing parenthesis if the matter referred to is within the parentheses. If there is more than one instance on the same page where a footnote is called for, a dagger or other reference mark is used. ‡

* The footnote is always preceded by an identical reference mark.

‡ If more reference marks are needed on a page, double marks are used. ■

Typesetting | Digital Design

While typesetting methods have changed over time, the criteria for judging good typography have not changed. Although you should know as much as possible about the various typesetting methods, it is more important to understand what constitutes a well-designed typeface and how type should be arranged on the page.

The following is a brief history of typesetting over the centuries and how the introduction of digital design revolutionized the industry.

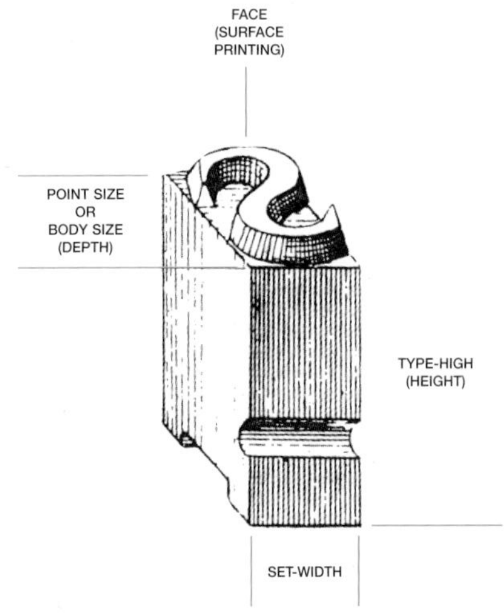

HANDSETTING

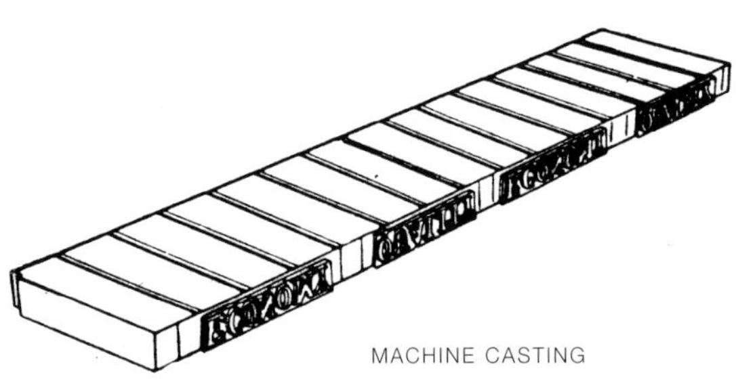

MACHINE CASTING

Typesetting Methods

Typesetting methods can be divided into four major categories: handsetting, machine casting, phototypesetting, and digital composition.

HANDSETTING | Handset type was introduced in the mid-fifteenth century by Johannes Gutenberg, and until the late nineteenth century, it was the only means of setting type.

In handset type (also called foundry type), every character was cast on a separate piece of metal and stored in a type case. The letters on metal type were reversed so they would appear correct when printed.

To set type, the compositor, or typesetter, held a composing stick in one hand and with the other selected the required pieces of type from the type case. When the job had been set, the type was "locked-up," inked, and printed.

The height of the metal type, referred to as type-high, had to be consistent in order to print evenly (.918 inches). If a piece of type was too low, it would not receive the ink; if too high, the type would press into the paper. After printing, the type characters were cleaned and redistributed into their proper compartments for future use.

Although the compositor worked quickly and instinctively, setting type by hand was slow and time-consuming. Today handsetting type is used mainly by private presses for limited-edition art books.

MACHINE CASTING | By the late nineteenth century, machines had been developed that could cast type either as individual characters (Monotype) or as entire lines (Linotype). To cast type, the typesetter operated a keyboard. As each letter was typed, molds (also called matrices) of the letters fell into position, and after each line was finished, the molds were filled with a molten lead alloy that solidified instantly to produce type. After printing, the type was melted down and reused.

Casting type was faster and more efficient than setting type by hand and therefore less expensive. The speed of the setting was limited only by the keyboard operator's typing ability, approximately 50 words per minute. Cast type did not totally replace handset type. They existed side by side, with the smaller text type being set by machine and the larger display type by hand.

Until the 1960s casting was the most widely used method of setting type, but it is no longer used commercially today.

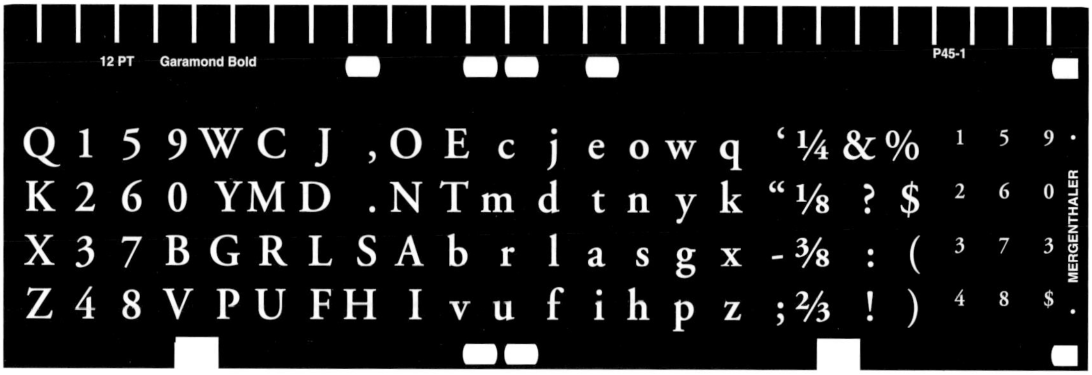

PHOTOTYPESETTING

PHOTOTYPESETTING | In the mid-1960s casting type in hot metal was replaced by the first form of "cold" type, called phototypesetting. This process involved the photographic projection of light through a film negative of the characters onto photosensitive film or paper. The characters to be set were input on a keyboard, stored on a tape, and controlled by large computers.

Since type was no longer restricted by the limitations inherent in metal, letterforms could be manipulated far more easily. Characters could be set close, touching, or overlapping. Furthermore, the letterforms were always exactly the same because the type was all shot from the same negative font. In spite of its many virtues, phototypesetting has been completely superseded by digital technology, which is even faster, more flexible, and less costly.

DIGITAL COMPOSITION | By the end of the 1980s, digital composition had become the most efficient method of typesetting. Digital typesetters, or laser imagers, are dramatically different in both storage and output from analog phototypesetting systems. In phototypesetting, characters were generated from photographic fonts. In digital composition systems, the characters are stored electronically as digital data in the computer's memory. The type is then generated as a series of dots or lines. Depending on the requirements, the output may be produced on virtually any surface or material.

The output devices for digital systems are high-speed type-generating machines capable of setting type at the rate of thousands of characters per second. The quality of the type is in direct relationship to the quality of the original drawings, their storage, and the speed of the output.

Because the type is digital, it can be electronically condensed, expanded, slanted, and manipulated. One of the great advantages of digital technology is the capacity to reproduce any image that can be digitized. This includes not only type but also photographs, illustrations, and other graphic images. This is accomplished through the use of a raster image processor (RIP), which converts the image into a digital file that can then be stored, manipulated, and output as necessary.

Digital Design

The revolution in digital design began with the advent of desktop publishing in 1982, when John Warnock and Charles Geschke developed Adobe PostScript, a standard computer language that could be used for manipulating visual information.

Using this technology in conjunction with the Aldus PageMaker program, Apple Computer began to market microcomputers that could be operated by people with minimal programming capabilities. Since that time there has been tremendous growth in the industry, with systems offering greater speeds, increased storage, and new programs.

Digital design has become more than just another typesetting or design method. It has essentially brought an end to the traditional typesetting industry by giving "desktop users" the ability to generate typography without relying on outside services. This has dramatically altered the designer's role.

Today the designer has become a combination artist and technician, often responsible for entire jobs ranging from editorial duties to production tasks.

DIGITAL TYPE ENLARGED

Digital programs give designers the ability to undertake projects in once highly specialized fields. Areas in typography, illustration, photography, moving images, and sound are no longer restricted to specific practitioners. Instead, processes in these disciplines are combined on a single platform.

Working with combined disciplines, or multimedia, is perhaps the most significant creative possibility in digital design. Typography can easily be part of an illustration, a photograph, or moving images; it no longer is generated as a separate element to be later combined in a final layout.

Even the printed page, once the major form of typographic expression, is being overshadowed by forms of communication like the World Wide Web. Because the digital process is universal to most forms of contemporary communication, digital typography moves easily between print, film, and Web design.

Although there are myriad aspects to working with computers, all the functions can be broken down into four principal areas: input, storage, manipulation, and output. Each of these functions is dependent on three things: the hardware, or equipment itself; the software, or computer applications; and the user's experience and capability.

INPUT | The entire process begins with some form of data that must be input and initially stored. Input may occur by typing text on a keyboard, scanning text or images, copying outside files, or even transcribing the spoken word through voice recognition programs. The objective is to turn analog data into digital data. Once converted and modified into compatible formats, the information can be stored and prepared to be manipulated.

STORAGE | One of the most significant developments in the computer industries has been the huge increase in the capacity to store data. Originally, 5-inch floppy disks and hard disk drives handled the storage for microcomputers. Early desktop systems held about 80K (80,000 bytes) of information internally and 20K on floppy disks.

Within a decade internal hard drives could hold a gigabyte (a billion bytes) of data, and optical disks nearly as much.

Today storage is so economical that it rarely poses a problem for the professional designer or studio to increase storage capacity.

MANIPULATION | Programming capabilities allow digital data to be reprocessed into the desired form. This includes the use and application of typography, photography, illustration, and even sound and moving images.

Computer data is manipulated using a combination of hardware and software. By working with a keyboard and a mouse, the user can call up programs, issue commands, select typefaces, reduce or enlarge design elements, and position copy. Other manipulating tools include touch screens, and styluses and tablets.

At the heart of the manipulation process is the operating system. The operating system controls most of the computer's basic chores and facilitates the use of the applications. In turn, the applications perform specific tasks. There are literally thousands of programs created for every purpose: word processing, design, page makeup, slide presentation, animation, video generation, three-dimensional rendering, and so on.

OUTPUT | As design progresses, the user has two basic ways to view it. First, the design can be viewed on a monitor, or screen, as it develops. For the designer this screen represents the desktop, or working environment. Second, hard copy can be generated through laser or inkjet printing, or another printing process. In fact, there are many methods of generating output, and in the packaging and product fields, even three-dimensional models can be produced.

When the job is completed and approved, it is prepared for final production and distribution. For the graphic designer this could mean printing, distribution through the Internet, or mass production in some digital format. All of these methods rely on varying levels of digital technologies. Some result in a tangible printed piece; others in fleeting images. ■

NOTE | Typesetting technology expands so rapidly that what is considered industry standard today can become quicky outdated.

Glossary

A

AA Author's alteration. An alteration to the original job that incurs additional charges. Compare to PE.

Accordion fold Series of parallel folds in paper in which each fold opens in the opposite direction from the previous fold—in a zigzag pattern.

Acetate Transparent plastic film used to cover presentations or to make indications over original art.

Adobe PostScript A computer imaging program language for page description.

A4 The international standard for business stationery. The approximate equivalent in the U.S. is 8 1/2 x 11 inches.

Against the grain Folding paper at right angles to the grain. See also Grain and With the grain.

Agate Unit of measurement used in newspapers to calculate column width. 14 agate lines equal 1 inch.

Align To line up, or place letters or words on the same horizontal or vertical line.

Alignment Arrangement of type in straight lines so that different sizes justify at the bottom (base-align) and ends of lines appear even on the page.

Alterations Any changes in copy after setting. See also AA and PE.

Ampersand Name of the type character "&" used in place of "and." Derived from the Latin word *et.*

Analog A language or process using a continuous and variable mechanical or electrical scale — rather than electrical pulses. For example, an electrical current. Compare to Digital. A dial phone is analog; a touch-tone phone is digital.

Antique finish A roughly finished book paper, usually in natural muted colors.

Application A computer program that is used to perform a specific task, such as word processing, page layout, or photographic manipulation.

Arabic numerals The figure zero and numerals 1 though 9, so called because they originated in Arabia. Compare to Roman numerals.

Art All original copy, whether prepared by an artist, camera, or other mechanical means. Loosely speaking, any copy to be reproduced.

Ascender The part of the lowercase letter that rises above the body, as in b, d, f, h, k, l, and t.

Asterisk Reference mark (*) used to indicate a footnote. Also used to indicate missing letters or words.

Author's alternation See AA.

B

Backbone Also called a *spine.* In binding, the part of a book that connects the front and back covers.

Backslant Typeface that slants backward; that is, opposite to italic.

Bad break A block of text with many hyphenations, a poorly designed rag, or a single word (widow) as the last line of text.

Baseline Horizontal line upon which all the characters in a given line stand.

Basis weight The weight of 500 sheets of paper (a ream) cut to a specific size.

Binary Anything made up of only two units, parts, or options. In computer systems, a base-2 numbering system that uses the digits 0 and 1.

Binary digit See Bit.

Binding The fastening together of printed sheets in the form of signatures into books, booklets, magazines, etc. Also, the covers and backing of a book.

Bit In computer systems, the smallest unit of information representing one binary digit, 0 or 1. The word is derived from the first two letters of binary and the last letter of digit.

Bitmapped display An image on the video screen in which each dot, or pixel, corresponds to one or more bits in the computer's random-access memory (RAM).

Black Letter Also called *Gothic.* A style of handwriting popular in the fifteenth century. Also, the class of typestyles based on this handwriting.

Bleed Area of image that extends beyond ("bleeds" off) the edge of the paper. Applies mostly to photographs or full areas of color. When a design involves a bleed image, the designer must allow from 1/8 to 1/4 inches beyond the intended trim size. A slightly larger sheet is required to accommodate bleeds when printing.

Blind embossing A bas-relief impression made with a regular stamping die, except that no ink or foil is used.

Blowup An enlargement of copy: photograph, artwork, type, or image.

Blueprint Also called *blues.* Inexpensive proofs made from a set of photo negatives, submitted for approval prior to platemaking.

Blurb Summary of contents of a book presented as jacket copy. Also, a short commentary, such as a caption or the text in comic strip balloons.

Body In composition, the metal block of a piece of type that carries the printing surface. It is the depth of the body that gives the type its point size.

Body copy Also called *body matter.* Regular reading matter, or text, as contrasted with display lines.

Body matter See Body copy.

Body size The depth of the body of a piece of type measured in points.

AMPERSANDS

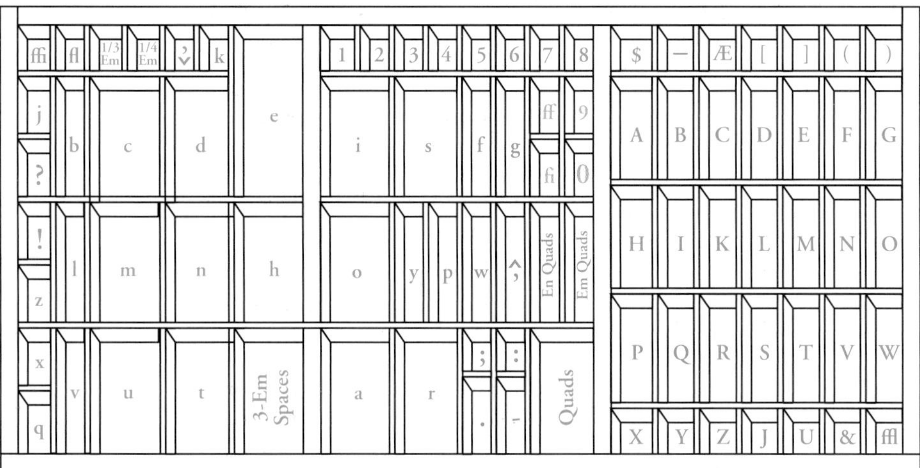

CALIFORNIA JOB CASE

Body type Also called *text type.* Type, from 6 points to 14 points, is generally used for body copy.

Boldface (bf) A heavier version of a regular typeface.

Bond paper A grade of writing and printing paper with a surface treated to take pen and ink well and have good erasure qualities.

BPS Bits per second.

Brackets Pair of marks [...] used to set off matter extraneous to the context.

Bullet A typographic element usually used to highlight specific lines of text.

Byte Eight bits. In most current systems, one character or symbol is represented by one byte.

California job case Used in traditional metal typesetting. Tray in which handset type is stored and from which it is set. The individual cubicles are logically arranged so that frequently used letters are most easily accessible.

Calligraphy Elegant handwriting, or the art of producing such handwriting.

Camera-ready art Physical copy assembled and suitable for photographing by a process camera or scanner. Mostly replaced by digitally prepared files.

C & sc Caps and small caps. See Caps and small caps.

Capitals Also called *caps* or *uppercase.* Capital letters of the alphabet.

Caps and small caps (C & sc) Capitals and small capitals. In composition, used to specify words that begin with a capital letter and have the remaining letters in small capitals, which are the same height as the body of the lowercase letters.

Caption Explanatory text accompanying illustrations.

Cardinal numbers Identifying sequence of numbers: one, two, three, etc. Compare to Ordinal numbers.

Casting An obsolete typesetting process in which molten metal is forced into type molds (matrices). Type can be cast as single characters or as complete lines.

Casting-off See Character counting.

Cathode ray tube In typesetting, electronic tube used to display letter image, in the form of dots (computer logic character formation) or lines (character projection), for exposure onto film, photographs, microfilm, or offset plates.

Centered type Lines of type of varying lengths set centered on the line measure.

Chapter heads Chapter title and/or number of the opening page of each chapter.

Character count The number of characters in a line, paragraph, or piece of copy.

Character counting Also called *casting-off.* Calculating the length of manuscript copy in order to determine the amount of space it will occupy when set in a given typeface and measure.

Character generation The electrode digital process of generating type and images. Usually by cathode ray tube and positive/negative charge.

Characters Individual letters, figures, punctuation, etc., of the alphabet.

Characters per pica (CPP) System of copyfitting that utilizes the average number of characters per pica as a means of determining the length of the copy when set in type.

Cicero Typographic unit of measurement predominant in Europe: approximately the same as the pica used in the U.S. and Asia.

Clip art Uncopyrighted images available in printed or digital form. Used when custom artwork is not viable because of cost or time.

CMYK See Four-color process.

Coated paper Paper with a surface treated with clay or another compound to improve the finish in terms of printing quality. A coated finish can vary from dull to very glossy and provides an excellent printing surface that is especially suited to fine halftones.

Collate To arrange sheets or signatures in proper sequence so the pages will be in the correct order before sewing and binding.

Colophon Inscription in a book that contains information relating to its production. Usually placed at the end of the book.

Color-matching system Method of specifying flat color by means of numbered color samples available in swatchbooks. The Pantone Matching System (PMS) is the most popular.

Color proof Printed color image that the designer and client check to make sure the color is accurate and in register prior to printing multiple copies.

Color separation The operation of separating artwork into the four process colors by means of filters in a process camera or by electronic scanners. The result is four continuous-tone films (negatives or positives), which are used to make printing plates.

Column inch A measure commonly used by smaller newspapers based on a space 1 inch deep and a column wide.

Composing stick In metal composition, a small metal tray-like device used to assemble type when it is being set by hand. It is adjustable so that lines can be set to different measures.

Composition The process of typesetting.

Comprehensive More commonly referred to as a comp. An accurate layout showing type and illustrations in position, suitable for use as a finished presentation.

Condensed type Narrow version of a regular typeface.

Continuous-tone copy Any image that has a complete range of tones from black to white: photographs, paintings, etc. Compare to Line copy.

Contour setting Type that takes the shape of a recognizable object.

Copy In design and typesetting, typewritten copy. In printing, all artwork to be printed: type, photographs, etc. See also Continuous-tone copy and Line copy.

Copyfitting Determining the area required for setting a given amount of typewritten copy in a specified typeface.

Counter Space enclosed by the strokes of a letter, such as the bowl of b, d, p, etc.

CPS Characters per second. A measurement referring to the output speeds of typesetting equipment.

CPU Central processing unit.

Crop To eliminate portions of an image or illustration so that it fits the page design better. Traditionally done by using cropmarks on the original copy to indicate to the printer where to trim the image.

Cropmarks In design, the lines that are drawn in the margins of the live image to indicate where the image or artwork should be trimmed.

CRT See Cathode ray tube.

Cursives Early italic typefaces that resemble handwriting but with the letters disconnected.

D

Data Information input, output, stored, or manipulated by a computer system.

Data bank A large store of information that can be selectively retrieved from a computer. A font library may be stored in a data bank.

Database A structured arrangement of data in a form that can be manipulated in a computer system.

Data processing A generic term for all systematic operations carried out on computer data.

Deckle edge Irregular, ragged edge on handmade papers, or the outside edges of machine-made paper.

Definition The degree of sharpness in a negative or print.

Delete A proofreaders' mark meaning "take out."

Descender That part of a lowercase letter that falls below the body of the letter, as in g, j, p, q, and y.

Desktop publishing The process whereby personal computers, peripherals, and suitable software are used to produce publication-quality documents.

Didot Typographic system of measurement used outside the U.S. Comparable to our point system.

Die-cutting A process of custom cutting using a steel die.

Digital A system for encoding a value using a sequence of digits. A computer is a digital device that uses sequences of bits to encode information. Compare to Analog.

Digital printing Plate-less printing direct from digital files.

Direct to plate Creating a plate directly from computerized copy without film.

Direct to press A digital process in which output is printed directly from computer files, bypassing traditional platemaking processes.

Disk An information storage medium. Traditionally available in floppy (portable) or hard (computer-installed) formats.

Display type Type used to attract attention, usually above 14 points in size.

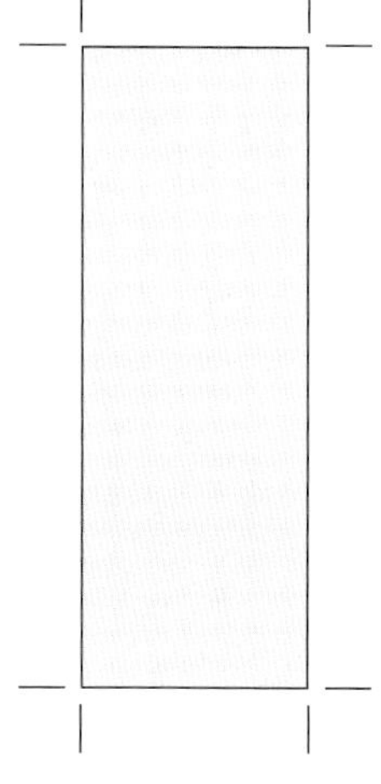

CROPMARKS

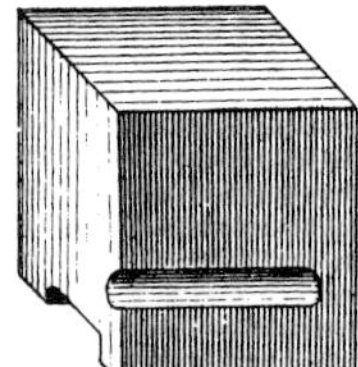
EM-QUAD

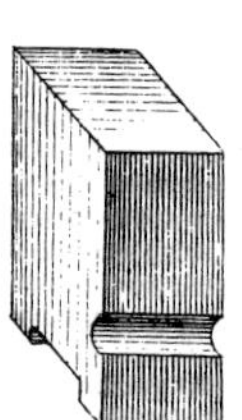
EN-QUAD

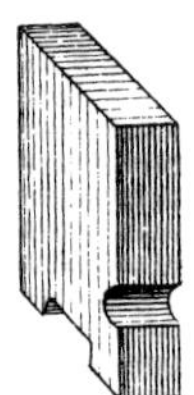
3-TO-THE-EM

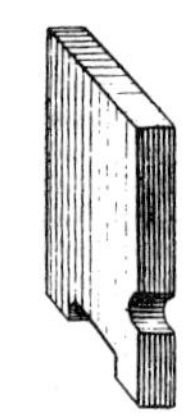
4-TO-THE-EM

Dithering A technique, similar to pointillist painting, of using small patterns of a few basic colors to simulate many more colors. Often used on inexpensive displays and printers, dithering reduces the resolution of an image and can introduce unwanted patterns.

DOS Disk operating system. Computer program code designed to handle the input, storage, manipulation, and output of data.

Dot leaders See Leaders.

Drop initial Display letter that is set into the text.

Dummy The preliminary layout of a printed piece showing how the various elements will be arranged. It may be either rough or elaborate, according to the client's needs. The term comp is used more frequently.

Duotone A photograph printed using two colors, usually black plus one color.

Editing Checking copy for fact, spelling, grammar, punctuation, and consistency of style.

Egyptian See Slab Serif.

Elite The smallest size of typewriter type: 12 characters per inch, as compared to 10 per inch on the pica typewriter.

Ellipses Three dots that indicate an omission or incomplete thought… often used when shortening copy.

Em Commonly used shortened term for em-quad. See also Em-quad.

Embossing Producing a raised image on a printed surface. See also Blind embossing.

Em-dash Also called a *long dash.* A dash the width of an em-quad.

Em-quad In handset type, a metal space that is the square of the type body size; that is, a 10-point em-quad is 10 points wide. The em gets its name from the fact that in early fonts the M was usually cast on a square body.

En Commonly used shortened term for en-quad. See also En-quad.

En-dash Slightly longer than a hyphen and takes the place of the word "to," such as 1970–2006.

En-quad The same depth as an em but one half the width: the en space of 10-point type is 5 points wide.

Expanded Also called *extended.* A wide version of a regular typeface.

Face The part of metal type that prints. Sometimes used as an abbreviation for typestyle or typeface.

Facsimile Full name for fax. A machine or modem capable of transmitting graphic information by phone or wireless method.

Family of type All the type sizes and typestyles of a particular typeface (roman, italic, bold, condensed, expanded, etc.).

Feathering A ragged, or feathered, edge on a printed type.

File Any collection of information stored on a disk; for example, a document, resource, or application.

Finish The surface properties of paper.

Fit Space relationship between two or more letters. The fit can be modified into a "tight fit" or a "loose fit" by adjusting the set-width or the tracking.

Flat color Generally refers to solid colors or tints rather than the four process colors.

Flop To turn over an image or photograph so that it faces the opposite way.

Flyer Advertising handbill or circular.

Folder An electronic file containing documents.

Folio Page number. Also refers to a sheet of paper when folded once.

Font Complete assembly of all the characters (uppercase and lowercase letters, numerals, punctuation marks, points, reference marks, etc.). Traditionally, a font referred to one size of one typeface; today a font is not size specific.

Format General term for style, size, and overall appearance of a publication.

Formatting The translation of specifications into formats or computer coding.

Foundry type Metal type characters used in hand composition.

Four-color process Method of reproducing full-color copy (original artwork, transparencies, etc.) by separating the color image into its three primary colors — magenta, yellow, and cyan — plus black.

Fractions In typesetting, a single keystroke or keystroke combination that builds customized fractions.

Full color Process color.

Galley In metal composition, a long tray that holds type prior to printing. Also the name of a proof pulled from a galley tray or any other unpaged proof.

Gatefold A page that folds into the gutter and, when unfolded, is about twice the size of a normal page.

Gigabyte (GB) 1,000 megabytes, or 1 billion bytes.

GIGO Garbage in, garbage out. Programming slang for bad input produces bad output.

Grain Predominant direction of the fibers in a sheet of paper. The direction of the grain is important when it is folded. A sheet folded with the grain folds easily; a sheet folded against the grain does not.

Gray scale A band of gray tones from white to black, often used as a test strip to measure the quality of a tonal range in photography and printing.

Grid The cross-ruled guidelines over which all parts of a page or book layout will be assembled.

Gutenberg, Johannes German inventor of movable type and letterpress printing (circa 1455) as we know it today.

Gutter Blank space where two pages meet at the binding or blank space between two columns of type.

Gutter margin Inner margin of a page on a spread.

H

Hairline A fine line or rule, 1/4-point in thickness.

Halftone The photomechanical reproduction of continuous-tone copy (such as photographs) in which the gradations of tone are created by the relative size and density of tiny solid dots.

Hanging indentation A type arrangement style in which the first line of copy is set full measure and all the lines that follow are indented.

Hard copy Typewritten copy or the printed version of a digital file.

Hard disk See Disk.

Hardware The mechanical and electronic parts that make up a computer. Compare to Software.

Head The top, as opposed to the bottom, or foot, of a book or a page.

Heading Bold or display type used to emphasize copy.

Headline The most important line of type in a piece of printing, enticing the reader to read further or summarizing at a glance the content of the copy that follows.

Head margin The white space above the first line on a page.

Hexadecimal A system used to specify RGB colors in graphics for the Web, specifically used in the programming language of HTML.

Hot type Slang expression for type produced by casting hot metal, now obsolete. Linotype was the most popular manufacturer.

Hyphenation. Determining where a word should break at the end of a line. In typesetting, computers are programmed to hyphenate.

I

Icon A symbol shown on the computer screen to represent an object, concept, or message; for example, a disk, folder, or document.

Ideographs Symbols representing an idea, not an object.

Illustration General term for any form of drawing, diagram, halftone, or color image.

Imposition In printing, the arrangement of pages in a press form so they will appear in correct order when the printed sheet is folded and trimmed.

Initial The first letter of a body of copy, set in display type for decoration or emphasis. Often used to begin a magazine article or a chapter of a book.

Input In computer composition, the initial data to be processed, usually in the form of text files. Also, any information received by the computer from storage, keyboard, mouse, scanner, etc.

Input device A scanner, keyboard, mouse, or other hardware that sends information to the computer.

Insert A separately prepared and specially printed piece that is inserted into another printed piece or a publication.

Italic A letterform style that slants to the right and is designed as a companion to the roman style of a typeface: *looks like this.* Also see Oblique.

Justified type Lines of type that align both left and right of the full measure.

Justify The act of justifying lines of type to a specified measure, flush right and left, by putting the proper amount of space between words in the lines to make them all even, or "true."

Kerned letters In metal type, characters in which a part of the letter extends, or projects, beyond the body or shank, thus overlapping an adjacent character.

Kerning Adjusting the space between letters so that part of one extends over the body of the next. Kerned letters are common in italic, script, and swash fonts.

Keyline See Mechanical.

Kill To delete unwanted copy or text.

Kilobyte (KB) 1,000 bytes.

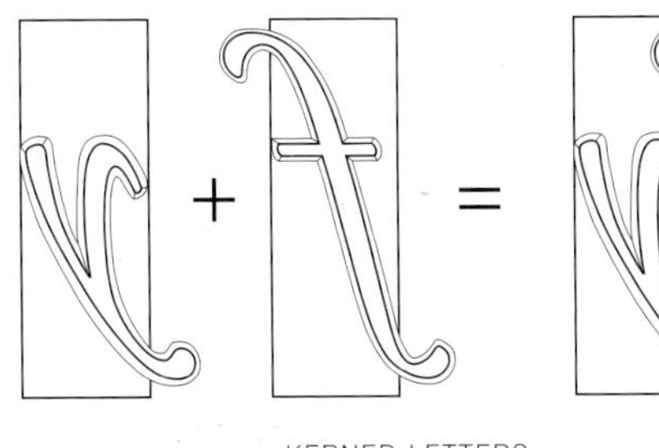
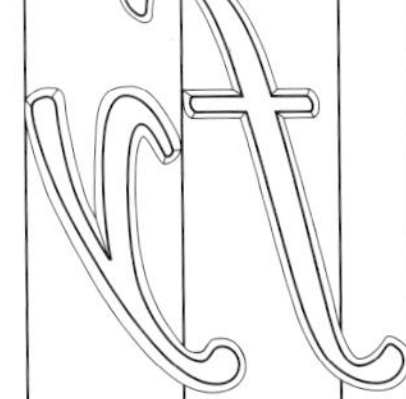

KERNED LETTERS

L

Laid paper Paper having a laid pattern: a series of parallel lines simulating the look of the handmade papers.

Layout Preliminary plan or blueprint of the basic design, usually showing the sizes and kind of type, illustrations, spacing, and general style in their proper positions. Used as a guide for the client or supplier.

LC Lowercase, or small letters, of a font.

Leaders A row of dots, periods, or dashes used to lead the eye across the page. Leaders are specified as 2, 3, or 4 to the em; in fine typography they are usually arranged to align vertically.

Lead-in The first words in a block of copy set in a contrasting typeface.

Leading (Pronounced ledding.) Also called *linespacing.* In metal type composition, the insertion of leads between lines of type. The term is still used to indicate space added between lines of type.

LIGATURES

Leads (Pronounced leds.) In metal type composition, the thin strips of metal (in thicknesses of 1 to 2 points) used to create space between the lines of type. Leads are less than type-high and so do not print.

Legibility The quality in typeface design that affects the speed of perception: the faster, easier, and more accurate the perception, the more legible the type.

Letterpress The printing method used to print directly from cast (hot-metal) type. It is based on relief printing, which means that the image area of the type is raised.

Letterspacing In composition, adding space between the individual letters in order to fill out a line of type to a given measure or to improve appearance.

Ligature Two or three characters joined as a single character; ﬁ, ﬂ, ﬄ, and ﬃ are the most common.

Lightface A lighter version of a regular typeface.

Line copy Any copy that is solid black, with no gradation of tones: line art, type, rules, etc. Compare to Continuous-tone copy.

Line gauge Also called a *type gauge* or *pica rule.* Used for copyfitting and measuring typographic materials.

Line length See Measure.

Linespacing In typesetting, an alternate term for leading.

Lining figures Also called *modern figures.* Numerals that are the same size as caps in a typeface and align on the baseline: 1, 2, 3, 4, 5, 6, 7, 8, 9, 0. Also see Old style figures.

Logotype A specific name or type arrangement trademarked and used as a company or corporate identifier. Usually shortened to logo.

Lowercase Small letters, also called as minuscules, as opposed to caps or majiscules.

M

Magnetic tape In typewriter composition and photocomposition, a tape or ribbon impregnated with magnetic material on which information may be placed in the form of magnetically polarized spots. Used to store data that can later be further processed and set into type.

Mainframe A large computer originally manufactured in a modular fashion.

Makeready The process of arranging the form on the press preparatory to printing so that the impression will be sharp and even.

Makeup Assembling the typographic elements (type and halftones) to form a page or a group of pages of a newspaper, magazine, or book.

Manuscript Copy to be set in type. Usually abbreviated to MS (sing.) and MSS (pl.). Can also refer to handwritten, as opposed to typewritten, material.

Markup In typesetting, to mark the type specifications on layout and copy for the typesetter. Generally consists of the typeface, size, line length, leading, etc.

Masthead Any design or logotype used to identify a newspaper or other publication.

Matrix Also called a *mat*. A metal mold from which type is cast.

Matte finish A coated paper with a dull finish. Also, in photography, a textured, finely grained finish on a photograph or photostat. As opposed to glossy.

Meanline The line that marks the tops of lowercase letters without ascenders.

Measure Also called *line length.* The length of a line of type, normally expressed in picas and points.

Mechanical Camera-ready assembly of all type and design elements pasted on artboard in exact position and containing instructions, either in the margins or overlays, for the platemaker.

Mechanical letterspacing Type set with automatic spacing between the characters.

Megabyte (MB) 1,000 kilobytes.

Memory The place in the computer's central processing unit where information is stored. See also RAM and ROM.

Menu A video display of programs and tasks.

Metric system Decimal system of measures and weights with the meter and the gram as the bases. Here are some of the more common measures and their equivalents:

KILOMETER	00.6214 mile
METER	39.37 inches
CENTIMETER	00.3937 inch
MILLIMETER	00.0394 inch
KILOGRAM	02.2046 pounds
GRAM	00.035 ounce
INCH	02.54 centimeters
FOOT	00.3048 meter
YARD	00.9144 meter
OUNCE	31.103 grams
POUND	00.4536 kilogram

Microchip Also called a *chip.* A silicon wafer typically containing millions of electrical components; chips make up the "brains" of the computer and perform such tasks as logical and numerical processing, data storage, and information management.

Minuscules Small letters, or lowercase.

Modem A hardware component that converts electronic computer signals into audible tones that can then be transmitted through telephone lines. A receiving modem then reconverts the audio tones back to digital data. In this way, files can be transmitted via telephone.

Modern Term used to describe the typestyle developed in the late eighteenth century.

Morgue A morbid name referring to a collection of reference material for the designer.

Mouse A hand-held device used to supplement the computer keyboard when working with computers. When it is moved across a flat surface, its motion is simulated on the screen by a cursor.

Mutton Also called a *mutt.* A nickname for the em-quad.

N

Network A collection of interconnected computers.

Newsprint A grade of paper containing about 85% ground wood and 15% unbleached sulfite. The weight is from 30 to 45 pounds and the surface is coarse and absorbent. Used for printing newspapers and low-cost flyers.

Noise Any undesirable signal occurring in an electronic or communications system. May also refer to an interfering pattern, such as the visible grain of a photograph.

Oblique Roman characters that slant to the right: *looks like this.* Compare to Italic.

OCR See Optical character recognition.

Offline Refers to equipment not directly controlled by a central processing unit or to operations conducted out-of-process. As opposed to online.

Old Style A style of type developed in the early sixteenth century.

Old style figures Numbers that vary in size, some having ascenders and others descenders: 1, 2, 3, 4, 5, 6, 7, 8, 9, 0. Compare to Lining figures.

Online Connected to the system and readily usable.

Opacity That quality in a sheet of paper that prevents the type or image printed on one side from showing through to the other: the more opaque the sheet, the less show-through it will have. Also, the covering power of an ink.

Optical center A point approximately 10% above the mathematical center of a page or layout.

Optical character recognition (OCR) The process of converting typewritten or printed documents into computer text. The document is scanned, then OCR software reads the text, and converts it into a word-processing file.

Optical disk A mass storage device using a laser to record and read digital data.

Ordinal numbers Sequence of numbers related to sequence: first, second, third, etc. Compare to Cardinal numbers.

Ornamented A typeface that is embellished for decorative effect.

Outline A typeface with the outline defined.

Output In typesetting, type that has been set.

Output device Any device that receives information from the microprocessor, most commonly the monitor.

ORNAMENTED LETTERS

Page description language The common computer language that ties together the various systems and output devices, such as monitors, keyboards, scanners, printers, and imagesetters.

Pagination Pages numbered in consecutive order.

Pantone Matching System (PMS) Brand name for a widely used color-matching system. See also Color matching system.

Paragraph openers Typographic elements used to direct the eye to the beginning of a paragraph. Often used when the paragraph is not indented.

Paste-up See Mechanical.

PC Personal computer.

CYAN

MAGENTA

YELLOW

BLACK

PROCESS COLORS

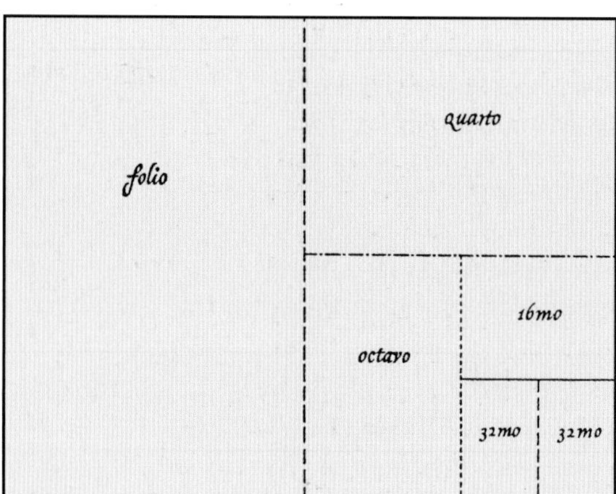

PRESS-SHEET OR FOLIO

PE Printer's error, or mistake made by the typesetter. Compare to AA.

Perfect binding A relatively inexpensive method of binding in which the pages are held together and fixed to the cover by means of flexible adhesive. Widely used for paperbacks, manuals, textbooks, and telephone books.

Peripheral An input, output, or storage device used in conjunction, and usually connected by cable, with a computer; for example, a printer, scanner, or zip drive.

Photocopy A duplicate image, made from the original.

Photostat Also called a *stat.* Trade name for a photoprint.

Phototypesetting Also known as *photocomposition* and erroneously as *cold type.* The preparation of manuscript for printing by projection of images of type characters onto photosensitive film or paper.

Pica A typographic unit of measurement: 12 points = 1 pica, and 6 picas = 1 inch. Also used to designate typewriter type 10 characters per inch (as opposed to elite typewriter type, which has 12 characters per inch).

Pi characters Special characters not usually included in a type font, such as special ligatures, accented letters, and mathematical signs.

Pixel Short for "picture element." One of the tiny squares or rectangles that make up a screen or printed image. Typical picture files may contain thousands or millions of pixels.

PMS See Pantone Matching System.

Point Smallest typographical unit of measurement: 12 points = 1 pica, and 1 point = approximately 1/72 of an inch. Type is measured in terms of points, the standard sizes being 6, 8, 10, 12, 14, 18, 24, 30, 36, 42, 48, 60, and 72 points in body size.

Point systems There are two major point measuring systems in use today: the English/American System, or pica system, used primarily by the English-speaking world, and the European Didot System, used by the rest of the world.

Preparation Also called *prep work* or *pre-press.* In printing, all the work necessary in getting a job ready for platemaking: preparing art, making mechanicals, shooting film, stripping, and proofing.

Pre-press proof Proof made directly from film before making printing plate.

Press proof A proof pulled on the actual production press.

Press-sheet Refers to a sheet of paper of specific size on which a job is printed. After printing, the sheets are gathered, folded, trimmed, and bound. With book production the full press sheet was traditionally referred to as a *folio* and with each fold the size and name changed.

Printer font In desktop publishing, a font a printer can use.

Printer's error See PE.

Process color Also called *full color.* Refers to the four-color process reproduction of the full range of colors by the use of four separate printing plates; one for each of the primary colors — magenta (process red), yellow, and cyan (process blue) — and one for black.

Program A collection of instructions and operational routines, necessary to complete computer commands or functions. See also Application.

Proofreader A person who reads the type that has been set against the original copy to make sure it is correct and who also may read for style, consistency, and fact.

Proofreaders' marks Shorthand symbols employed by copyeditors and proofreaders to signify alterations and corrections in the copy.

Proof(s) A trial print or sheet of printed material that is checked against the original manuscript and upon which corrections are made. A proof also refers to any output that can be inspected prior to final production.

Quad A piece of type metal less than type-high used to fill out lines where large spaces are required. An em-quad is the square of the particular type size: a 10-point em-quad is 10 x 10 points. An en-quad is half the width of an em.

Rag Also called *ragged edge.* Refers to the pattern formed by the words on the edge of a text block that is not set justified.

Rag papers Papers containing a minimum of 25% rag or cotton fiber. These papers are generally made up in the following grades: 25%, 50%, 75%, and 100%.

Random access memory (RAM) Memory chips that temporarily store data or instructions for immediate processing; when the computer is turned off, the RAM information is lost forever. To save information from RAM, it must be transferred to a permanent storage device such as a hard drive or disk.

Raster image processing (RIP) The conversion of type and images to an arrangement of dots that can be stored in a computer and called up on the screen and manipulated as necessary.

Rasterization The process of converting image data into output data.

Reader's proof Also called a *printer's proof.* A galley proof, usually the specific proof read by the proofreader, that will contain queries and corrections to be checked by the client.

Recto The right-hand page of an open book, magazine, etc. Page 1 is always on a recto, and rectos always bear the odd-numbered folios. Compare to Verso.

Registration marks Devices, usually a cross in a circle, applied to original copy and film reproductions. Used for positioning negatives in perfect register or, when carried on press plates, for the register of two or more colors in printing.

Resolution The fixed number of pixels or dots available on an output device (display screen, printer, imagesetter, etc.).

Reversed type In printing, refers to type that drops out of the background and assumes the color of the paper.

Read only memory (ROM) Memory chips that store information permanently. ROM doesn't vanish when the system is turned off, but it cannot be changed. Information the computer uses for its most basic operations, such as establishing the user interface (or main window) is stored in ROM.

Roman An upright letterform with serifs derived from Roman stone-cut letterforms.

Roman numerals Roman letters commonly used as numerals until the tenth century C.E.: I=1, V=5, X=10, L=50, C=100, D=500, and M=1,000. Compare to Arabic numerals.

Rough A sketch or thumbnail, usually done on tracing paper, giving a general idea of the size and position of the various elements of the design.

Rule A black line used for a variety of typographic effects, including borders and boxes.

Runaround Type that surrounds an image, display type, or space.

Run in To set type with no paragraph breaks or to insert new copy without making a new paragraph.

Running foot A book title, chapter head, or other head "run" at the bottom of every page in a book.

Running head A book title, chapter head, or other head "run" at the top of every page in a book.

Scaling The process of calculating the percentage of enlargement or reduction of the size of original artwork to be reproduced. This can be done by using the geometry of proportions or by the use of a proportion wheel or calculator.

Scanner Photoelectric equipment for digitizing images (turning hard copy into digital files). Also to produce color separations from full-color copy.

Script A typeface based on handwritten letterforms. Scripts come in formal and informal styles and in a variety of weights.

Self-cover Booklets or pamphlets that have the same stock (paper) for both cover and text. Used when the cover stock does not have to be particularly strong or to save cost.

Self-mailer A printed piece designed to be mailed without an envelope.

Serifs The opening and closing cross-strokes in the letterforms of some typefaces. Sans serif typefaces, as the name implies, do not have serifs but open and close with no curves and flourishes.

Service bureau Graphic production facility where black and white or color output, mounting, scanning, and other services are produced for the designer.

Set-width Also called *set.* In metal type, the width of the body upon which the type character is cast. In digital typesetting, the width of the individual character, including a normal amount of space on either side.

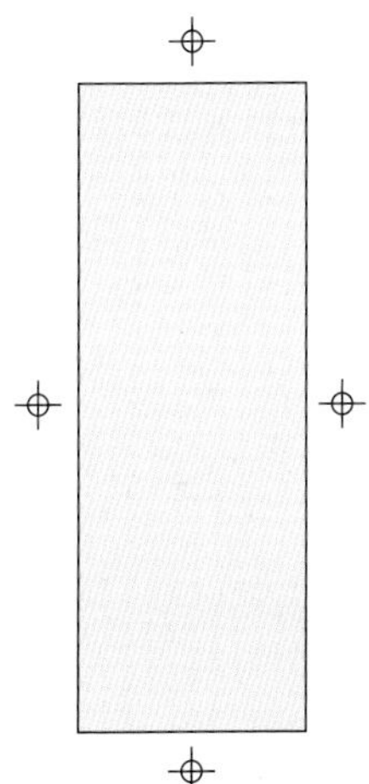

REGISTRATION MARKS

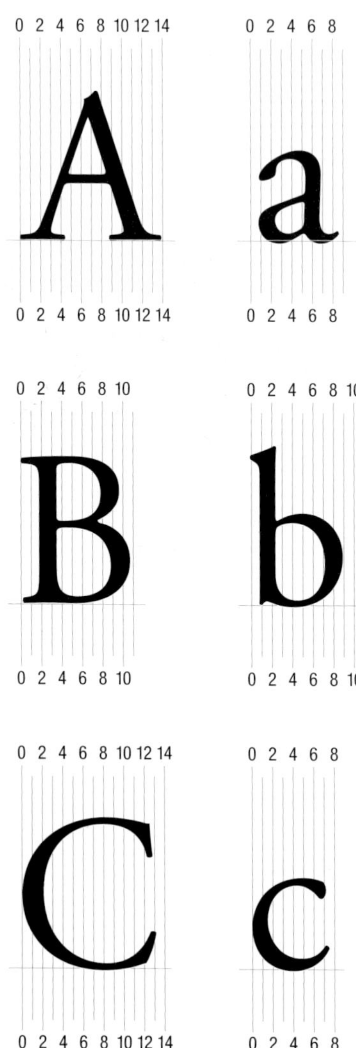

UNITS MEASURE THE SET-WIDTH

Show-through The phenomenon in which printed matter on one side of a sheet shows through on the other.

Signature A printed sheet that is folded, gathered, and trimmed.

Slab Serif Also called *Egyptian* and *square serif.* Typestyle recognizable by its heavy, square serifs.

Small caps (sc) A complete alphabet of capitals that is the same size as the x-height of the normal typeface: AA, BB, CC, etc.

Software Computer programs, consisting of instructions telling the computer how to do the different tasks it performs. Application programs, utilities, operating systems, etc., are all software. Compare to Hardware.

Solid In composition, refers to type set with no leading between the lines.

Solid color In printing, refers to a blended ink and not a color built up by mixing values of CMYK.

Spec To specify type or other materials in the graphic arts.

Spread A pair of facing pages.

Square halftone Also called a *square-finish halftone.* A rectangular—not necessarily square—halftone, i.e., one with all four sides straight and perpendicular to one another.

Square serif A typeface in which the serifs are the same weight or heavier than the main strokes.

SS Abbreviation for "same size."

Stet A proofreader's mark that indicates copy marked for correction should stand as it was before the correction was made. Copy to be stetted is always underlined with a row of dots, usually accompanied by the word *stet.*

Stock Also called *substrate.* Any material used to receive a printed image: paper, board, foil, etc. In papermaking, pulp that has been beaten and refined and after dilution is ready to be made into paper.

Storage A device, such as a hard disk, diskette, tape, drive, etc., onto which data may be written for retrieval at a later time.

Swash A capital letter with an ornamental flourish.

T

Text The body copy in a book or on a page, as opposed to the headings.

Text type Main body type, usually 14 points or smaller.

Thumbnails Small, rough sketches.

Tint A color obtained by adding white to the solid color. In printing, a photomechanical reduction of a solid color by screening.

Tracking Used in digital typography to mean overall letterspacing.

Transitional A typestyle that combines features of both Old Style and Modern (such as Baskerville).

Transpose (tr) Commonly used term in both editorial and design to designate that one element (letter, word, picture, etc.) and another should change places.

Trim To cut off and square the edges of a printed piece or of stock.

Trim size The final size of a printed piece after it has been trimmed. When the form is imposed for printing, allowance must always be made for the final trim size.

Type The letters of the alphabet and all the other characters used, singly or collectively, to create words, sentences, blocks of text, etc.

Typecasting Setting type by casting it in molten metal either in individual characters (Monotype) or as complete lines of type (Linotype).

Type family A range of typeface designs that are all variations of one basic style of the alphabet.

Type gauge A rule calibrated in points and picas on one edge and inches on the other. Used to measure line length or baseline to baseline when working with columns of type.

Type-high The height of a standard piece of metal type: 0.918 inch (U.S.).

Typewriter composition Also called *strike-on* or *direct impression composition.* Composition for reproduction produced by a typewriter.

Typographic errors Also called *typos.* Errors made in copy while inputting copy.

Typography The art of designing with type. By mechanizing much of the art, technology is rapidly making typography a science as well as an art.

U&lc Commonly used abbreviation for uppercase and lowercase. Used to specify text that is to be set in caps (usually initial caps) and lowercase letters as written.

Uncoated paper The basic paper, produced on the papermaking machine with no coating operations.

Unit A measurement based on the division of the em into equal increments.

Unjustified type Lines of type set at different lengths and aligned on one side (left or right) and left ragged on the other.

Uppercase The capital letters of a type font: A, B, C, etc.

User-friendly Any part of a computer system that is easy to use.

Value The degree of lightness or darkness of a color or a tone of gray, based on a scale of graduated tonal values running from pure white through all the gradations of gray to black.

Verso The left-hand side of a spread, as opposed to the recto, which is the right-hand side of a spread. The verso always carries an even-numbered folio. Also refers to the reverse side of a printed sheet.

Visual A layout or comp.

Visual display A visual representation of computer output.

WF See Wrong font.

Window A panel on the computer screen showing toolboxes, menus, icons, etc., that allow the user to easily start programs, open files, and perform specific actions within a program. It is possible to layer multiple windows on the screen, although only the top one is active at any time.

With the grain A term used to describe the directional character of paper, often applied to the folding of a sheet of paper parallel to the grain. Paper folds more easily and tears straighter with the grain than against the grain. See also Grain and Against the grain.

Woodtype Type made from wood. Formerly used for the larger display sizes more than 1 inch where the weight of the metal made casting impractical.

Wordspace The space between words.

Wove paper An uncoated paper that has a uniform surface with no discernible marks.

Wrong font (wf) An error in typesetting in which the letters of different fonts become mixed.

Xerography Also called *photocopy.* An inkless printing process that uses static electricity. Xerox, a trade name for this process, is a good example.

X-height Height of the body of lowercase letters, exclusive of ascenders and descenders.

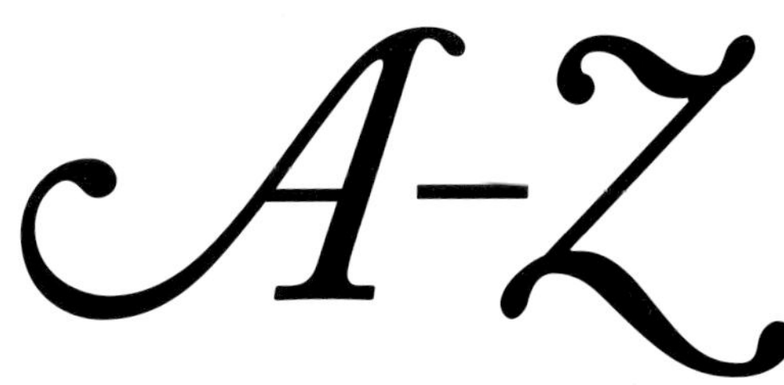

SWASH INITIALS

The following is a partial list of the many excellent books on typography and graphic design. Several of the book listed may be out of print but are worth reviewing in libraries.

For a more complete listing of graphic design and typographic books, magazines, organizations, and Web sites, visit: **www.designingwithtype.com/5.**

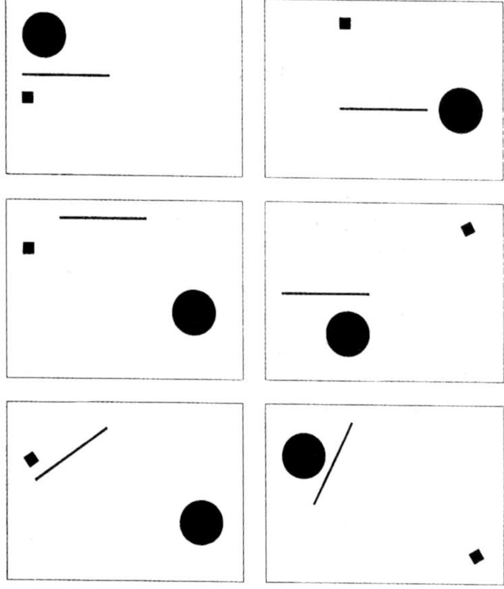

ILLUSTRATION FROM *THE NEW TYPOGRAPHY* BY JAN TSCHICHOLD

Afrikan Alphabets
Saki Mafundikwa

An Alpabet Source Book
Oscar Ogg

American Typography Today
Robert Carter

American Wood Type
Rob Roy Kelly

Asymmetric Typography
Jan Tschichold

Compendium for Literates: A System for Writing
Karl Gerstner

The Complete Manual of Typography
James Felici

The Design of Books
Adrian Wilson

Design with Type
Carl Dair

The Designer and the Grid
Lucienne Roberts and Julia Thrift

Designing
Ivan Chermayeff, Tom Geismar, and Streff Geissbuhler

Designing Books
Jan Tschichold

Designing Books
Jost Hochuli and Robin Kinross

Designing Programmes
Karl Gerstner

Designing Typefaces
David Earls

Education of a Typographer
Steven Heller

The Elements of Typographic Style
Robert Bringhurst

Expressive Typography and New Media
George Kepes

Finer Points in the Spacing and Arrangements of Type
Geoffrey Dowding

Form of the Book: Essays on the Morality of Good Design
Jan Tschichold

Forms and Counterforms
Adrian Frutiger

Gestalt
George Kepes

The Graphic Artist and His Design Problems
Josef Müller-Brockmann

Graphic Design Manual: Principles and Practice
Armin Hofmann

Graphic Design Sources
Kenneth Hiebert

Grid Systems in Graphic Design
Josef Müller-Brockmann

A Handbook for Modern Designers
Stanley Morison

Helvetica: Homage to a Typeface
Lars Müller

A History of Graphic Design
Philip B. Meggs

Hot Designers Make Cool Fonts
Allan Haley

Information Graphics
Peter Wildbur and Michael Burke

Irish Type Design
Dermot McGuinne

Looking Closer: Critical Writings on Graphic Design
Michael Bierut, William Drenttel, Steven Heller, and D. K. Holland

Typography: Macro and Microesthetics
Willi Kunz

Making Digital Type Look Good
Bob Gordon

Manuale Typographicum
Herman Zapf

Modern Typography
Robin Kinross

The New Typography: A Handbook for Modern Designers
Jan Tschichold

Paul Rand
Steven Heller

Pioneers of Swiss Graphic Design
Josef Müller-Brockmann

Printing Types: Their History, Forms and Use
D. B. Updike

Reviving the Rules of Typography
David Jury

Stop Stealing Sheep & Find Out How Type Works
Erik Spiekerman

Thinking with Type
Ellen Lupton

Typographic Design: Form and Communication
Rob Carter, Ben Day, and Philip Meggs

The Visual Display of Quantitative Information
Edward R. Tufte

Index

Colophon

The authors invite comments and suggestions for future editions. Attempts to credit designs have been made where possible, and any corrections or additions are welcome.

TYPE | The text is set in 8.5-point Helvetica Neue Roman.
The main headings are set in 16-point Helvetica Neue Light.
The subheadings are set in 9-point Helvetica Neue Black.
The captions are set in 8-point Helvetica Neue Roman.
The identifying captions are set in 6-point Helvetica Neue Light.

DESIGN | James Craig and Irene Korol Scala

PUBLISHED | Watson-Guptill Publications, New York
Candace Raney, Executive Editor
Susan E. Meyer, Editor (first edition through fourth edition)
Alison Hagge, Editor (fifth edition)
Ellen Greene, Production Manager